Fiscal Policy for Sustainable Development in Asia-Pacific

Lekha S. Chakraborty

Fiscal Policy for Sustainable Development in Asia-Pacific

Gender Budgeting in India

Lekha S. Chakraborty
National Institute of Public Finance
and Policy
New Delhi, Delhi, India

ISBN 978-981-19-3280-9   ISBN 978-981-19-3281-6 (eBook)
https://doi.org/10.1007/978-981-19-3281-6

© The Editor(s) (if applicable) and The Author(s), under exclusive license to Springer Nature Singapore Pte Ltd. 2022
This work is subject to copyright. All rights are solely and exclusively licensed by the Publisher, whether the whole or part of the material is concerned, specifically the rights of translation, reprinting, reuse of illustrations, recitation, broadcasting, reproduction on microfilms or in any other physical way, and transmission or information storage and retrieval, electronic adaptation, computer software, or by similar or dissimilar methodology now known or hereafter developed.
The use of general descriptive names, registered names, trademarks, service marks, etc. in this publication does not imply, even in the absence of a specific statement, that such names are exempt from the relevant protective laws and regulations and therefore free for general use.
The publisher, the authors and the editors are safe to assume that the advice and information in this book are believed to be true and accurate at the date of publication. Neither the publisher nor the authors or the editors give a warranty, expressed or implied, with respect to the material contained herein or for any errors or omissions that may have been made. The publisher remains neutral with regard to jurisdictional claims in published maps and institutional affiliations.

This Palgrave Macmillan imprint is published by the registered company Springer Nature Singapore Pte Ltd.
The registered company address is: 152 Beach Road, #21-01/04 Gateway East, Singapore 189721, Singapore

For my mom.

Foreword

The public budget of a country is one of the earliest economic tools that economists and accountants have had available over the years for their theorizing and their analysing. Public budgets became available when the public accounts of countries could be separated from the private accounts of those who ran the countries (kings or other rulers).

The early, original budgets were limited in their size and had few explicit objectives to promote. These included national defence, domestic security (with police and justice), some essential public infrastructure, administration, and a few others. Equity objectives generally played very limited if any role in old budgets. The situation started changing in the twentieth century, especially in the second half, when countries became more democratic, and when the pursuit of equity and other social goals progressively entered the public budgets. Access to higher public revenue had also become easier, due to changes in the economic structures and to the growing acceptance of the principle of ability to pay in taxation. These changes made the pursuit of utilitarian objectives more achievable, through public budgets.

Budgets became progressively more ambitious in the goals that they promoted. Budgets became also more detailed documents, and generally more complex. Their marksmanship moved from the abstract concept of the "country" to the more specific one of its "inhabitants", generally defined as nucleuses of families and with some stratifications among different classed or categories of citizens. The social-utilitarian objective became progressively more important.

As time passed, the past uniformity in objectives of public budget started to give way to new considerations. The need to educate the young, and to increase the countries' "human capital" directed more budgetary attention to the needs of the young. The lengthening of life expectancy, that increased the share of older components of the populations, directed the allocation of some spending to the protection of the old. The breaking up of large, extended families created increasing public needs to deal with invalids and individuals needing special attention.

In countries with individuals from different races, racial equity started to attract attention. In countries with high shares of foreign born, the treatment of immigrants attracted some importance. Finally, the realization that men and women may be subjected to different stresses in most countries, and in some more than in others, could not fail to become an area of interest to the budget.

This book is especially focused on the roles that men and women play in the economies of many countries and in the ways in which budgets have ignored or have accommodated those roles. It provides the most comprehensive survey now available of what is known in this area and on what has been achieved so far in several, different countries, including India. "Gender budgeting" has become progressively more common in the world but the author argues that it has not become common enough. Many countries' budgets continue to implicitly discriminate against women, especially in some countries, and especially in developing countries.

In some of these countries, women have often responsibilities within families that demanding but are not officially measured. These responsibilities may include having to get drinking water or fuel for burning from far away sources. Because of these burdens, girls often are not able to attend schools thus making more difficult for them to raise their life incomes. In these cases, public spending that provided families with running water and burning fuel would remove this significant "gender bias". But such cases would require higher public resources. Thus often difficult choices must be made. The choices must pay attention to gender considerations.

The eleven chapters that form this book are full of information on these issues and on attempts by various countries and by some sub-national jurisdictions to deal with gender-relevant issues in their budgets. The book provides a lot of statistical evidence and useful discussion of the connection between gender budgeting and the UN sustainable development goals. The book recognizes that the "mechanism design" that is needed to achieve various social goals is often inadequate and needs reforms. Sen's concern about the many statistically "missing women" in countries such as China and India also attracts some discussion.

The book highlights the difference between "ex ante gender budgets" and "ex post gender budgets", recognizing that inefficiency or even corruption may distort the budgetary interventions away from the original intentions. Australia is mentioned as having been a pioneer in developing a gender-sensitive budget statement. The need for using a "budget lens" is now increasingly recognized and countries are becoming increasingly aware of the need for such lens. The book reports that as many as 90 countries are now pursuing some form of "gender budgeting". This trend has created an increasing need for statistics that are disaggregated by gender. Such reliable statistics often do not exist.

Lekha Chakraborty's new book is a welcome addition to an area of public finance that is still relatively unknown to many. It is an area that is likely to grow in importance. This book should help in attracting increasing attention to this area.

Vito Tazi
Former Director,
IMF Fiscal Affairs
Washington DC, USA

Preface

Fiscal policy is prima facie gender-neutral. But it can turn gender blind due to the socio-economic asymmetries in development across gender. The role of public policy is to ensure "Leave No One Behind" in the journey towards sustainable economic growth. Gender budgeting, as a Public Financial Management (PFM) tool, is about applying a "gender lens" in fiscal policy frameworks to redress gender inequalities by ensuring fiscal transparency and accountability.

In 2016, the International Monetary Fund (IMF), for the first time ever, asked its member nations to integrate gender budgeting into PFM. Gender budgeting has reached the world stage when United Nations Secretary-General (UNSG) High-level Panel on Women's Economic Empowerment in 2016 identified gender budgeting as one of the tools to ensure gender equality.

Extraordinary times require extraordinary policy responses. In the times of global uncertainties and the COVID-19 pandemic, it is opportune to unpack what gender-responsive fiscal policy entails. With many governments preparing public finance strategies for the post-pandemic fiscal year, we now have a renewed opportunity to strengthen gender budgeting as an effective PFM tool to redress mounting inequalities. In Asia-Pacific, gender budgeting has evolved as a fiscal innovation, that translates gender-related commitments to fiscal commitments through identified processes, resources, and institutional mechanisms, impacting both the spending and revenue sides of the budget. In a country like

India, where it is well known that gender discrimination starts even before birth resulting in adverse sex ratios at birth, gender budgeting is a powerful tool to redress gender inequalities.

The National Institute of Public Finance and Policy (NIPFP), an independent think tank of the Ministry of Finance, is the pioneering institute to conduct gender budgeting in India. Since 2004, at national and selected subnational levels, gender budgeting has been institutionalized within the Ministry of Finance using NIPFP methodology for preparing the analytical matrices. India is a leading example of sustainable gender budgeting in Asia-Pacific region.

Korea has integrated gender budgeting within National Finance Law in 2006, within the legal fiat. In the Philippines, gender budgeting was made mandatory by legally earmarking 5% of all sectoral expenditure on women. However, the "earmarking" can only be a second-best principle of gender budgeting. The fiscal marksmanship—possibility of fiscal forecasting errors—of gender budgeting is a crucial determinant to understand why higher budgetary allocation does not automatically ensure higher public expenditure for women's empowerment.

The overall macroeconomic environment of Asia-Pacific region—especially the procedures that relate to "fiscal rules" and avoiding fiscal austerity—plays a crucial role in ensuring gender equitable outcomes of gender budgeting.

I hope my book will interest students, economists, media professionals, and policymakers who are searching for understanding gender budgeting, and how countries can promote greater gender equality through public finance management.

New Delhi, India   Lekha S. Chakraborty

Acknowledgements

I would like to thank the National Institute of Public Finance and Policy (NIPFP) for the enabling environment to write this book. I express my gratitude to NIPFP, International Monetary Fund (IMF) and Levy Economics Institute of Bard College, New York for granting me permission to use my selected working papers in this book.

I benefitted immensely from my presentations in international meetings—including the American Economic Association Meetings in Atlanta—and from my professional interactions with eminent scholars and policymakers, to write the book. I would particularly like to thank the Governing Board of Management of the International Institute of Public Finance Munich, where I am a Member; the International Working Groups on Gender, Macroeconomics and International Trade; Econometric Society of India and the Research Group on Employer of Last Resort for enabling academic deliberations.

I express my sincere gratitude to my mentors and colleagues at NIPFP, Levy Economics Institute, Centre for Development Studies, American University, University of Utah, Uppsala University, Carleton University; IMF, World Bank, and various UN entities where I worked on short stints. I must record my appreciation for my research interns for their help in analysis, at various stages of my book.

I express my gratitude to two anonymous reviewers of the book to whom it was sent by the Palgrave Macmillan. I immensely benefitted from their comments.

I express my love to my family—particularly my son—for their immense support.

Contents

1	**Introduction**	1
	The Macroeconomic Backdrop	2
	The Rationale	6
	The Analytical Framework	7
	Ex Ante and Ex Post Frameworks of Gender Budgeting	10
	The Structure	13
	References	15
2	**Macroeconomic Policy Coherence for Gender Equality in Asia-Pacific**	19
	Fiscal Policy Stance	21
	Effective Fiscal Management and Governance	25
	Inequalities in Fiscal Policy	25
	Linking Resources to Results: Outcome Budgets	26
	Normative Framework and Methodology to Analyse the Fiscal Policy for Gender Equality	29
	Monetary Policy Stance	30
	Structural Reforms	33
	Mapping of Macro Policies in Asia-Pacific	36
	Identifying Specific Policy Tools	37
	References	33

3	**Gender-Budgeting and Gender Equality Outcomes: Evidence from Asia-Pacific**	43
	Measuring Gender Equality	46
	Interpreting Data	51
	The Empirical Investigation	54
	The Significance to Go Beyond Models	58
	References	59
4	**Gender Budgeting and the Efficacy of Measuring Unpaid Care Economy**	63
	Statistical Invisibility of Unpaid Care Economy	65
	Time-Use Pattern Across Gender and Geography in India	70
	Valuation of Unpaid Care Economy: An Illustration	83
	Gender Budgeting: The Link Between Public Investment and Time Allocation	88
	References	94
5	**Determining Gender Equality in Fiscal Federalism: Evidence from India**	97
	Theoretical and Empirical Literature	98
	Fiscal Federalism in India: Institutional Details	101
	Fiscal Federalism Arrangements and Gender Equality	106
	The Empirical Models and Results	108
	References	115
6	**Fiscal Decentralization and Ex Ante Gender Budgeting: Case Studies of Selected Countries Including India**	119
	Fiscal Decentralization and Gender Frameworks	121
	Third Tier Institutional Details: Fiscal Devolution Through a Gender Lens	127
	Fiscal Decentralization and Local Level Gender Budgeting: Case Studies	133
	The Philippines	133
	India	135
	Kerala	138
	Karnataka	144
	West Bengal	145
	Fiscal Decentralization and Local Level Gender Budgeting in Other Countries: Case Studies	148

	Morocco	148
	South Africa	151
	Ethiopia	155
	Nepal	155
	IMF Government Finance Statistics (GFS): Analyzing "General Government" Data	157
	References	161
7	**Fiscal and Regional Context of Gender Budgeting in Asia**	165
	Overview of Gender Budgeting in Asia	169
	Country-Specific Gender Budgeting Efforts in Asia Pacific	172
	Australia	173
	Initial Project on Gender Budgeting	173
	A Backlash: Office of Status of Women demoted from Prime Minister's Office	175
	Abrupt End to Gender Budget Statements	175
	Korea	176
	Legal Backing for Conducting Gender Budgeting	176
	Institutionalizing Gender Budgeting	178
	Gender Budgeting in Infrastructure	180
	Local Level Gender Budgeting	180
	Challenges	181
	Summary of Prominent Gender Budgeting Efforts	181
	The Philippines	182
	Fiscal Decentralization and Gender Budgeting	183
	Bangladesh	185
	Sri Lanka	186
	Indonesia	187
	Pakistan	188
	Country-Specific Outcomes	189
	Positive Outcomes of Gender Budgeting	190
	References	192
8	**Gender Budgeting, as Fiscal Innovation in India**	197
	Gender Budgeting, as a Fiscal Innovation	198
	Integrating Gender in Intergovernmental Transfers	204
	Tax Side Gender Budgeting and Tax Incidence Analysis	205
	Strengthening Accountability Mechanisms and Capacity Building and Gender Mainstreaming	206

	Phase 1: Country-Specific Gender Diagnosis and Intergovernmental Fiscal Framework Models	207
	Phase 2: Intergovernmental Institutional Design	208
	Phase 3: Capacity Building	209
	Phase 4: Accountability Mechanisms	210
	Public Expenditure Tracking	210
	Gender Equality Outcomes Across Indian States	211
	References	216
9	**The Political Economy of Gender Budgeting in India and Fiscal Marksmanship**	219
	Fiscal Rules and Financing of Deficits in India	220
	The Intergovernmental Fiscal Transfers in India, 2021–2022	232
	Applying "Gender Lens" to Union Budget 2021–2022	236
	Fiscal Marksmanship	244
	References	253
10	**Gender-Budgeting Outcomes and Public Expenditure Benefit Incidence**	255
	The Analytical Framework	256
	The Public Expenditure Benefit Incidence Analysis (BIA) Methodology	261
	Estimating Unit Cost	261
	Identifying the Users	261
	Aggregating Users into Groups	261
	Calculating the Benefit Incidence	262
	International Classification of Diseases (ICD)—Benefit Incidence	262
	Quintile-Wise Benefit Incidence and Polarization Ratio	269
	References	285
11	**COVID-19 Context and the Way Ahead**	287
	Constraints of Rules-Based Policy Space	288
	Obsession with "Economic Growth" Frameworks	288
	Fiscal Sustainability in Low Interest Rate Regime	289
	Strengthening Fiscal Marksmanship	289
	Innovative Financing of Deficits	290
	Incorporating Unpaid Care Economy into Macro Policy	290

Acknowledging Intersectionality Issues in Gender Budgeting	291
Fiscal Decentralization: Move Ahead from "One Size Fits All" Gender Budgeting	291
Link Between Fiscal Policy and Gender Equality Outcomes	292
Public Expenditure Tracking and Fiscal Incidence Analysis	292
Measuring Gender-Aware Human Development Outcomes	293
Second Generation Reforms of Gender Budgeting	293
Integrating Gender in Intergovernmental Fiscal Mechanisms	293
Gender Budgeting and Feminization U	294
Strengthening Gender Budgeting on Taxation Side	294
Fiscal Transparency and Accountability Through Gender Budgeting	294
Political Will for Sustainable Gender Budgeting as PFM	295
References	295

Abbreviations

AAAA	ADDIS ABABA ACTION AGENDA
ADB	Asian Development Bank
AEA	American Economic Association
BCC	Budget Call Circular
BEE	Black Economic Empowerment
BIA	Benefit Incidence Analysis
CAG	Comptroller and Auditor General
CEDAW	Convention on the Elimination of All Forms of Discrimination Against Women
CEE	Commission of Employment Equity
CGE	Commission of Gender Equality
DBT	Direct Benefit Transfers
DILG	Department of Interior and Local Government
EPWP	Expanded Public Works Programme
EWR	Elected Women Representatives
FC	Finance Commission
FR	Fertility Rate
FSLRC	Financial Sector Legislations Reforms Commission
GAD	Gender and Development
GDI	Gender-Related Development Index
GDI	Gender Development Index
GE	Gender Equality
GEAR	Growth, Employment and Redistribution
GEM	Gender Empowerment Measure
GFS	Government Finance Statistics
GII	Gender Inequality Index

GST	Goods and Services Tax
HDI	Human Development Index
HDR	Human Development Report
ICD	International Classification of Diseases
IGFT	Intergovernmental Fiscal Transfers
IHDI	Inequality Adjusted Human Development Index
ILO	International Labour Organisation
IMF	International Monetary Fund
JMC	Joint Monitoring Committee
KWDI	Korean Women's Development Institute
LFPR	Labour Force Participation Rate
LGC	Local Government Code
LGU	Local Government Unit
MGNREGA	Mahatma Gandhi National Rural Employment Guarantee Act
MMR	Maternal Mortality Ratio
MPCE	Monthly Per Capita Expenditure
MTFF	Medium Term Fiscal Framework
MWCD	Ministry of Women and Child Development
NCRFW	National Commission on the Role of Filipino Women
NIPFP	National Institute of Public Finance and Policy
NITI	National Institution for Transforming India
NSO	National Statistical Organisation
NSS	National Sample Survey
OECD	Organisation for Economic Cooperation and Development
OSW	Office of Status of Women
PEFA	Public Expenditure Financial Accountability
PFM	Public Financial Management
PSBR	Public Sector Borrowing Requirement
RGI	Registrar General of India
RMSE	Root Mean Squared Error
SDG	Sustainable Development Goal
SDP	State Domestic Product
SE	Secondary Education
SFC	State Finance Commission
SGSY	Swarnajayanti Gram Swarozgar Yojana
SHG	Self Help Group
SNA	System of National Accounting
SPRSM	Strengthening Poverty Reduction Strategy Monitoring
SRS	Sample Registration System
TFP	Total Factor Productivity
TLLSS	Timor-Leste Living Standards Survey
TOR	Terms of Reference
TUS	Time Use Survey

UBI	Universal Basic Income
UDAY	Ujjwal Discom Reassurance Yojana
UN ESCAP	United Nations Economic and Social Commission for Asia and the Pacific
UNDP	United Nations Development Program
UNIFEM	United Nations Development Fund for Women
UNRISD	United Nations Research Institute for Social Development
UNSD	United Nations Statistical Division
VAT	Value Added Taxes
WBI	Women's Budget Initiative
WCP	Women's Component Plan
WER	Women Elected Representatives
WHO	World Health Organisation

List of Figures

Fig. 3.1	Gross secondary enrolment ratio in Asia-Pacific (*Source* World Bank, World Development Indicators database; and authors' estimates)	51
Fig. 3.2	Under 5 child mortality in Asia-Pacific (*Source* World Bank, World Development Indicators database; and authors' estimates)	52
Fig. 3.3	Maternal mortality ratio in Asia-Pacific (*Source* World Bank, World Development Indicators database; and authors' estimates)	53
Fig. 3.4	Labour force participation rate in Asia-Pacific (*Source* World Bank, World Development Indicators database; and authors' estimates)	54
Fig. 3.5	Women in national parliaments in Asia-Pacific (*Source* World Bank, World Development Indicators database; and authors' estimates)	55
Fig. 3.6	GDI, time consistent version (*Source* Authors' estimates)	56
Fig. 9.1	Distribution of the Gender Budget in the Total Budget, India (*Source* [Basic Data], Expenditure Budgets Union Budget 2021–2022, Government of India [2019])	236
Fig. 10.1	Concentration curves, public expenditure incidence, and targeting: Pictorial representation (*Source* Davoodi et al. [2003])	257
Fig. 10.2	Gender Differential in Benefit Incidence: All ICD Combined (*Source* Government of India [2015], National Sample Survey 75th Round on Health)	275

Fig. 10.3 Gender Differential in Benefit Incidence: Certain infectious and parasitic diseases (ICD-I) (*Source* Government of India [2015], National Sample Survey 75th Round on Health) 276

Fig. 10.4 Gender Differential in Benefit Incidence: Neoplasms (ICD-II) (*Source* Government of India [2015], National Sample Survey 75th Round on Health) 276

Fig. 10.5 Gender Differential in Benefit Incidence: Diseases of the blood and blood-forming organs and certain disorders involving the immune mechanism (ICD-III) (*Source* Government of India [2015], National Sample Survey 75th Round on Health) 277

Fig. 10.6 Gender Differential in Benefit Incidence: Endocrine, nutritional, and metabolic diseases (ICD-IV) (*Source* Government of India [2015], National Sample Survey 75th Round on Health) 278

Fig. 10.7 Gender Differential in Benefit Incidence: Mental and behavioural disorders (ICD-V), and Diseases of the nervous system (ICD-VI) (*Source* Government of India [2015], National Sample Survey 75th Round on Health) 278

Fig. 10.8 Gender Differential in Benefit Incidence: Diseases of the eye and adnexa (ICD-VII) (*Source* Government of India [2015], National Sample Survey 75th Round on Health) 279

Fig. 10.9 Gender Differential in Benefit Incidence: Diseases of the ear and mastoid process (ICD-VIII) (*Source* Government of India [2015], National Sample Survey 75th Round on Health) 279

Fig. 10.10 Gender Differential in Benefit Incidence: Diseases of the circulatory system (ICD-IX) (*Source* Government of India [2015], National Sample Survey 75th Round on Health) 280

Fig. 10.11 Gender Differential in Benefit Incidence: Diseases of the respiratory system (ICD-X) (*Source* Government of India [2015], National Sample Survey 75th Round on Health) 281

Fig. 10.12 Gender Differential in Benefit Incidence: Diseases of the digestive system (ICD-XI) (*Source* Government of India [2015], National Sample Survey 75th Round on Health) 281

Fig. 10.13	Gender Differential in Benefit Incidence: Diseases of the skin and subcutaneous tissue (ICD-XII) (*Source* Government of India [2015], National Sample Survey 75th Round on Health)	282
Fig. 10.14	Gender Differential in Benefit Incidence: Diseases of the musculoskeletal system and connective tissue (ICD-XIII) (*Source* Government of India [2015], National Sample Survey 75th Round on Health)	282
Fig. 10.15	Gender Differential in Benefit Incidence: Diseases of the genitourinary system (ICD-XIV) (*Source* Government of India [2015], National Sample Survey 75th Round on Health)	283
Fig. 10.16	Gender Differential in Benefit Incidence: Pregnancy, childbirth and the puerperium (ICD-XV), and Certain conditions originating in the perinatal period (ICD-XVI) (*Source* Government of India [2015], National Sample Survey 75th Round on Health)	283
Fig. 10.17	Gender Differential in Benefit Incidence: Injury, poisoning, and certain other consequences of external causes (ICD-XIX) (*Source* Government of India [2015], National Sample Survey 75th Round on Health)	284
Fig. 10.18	Gender Differential in Benefit Incidence: External causes of morbidity and mortality (ICD-XX) (*Source* Government of India [2015], National Sample Survey 75th Round on Health)	284
Fig. 10.19	Gender Differential in Benefit Incidence: Factors influencing health status and contact with health services (ICD-XXI) (*Source* Government of India [2015], National Sample Survey 75th Round on Health)	285

List of Tables

Table 3.1	Determinants of GDI, GII, and sectoral spending: panel estimates	57
Table 4.1	Time allocation in SNA and Non-SNA, India 2020	71
Table 4.2	Distribution (%) of time use into SNA and Non-SNA, India 2020	72
Table 4.3	Age-disaggregated time allocation in SNA and Non-SNA in India, 2020	73
Table 4.4	Age-disaggregated distribution (%) of time allocation in SNA and Non-SNA, India 2020	76
Table 4.5	Time allocation of men and women in a day in different activities in India, 2020	78
Table 4.6	Time allocation by men and women of different levels of education in India, 2020	79
Table 4.7	Time allocation in different activities by geography, 2020	81
Table 4.8	Distribution (%) of time, by geography and gender, in India, 2020	82
Table 4.9	Percentage of men and women participating in different activities (usual principal activity status)	84
Table 4.10	Time allocation by women and men, selected states of India (weekly average time in hours)	86
Table 4.11	Distribution (%) of time use in SNA and Non-SNA: Selected states in India	87
Table 4.12	Valuation of unpaid care economy: Selected states of India	88

Table 4.13	Time-use pattern by men and women in water sector (weekly average time in hours)	89
Table 4.14	Econometric Link between Infrastructure and Time Allocation	92
Table 5.1	Descriptive statistics	109
Table 5.2	Impact of intergovernmental fiscal transfers on gender equality, with lagged gender budgeting dependent variable: GMM estimates	113
Table 5.3	Impact of IGFT and gender budgeting on fiscal spending, with lagged de-pendent variable—GMM estimates	114
Table 6.1	Criteria of gender responsive budgeting and scores in Nepal	156
Table 6.2	General government finance: Expenditure (% of GDP) by functions of government, IMF GFS 2019	158
Table 6.3	General Government Finance: Expenditure (% of GDP) by Economic Classification, IMF GFS 2019	159
Table 6.4	General Government Finance: Revenue (% of GDP), 2019	160
Table 7.1	Fiscal context of gender budgeting in Asia	166
Table 7.2	Legal Fiat of Gender Budgeting	170
Table 7.3	Revenue-Side Gender Budgeting	171
Table 7.4	Institutionalizing Gender Budgeting in Korea	176
Table 8.1	Phases of gender budgeting in India	199
Table 8.2	Gender Inequality Index (GII) across Indian States/Union Territories, 2017–2018	212
Table 8.3	HDI and GDI across Indian States/Union Territories, 2017–2018	214
Table 9.1	Levels of deficit (Rs. crores)	221
Table 9.2	Sources of Financing Fiscal Deficit (Rs. crores)	223
Table 9.3	The composition and fiscal marksmanship of revenue receipts	224
Table 9.4	Anatomy of revenue expenditure	229
Table 9.5	Intergovernmental fiscal transfers—conditional and unconditional	233
Table 9.6	Part A: Specifically Targeted programmes for Women in Union Budget 2021–2022, India	237
Table 9.7	Part B: Sectoral Composition of Gender Budgeting, 2021–2022	239
Table 9.8	Fiscal marksmanship: The Sources of Fiscal Forecasting Errors	245
Table 9.9	Fiscal marksmanship of Gender Budgeting: Part A	248

Table 9.10	Fiscal Marksmanship of Part B Allocations of Gender Budgeting, 2020–2021	250
Table 10.1	WHO International Classification of Diseases (ICD) to Indian National Sample Survey Mapping	263
Table 10.2	Unit Utilized in Health Sector: As per income quintiles across gender, India 2019	265
Table 10.3	Average medical expenditure for Ambulatory Health Services across Indian States, 2019 (in Rs.)	266
Table 10.4	Disease-specific Morbidity: Unit Utilized Pattern of Hospitalization across Plausible ICD-10 Mapping, India 2019	268
Table 10.5	Polarization Ratio	270
Table 10.6	Quintile-wise Behavioural Access to Health Care in Rural and Urban India Across Gender	272

CHAPTER 1

Introduction

Extraordinary times require extraordinary policy responses. In the time of COVID-19 pandemic, with the widespread lockdowns, women have disproportionately borne the socio-economic brunt of the pandemic. With many governments preparing public finance strategies for the post-pandemic fiscal year, we now have a renewed opportunity to strengthen gender budgeting as an effective public finance management tool to redress these mounting inequalities (Polzer et al., 2021; Sayeh et al., 2021). Gender budgeting is a fiscal innovation, encompassing all phases of public financial management (Chakraborty, 2014). Ideally, gender budgeting is an approach to fiscal policies and administration that translates gender-related commitments into fiscal commitments through identified processes, resources, and institutional mechanisms, impacting both the spending and revenue sides of the budget.

Prima facie, the fiscal policies may appear to be gender-neutral. It can turn gender-blind due to differences in the socially determined systemic roles played by women and men. As a consequence, gender-neutrality of fiscal policies can turn to gender blindness (Elson, 2000; Elson & Cagatay, 2000). This is due to the fact that women and men are at asymmetric levels of development on the socio-economic scale. The UN's COVID-19 Global Gender Response Tracker revealed that more than a thousand fiscal policy measures have been implemented by different countries—as part of fiscal stimulus packages—to tackle the widening gender inequalities. However, adopting such policies is only a partial approach to tackling gender inequalities. This is primarily because the fiscal stimulus packages are short run in nature. Ideally, there should be a coherent long-term macroeconomic policy framework to integrate gender concerns, and to translate the gender equality commitments into fiscal commitments. This is the core of gender budgeting, to ensure a sustained fiscal space for gender equality through transparency and accountability.

Gender budgeting is emerging as an important Public Financial Management tool to analyze the efficacy of the fiscal policies on gender equality. Gender budgeting does not mean making separate budgets for women nor is it confined to the analysis of earmarked funds for programmes exclusively targeted at women within budgets (Chakraborty, 2016a; Kolovich, 2018; Stotsky, 2016). It refers to an analysis of the entire budget through a gender lens to identify gender-differential impacts and translate gender commitments into budgetary commitments (Çağatay et al., 1995; Cagatay et al., 2000). Integrating gender in fiscal policy enhances transparency and accountability. Gender budgeting is an analysis of budgets to ascertain the relative benefits (or losses) derived by each gender from a particular fiscal programme/project. Gender budgeting has reached the world stage when the United Nations Secretary General's High-level Panel identified gender budgeting as one of the specific policy tools for Women's Economic Empowerment in 2016. The commitment of IMF in 2016 for the first time ever to conduct gender budgeting within the Public Financial Management (PFM) also strengthen the efficacy of gender budgeting on gender equality outcomes.

THE MACROECONOMIC BACKDROP

The macroeconomic uncertainty in times of the COVID-19 pandemic is hard to measure. The economic stimulus packages are short run in nature and the "normalization" process will begin by phasing out the COVID-19 stimulus announcements. In such contexts, long term Public Financial Management (PFM) tool like gender budgeting has significance to correct the exacerbating gender inequalities. Gender-budgeting frameworks also push the frontiers ahead of the economic growth paradigm. The economic growth per se will not "trickle down" to better human development outcomes.

The macroeconomic frameworks are rules-based across countries—both for fiscal and monetary stance. The monetary stance is based on inflation targeting rules—where the policy rates are pegged on the basis of deviation of inflation anchor from inflationary expectations and the output gap. The inflationary expectations and output gap are unobserved variables. The inflationary expectations are constructed on the basis of expectations surveys. The inflationary expectations data is gender neutral.

The output gap is the difference between potential output and actual output. The potential output is not inclusive of the economic activity outside the purview of Systems of National Accounts (SNA). The potential output is constructed by decomposing the output into trends and cycles. The unpaid care economy is not taken into consideration while constructing the potential output. Such underestimates of potential output are generated through econometric methodologies—mostly filters—which eliminate the cyclicality elements of GDP and arrive at the potential component using the trend elements of the series. If the fastest and smartest way to increase the potential GDP is by incorporating the economic activity done by women, conscious public policies related to care economy infrastructure are crucial.

Economists and policymakers use the variable "output gap" to capture the macroeconomic uncertainties. This deviation between potential output and actual output is a standard representation of a "cycle". It is based on business cycle theories. However, the business cycle always is not a "cycle" (Aguiar & Gopinath, 2007). When the COVID-19 pandemic and other macroeconomic crises tend to "permanently" push down the level of a country's GDP, it is inappropriate to assume that output will bounce back to prior-pandemic levels. The hysteresis (the dependence of economic path on history) in analysing the output dynamics in COVID-19 pandemic crisis is significant for designing appropriate fiscal and monetary policies to tackle the COVID-19 pandemic. This is because of the persistence of sluggish growth and weak macroeconomic recovery.

The assumption that recessions are followed by quick rebounds is not always correct. The economic recovery can be uneven if fiscal and monetary policy stances do not integrate gender-aware human development components into the policy processes. The economic stimulus packages have two components—instantaneous firefighting packages and structural reforms. It is important to apply a "gender lens" in both these components of economic stimulus packages to pre-empt exacerbating gender inequality outcomes.

The central banks so far have not integrated a "gender lens" into the monetary policy reaction function. However, the debate on whether climate change can be part of monetary policy has begun. Many central banks have started assessing the climate change risks and uncertainties through green stress tests of investment decisions, as these climate change related risks can in turn affect the financial stability (Chakraborty, 2022). The significant policy tool of the central bank is policy rates. During the times of COVID-19 pandemic, the central banks have kept the policy rates lower for the sustained growth recovery process. However, with mounting inflation against the backdrop of Russia's war in Ukraine and the energy price volatility, central banks have huge pressure to raise the interest rates. If the central banks "bite the bullet" and hike the interest rates, it can dampen the growth recovery process (Roubini, 2022). If central banks do not increase the interest rates, it can lead to the de-anchoring of inflationary expectations and lead to the reputation risk of the central banks. With zero lower bound and negative real interest rates, the monetary policy has proved inefficacious as a countercyclical policy tool to reset the economy to pre-crisis growth levels. The fiscal re-dominance at the same time, though desirous, has been bound to the fiscal austerity wave and tight fiscal rules.

The world nations will miss the chance to reset the economy to the pre-crisis levels in terms of growth and gender-aware human development, if fiscal policy space does not remain accommodative in the times of pandemic crisis. Fiscal rules insist that the level of fiscal deficit to GDP ratio needs to be maintained at 3 per cent. However, there is a fundamental rethinking of the efficacy of fiscal rules against the backdrop of a pandemic (Chakraborty & Harikrishnan, 2022). High public debt has no fiscal costs if the real rate of interest is not greater than the real rate of growth of the economy (Blanchard, 2019). High public debt is not catastrophic if "more debt" can be justified by clear benefits like public investment or "output gap" reduction. Blanchard (2019) highlighted the "hysteresis effects" (the persistent impact of short-run fluctuations on the long-term potential output) and suggested that a temporary fiscal expansion during a contraction could even reduce debt on a longer horizon. There is increasing recognition of the fact that gender-aware human capital formation and physical infrastructure have suffered from fiscal consolidation measures. In the context of emerging economies, public investment is a significant determinant of "crowd-in" private corporate investment (Chakraborty, 2016b, 2022). If we are worried about a "bad equilibrium", it is better to have a "contingent fiscal rule" (which may not need to be used) rather than steady fiscal consolidation.

If the path towards fiscal consolidation is through expenditure compression than tax buoyancy, the quality of fiscal consolidation will suffer. The financing pattern of fiscal deficits also need to be analysed to understand the efficacy of gender budgeting. There is a transition in the financing pattern of deficits from seigniorage financing (monetized deficits) towards bond financing. However, there is limited evidence on the earmarking of market borrowings towards specific sustainable development goals. Green bonds—earmarking a portion of sovereign debt bond towards green energy infrastructure—is increasingly getting attention. However, the "gender bonds"—as a transformative financing for gender equality goals—need more calibrated processes.

There is increasing attention towards money financing of fiscal programmes. However, due to its inflationary potential, governments have been reluctant to resort to monetary financing of fiscal deficits. However, if the real rate of interest is above the real growth of the economy, public debt may become unsustainable. In such situations, the eventual monetization of deficit is crucial. A finite money financing of fiscal programmes—for a judicious mix of specific fiscal programmes like gender budgeting, Employer of Last Resort (ELR) policies—where the government guarantees jobs; and targeted cash transfers to people in low-income quintiles to avert the livelihood crisis—is significant in the times of macroeconomic uncertainties.

Fiscal policy has a significant role to catalyse aggregate demand in times of crisis. The assumption that demand shocks have only a transitory impact on the economy in the times of COVID-19 pandemic needs a relook. Even demand shocks can have a permanent impact on output. When there are no clear economic cycles, especially when the drop in GDP is a "permanent scar" rather than a transient deviation, the role of fiscal and monetary policy as counter-cyclical policy tools might not operate to help the economy to rebound to a prior-crisis growth path. Economic cycles are defined as a succession of crises that followed periods of prosperity, though these peaks and troughs do not follow a given frequency or periodicity.

With the persistence of cyclicality, the economy will not rebound to prior pandemic levels of economic growth. This persistence of cyclicality are the permanent "scars" left by COVID-19 pandemic. Unless fiscal and monetary policies incorporate these aspects, the impact of economic stimulus packages to tackle the pandemic will be partial. The predominant form of pandemic responses was in the form of liquidity infusion.

However, credit-related economic stimulus packages have limited multiplier effects (Stiglitz & Rashid, 2020). If there is no corresponding growth in the economy, a huge credit infusion can accentuate non-performing assets.

From a gender perspective, the uneven access to credit is a matter of concern. Lowering of interest rates by the monetary policy authorities have made credit cheaper for boosting the investment. However, from a gender perspective, in the debate on cost of credit versus access to credit, it is the latter that matters more for women. Access to formal financial systems has become tough for women due to a lack of collateral. The financial inclusion has happened on a limited scale due to peer monitoring models through self-help groups. However, when the markets are uncertain, the pressure of credit repayment can compel women to engage in Ponzi finance with the indigenous money lenders at higher rates of interest.

The Rationale

The dual rationale for integrating a gender lens into macroeconomic policy are its equality and efficiency dimensions. Where there is increasing recognition that problems of inequality cannot be resolved by trickle-down effects of economic growth, the concerns about gender inequality need to be built into the macroeconomic policy framework. Apart from the "social justice" and "human rights" dimensions, gender equality can benefit the economy through efficiency gains (Lahiri et al., 2002; Sharp, 2003). From an efficiency perspective, what is important is the social rate of return on investment in women, which can be shown in some cases to be greater than the corresponding rate for men (Elson, 1999). Gender budgeting, within a rights-based approach, is increasingly recognized as a tool to address gender discrimination (Elson, 2006). A rights-based approach, among other things, looks at the resource requirements (budgets) for human development. A "human rights" approach provides values against which to assess budgets; it assists in choosing between different budgetary and policy options and strengthens the demand for budget transparency and fiscal accountability. Gender budgeting is also based on the premise of ensuring transparency in the budgetary allocation for women, protecting these provisions from re-appropriation and thereby enhancing accountability ("voice").

Economic growth is often cited as an outcome of reducing gender inequality (SDG 5), which serves to close inefficient gender gaps in workforce participation, education, and health (Berik, 2006; Berik et al., 2009; Dollar & Gatti, 1999; Klasen, 1999, 2002; Seguino, 2008). Another motivation for SDG5 (gender equality) is its perceived potential to promote equitable development, distinct from economic growth. There are two facets to this motivation: at a basic level, women and girls tend to suffer greater disadvantages across a range of social and economic indicators, therefore alleviating these development disparities through gender-budgeting programmes has been seen as a valid development end in itself (Chakraborty et al., 2017). Secondly, policymakers and academics have long highlighted the value of gender equality as a precursor to, or tool for promoting, economic development more broadly (Chakraborty et al., 2017; Palmer, 1995; Sen, 2000; World Bank, 2011). Once the policy commitment is set, the success of these attempts becomes crucial for economic "institutions".

The Analytical Framework

The analytical framework of gender budgeting rests on the role of the government to design an ideal "mechanism design" for better gender equality outcomes. Intertemporally, the role of government has widened from the strict confinements of security, law and order functions of the State to redistributive justice and equity issues. There is an increasing recognition of the role of institutions in analysing the processes of growth and financing sustainable development goals (SDGs). From this perspective, the gender aware human development has become a function of fiscal policy.

Theoretically, an ideal mechanism design is based on the ability of a government to achieve simultaneously Pareto optimality, incentive compatibility (of what government provides and what citizens desire from the government) and a balanced budget. However, as Hurwicz (1952) in his work on mechanism design had rightly pointed out that the simultaneity of these three conditions is unattainable, leave alone the chances of any two of these conditions likely to be attainable.

The government, as a mechanism designer, at the outset, if aware of the set of policy priorities required for optimal outcomes can subsequently design mechanisms for achieving it. Unpacking the algorithms, researchers have analysed the existence of any "Wicksellian links" in the economy. The Wicksellian links suggest that the unit of tax paid by the citizens and the unit of satisfaction derived by the citizens from the public provisioning are interconnected. If not, the Wicksellian connection breaks. Empirical evidence suggests that the Wicksellian links in the context of emerging and developing economies are weak. This evidence is based on the empirical literature on tax evasions and non-compliance with taxes by the citizens. The citizens prefer to reveal their demand from public provisioning of goods "strategically" than "sincerely" to avoid paying taxes. When citizens reveal their preferences as more "strategic than sincere", the public financing of goods and services becomes difficult. The Lindahl–Wicksell mechanism had suggested an atomized taxation regime to break this policy uncertainty. These atomized taxes are also to solve the mechanism design issues. The Lindahl–Wicksell mechanism of "atomized taxes" works as follows—increase the tax rate for those who reveal a strong demand and decrease the tax rate for those who reveal a weak demand, so that in the course of time, the demand will increase from those who are taxed less and the demand will decrease from those who are taxed more and an equilibrium mechanism design can be theoretically attained. However, an atomized taxation regime cannot be an ideal mechanism design for financing gender equality goals. The moment a citizen reveals his/her preferences strategic than sincere—for instance, gender aware human development financing is of no priority—the public financing of this priority rise to a level of devastating dimension.

While these algorithms of mechanism design remained inconclusive, the narratives that have catalyzed the notion of institutionalizing gender budgeting are based on the premise that institutions are the "rules of the game" in a society and these are the humanly devised constraints that shape human interaction (North, 1991). Acemoglu and Robinson (2013) argued that institutions, and they alone, determine the prosperity of a nation. They emphasized the significance of "inclusive economic institutions" that enforce property rights and create a level playing field in a pluralistic manner. Gender budgeting from that perspective can be a transformative financing for gender equality (Chakraborty, 2016c). Maskin (2008) in his Nobel prize lecture "Mechanism Design: How to Implement Social Goals?" Narrated that mechanism design begins by identifying desired outcomes (goals)—where he asks whether economic institutions (mechanisms) could be designed to achieve social goals—if so, what forms would institutions take? This is quite contrary to the "positive" approach that usually macroeconomists prescribe which excludes gender development-conscious economic growth (Chakraborty, 2016c). The government is the mechanism designer which chooses the institution (procedure, mechanism or game) that determines outcome (gender equality).

The outcomes are context-dependent and depend on the choice and priorities of the government. Why explorations on the role of mechanism design (institutions, procedures and public policies) in analysing the "endemic social constructs" including patriarchy remain elusive? What makes gender budgeting compelling? Recall the debate set off by Amartya Sen when he claimed that millions of women were "missing". This is a human catastrophe. There is a need to analyze the role of public policy and institutions in correcting these blatantly oppressive prejudices that run deep in the society and results in female survival disadvantage, as well as the role of institutions in upholding the "right to life" for girl children and women (Chakraborty, 2016c).

Obvious things are often the most invisible. Surpassing the blatant reality, mainstream economists have always searched for "economic reasons" for integrating gender into macroeconomic policies for enhancing growth (Chakraborty, 2016c). On the other hand, economic growth per se does not gender equality outcomes. The relationship between gender equality and economic growth is an asymmetrical one (Kabeer & Natali, 2013). The dynamic interaction between the statistically invisible care economy segment of the economy, viz., the household and community production of non-marketed goods and services included as per the United Nations Statistical Division (UNSD) revisions in the Systems of National Accounts (SNA) 1993, and that of the market economy have marked the market-oriented foundations of engendering macroeconomic policies (Chakraborty, 2016c). These dynamics capture the intra-household intensity and allocation of time between the dual sets of economic activity. In recent years, "time deficits" in the invisible care economy due to the deficiency in public infrastructure investment and related public policies itself have become the prominent research agenda globally.

The macroeconomic policies for gender development—especially gender budgeting as "institutional reforms"—have started earning recognition. The government can announce a national finance law mandating that choice. Gender budgeting has been mandated by law in many countries including Mexico (Oaxaca), Korea and the Philippines. In Oaxaca, gender-disaggregated taxation policies were mandated by law. In Korea,

National Finance Law incorporated Articles on gender budgeting, as a Public Financial Management (PFM) tool (Chakraborty, 2016a). In the Philippines, gender budgeting was mandated by law to earmark a specific component of developmental budgets for gender development projects, which they referred to as Gender and Development (GAD) budgets. Budget Call Circulars have been used in several countries to make gender budgeting mandatory (Budlender, 2015).

An "ought-to-be" reforms package may be designed by the highest policymaking body with gender budgeting as one of the high policy priorities (Chakraborty, 2016c). Unpacking the social content of macroeconomic policies is pertinent for rapid economic growth. Right institutions and innovative tools should be adopted to strengthen the "gender lens" of public spending decisions and how gender differential outcomes of fiscal policy are measured. The role of the Ministry of Finance in owning such gender equity considerations from a fiscal policy perspective is significant. However, the uncertainties involved in fiscal innovation, the inability of the economic agents to clearly visualize the appropriate measures, data paucity, and the efficacy of the new institutional mechanisms to take it to logical outcomes were the formidable challenges posed to the gender-budgeting process (Chakraborty, 2016c).

While social mores cannot be fully transformed by fiscal fiats, a proactive mechanism design by the State is called for. Here, the crucial question that confronts one's mind is, "to design policy for what?"—for "economic growth" or for human development-conscious growth? (Chakraborty, 2016c).

Ex Ante and Ex Post Frameworks of Gender Budgeting

The analytical framework for preparing gender budgeting can be broken down into: (a) ex ante gender budgeting, in which the needs of the women are identified first and then incorporated into the budget and (b) ex post gender budgeting, in which the existing budget is analysed through a gender lens. Ex ante gender budgeting is articulated as the identification of gender needs in the planning process which is essential for the budgeting (Chakraborty, 2014). Ex ante instruments include gender-budget statements (e.g. in gender needs assessments) and policies such as budget allocations for specific sectors (Polzer et al., 2021). Governments employ concurrent policies and tools when they consider a gender perspective during their resource allocation, for example through programme-based budgeting or tracking the progress of gender spending. Ex post approaches include tools (e.g. spending reviews and gender audits) or focus on policy analyses (e.g. causes of gender gaps) (Polzer et al., 2021). Comprehensive gender-budgeting systems encompass all three stages of the budgeting process.

An ex post gender-budget analysis begins with the identification of three categories of public expenditure: (i) Expenditure specifically targeted to women and girls (100 per cent targeted for women); (ii) Pro-women allocations; which are the composite expenditure schemes with a women component (that is, a scale of 100 to 30—at least 30 per cent targeted for women); and (iii) Mainstream public expenditures that have gender-differential impacts (that is, a scale of 0–30). It is relatively easy to identify the specifically targeted programmes for women across ministries from the Expenditure Budget documents (Chakraborty, 2016a). But the challenge is that discerning what component of mainstream budget programmes has a "pro-women" or gender-equality impact is not easily done from simple perusal of the budget documents. The ex post gender budgeting can be extended to gender-disaggregated benefit incidence analysis. The public benefit incidence (BIA) analysis is one of the tools identified for gender budgeting. BIA is a relatively simple and practical method for estimating the distributional impact of public expenditure across different demographic and socio-economic groups. BIA can identify how well public services are targeted to certain groups in the population, across gender, income quintiles and geographical units (Austen et al., 2013; Budlender et al., 2002; Demery, 2000).

Apart from public expenditure incidence analysis, Elson (1999) described some other tools for conducting gender budgeting, which include gender-aware policy appraisal of macroeconomic strategy and Medium-Term Economic Policy Framework; gender-disaggregated beneficiary assessments; sex-disaggregated analysis of the impact of the budget on time use; gender-aware Medium-Term Economic Policy Framework; gender-aware Budget Statement; and tax incidence analysis. A gender-aware policy appraisal of the overall macroeconomic strategy and Medium-Term Economic Policy Framework depends on the macro-fiscal strategy and the sustainability of public debt. The sustainability of public debt is a condition where the real rate of interest is not greater than the real growth of the economy (Chakraborty, 2016b). If the fiscal consolidation path takes place through expenditure compression than through tax buoyancy, the human development related expenditure may decline. This expenditure compression path affects gender budgeting negatively.

The gender-disaggregated beneficiary assessment is a qualitative methodology by which the citizens are asked to assess how far fiscal policies are beneficial for them, as they perceive them through opinion polls, attitude surveys, group discussions or interviews. This participatory budget process offers inferences for redistribution and more budget accountability. The gender-disaggregated impact analysis of budget on time use is based on the realization that women contribute disproportionately larger amounts of their time to unpaid care economy activities. Therefore, the fiscal policies relate to tax credits for child care, parental leave, child benefits and single-parent allowances have positive impacts on the unpaid care economy. Women had to travel greater distances to collect fuel, and therefore integrating gender budgeting in energy sector by providing clean fuel to poor income households can impact positively their health status and time stress.

The gender-aware Medium-Term Economic Policy Framework is used to assess the impact of economic policies on women, including both fiscal and monetary policies. This is a useful tool in times of pandemic to assess the impact of economic stimulus packages on women and to design a medium-term strategy. Linking policy, planning and budgeting, the medium-term economic policy framework usually for a three-year rolling budget, describes a government's policy goals, explains the economic scenario within which those goals are being addressed, and focuses on the resource requirements. The integration of gender analysis into the medium-term budget process goes beyond impact analysis of economic policies, as it is linked to the principles of participatory budgeting.

A gender-budget statement is prepared by the government by applying a gender lens to the budget and identifying the intensity of the gender component in public expenditure. For instance, in India, Gender Budget Statements have been released since 2005–2006 including the specifically targeted programmes for women, and the gender components in mainstream spending. This is mandated through Budget Circular across countries. Gender budgeting is not confined to public expenditure analysis. It is also applicable to taxes at various levels of government and intergovernmental tax transfers—both conditional and unconditional fiscal transfers (Anand & Chakraborty, 2016; Chakraborty, 2021; Chakraborty & Singh, 2017; Stotsky, 2021). Global income taxes are typically a source of gender bias, in the countries where couples filing joint returns incur a greater tax liability than they would if they filed as individuals (Grown & Valodia, 2010). The indirect taxes may seem to be gender-neutral, however, they can have significant gender-differential impacts based on the household income and the consumption patterns (Chakraborty et al., 2010). Nature resource taxation can have gender-differential impacts. If a portion of natural resource taxes are not earmarked for the human development of the regions they are extracted from, it can accentuate inequalities.

The Structure

The book is organized into 11 chapters. Chapter 2 analyses how macroeconomic policy coherence is closely linked to achieving gender equality in the context of Asia Pacific. Specifically, the chapter attempts to identify the significant constraints in the macro policymaking to integrate gender perspectives. There is a transition in the macro policymaking from discretion to rules. Integrating gender perspectives within a rules-based framework is challenging. These constraints in the monetary and fiscal policies are analysed in the chapter. How policy tools can be used in the region to integrate "Leave No One Behind" (LNOB)? An inventory analysis of these policy imperatives is captured in the chapter.

Economic growth per se cannot capture the human development outcomes. Measuring gender-aware human development is challenging. Chapter 3 provides the measurement issues related to gender-aware human development outcomes and focusses on establishing the analytical links between macro-fiscal policy and the gender equality outcomes, in the context of Asia Pacific countries. It provides the macroeconomic channels through which these links are established.

The statistical invisibility of care economy work—especially the unpaid or unmonetized work in the household—is a matter of concern. Gender-budgeting frameworks provide significance to the efficiency and allocation of time spent in the care economy sector. Using Time Use Survey 2020 in India, Chapter 4 presents an analysis of gender-disaggregated time allocation under SNA (Systems of National Accounts) and Non-SNA. The chapter also provides an overview of how to use macro-fiscal policies—in particular the policies related to public infrastructure—to minimise the private costs. From a public finance perspective, gender-budgeting analysis often rests on the assumption that mainstream expenditures, such as public infrastructure, cannot be gender-partitioned. However, analysis in Chapter 4 reveals how a gender lens can be applied to infrastructure investment decisions.

Intergovernmental fiscal transfers (IGFT) are, in theory, neither good nor bad for tackling gender inequalities. The asymmetry in revenue and expenditure assignments leads to vertical and horizontal imbalances in fiscal federalism. Chapter 5 analyses the plausibility of incorporating gender criteria into the tax transfers which are designed to redress such vertical and horizontal imbalances.

The principle of subsidiarity—which emphasises that the policy decisions can be efficiently taken at a level of government closest to the people—is crucial for conducting gender budgeting. Chapter 6 discusses selected local level fiscal decentralisation and gender-budgeting experiments. The feminization of local governance at the third tier may alter the public expenditure decisions—through gender-budgeting experiments—that correspond more closely to the revealed preferences of women.

Gender budgeting is a fiscal innovation. A fiscal innovation encompasses four distinct phases—model building and knowledge networking, setting up institutional mechanisms, strengthening capacity building and ensuring accountability mechanisms. The gender-budgeting efforts in the Asia-Pacific, within the Public Financial Management frameworks, are captured in Chapter 7.

The Ministry of Finance played a significant role in the sustainability of gender-budgeting experiments. India is a leading example of gender budgeting, integrating gender budgeting in Budget Circulars, Expenditure Budgets, and the Outcome Budget (Stotsky, 2021; UNDP, 2010). Chapter 8 reveals the path of gender budgeting in India covering those attempts in public expenditure, taxation and intergovernmental fiscal transfers. The National Institute of Public Finance and Policy (NIPFP), an independent research institute of the Ministry of Finance—the pioneer in gender budgeting in India—provided the analytical matrices to conduct gender budgeting in national and subnational governments of India.

Gender budgeting is not a technocratic exercise. It has political economy contexts. Chapter 9 analyses the political economy of gender budgeting using Union Government 2021–2022 data through a gender lens, incorporating fiscal marksmanship analysis. Fiscal marksmanship analysis captures the extent of errors in budgetary forecasting.

Chapter 10 analyses the distributional impact of public expenditure across income quintiles on women, based on public expenditure benefit incidence analysis. The International Classification of Diseases (ICD) codes are used to map the National Sample Survey 2019 data on health sector incidence across income quintiles, gender and geography. Chapter 11 concludes and suggests the way forward.

REFERENCES

Acemoglu, D., & Robinson, J. A. (2013). Economics versus politics: Pitfalls of policy advice. *Journal of Economic Perspectives, 27*(2), 173–192.

Aguiar, M., & Gopinath, G. (2007). Emerging market business cycles: The cycle is the trend. *Journal of Political Economy, 115*(1), 69–102.

Anand, A., & Chakraborty, L. (2016). *Engendering' intergovernmental transfers: Is there a case for gender-sensitive horizontal fiscal equalization?* (Working Paper 874). The Levy Economics Institute of Bard College.

Austen, S., Costa, M., Sharp, R., et al. (2013). Expenditure incidence analysis: A gender-responsive budgeting tool for educational expenditure in Timor–Leste? *Feminist Economics, 19*(4), 1–24.

Berik, G. (2006). *Growth with gender inequity: Another look at east Asian development.* (Working Paper 2006_03). University of Utah, Department of Economics, 26.

Berik, G., Yana van der Meulen, R., & Stephanie, S. (2009). Feminist economics of inequality, development, and growth. *Feminist Economics, 15*, 1–33.

Blanchard, O. (2019). Public debt and low interest rates. *American Economic Review, 109*(4), 1197–1229.

Budlender, D. (2015). Budget call circulars and gender budget statements in the Asia Pacific: A review. UN Women.

Budlender, D., Elson, D., Hewitt, G., & Mukhopadhyay, T. (2002). *Gender budgets make cents. Understanding gender responsive budgets.* Commonwealth Secretariat/London.

Çağatay, N., Elson, D., & Grow, C. (1995). Introduction. *World Development, 23*(11), 1827–1836.

Catagay, N., et al. (2000). *Budgets as if people mattered: Democratizing macroeconomic policies.* UNDP/SEPED.

Chakraborty, L. (2014). *Gender budgeting, as fiscal innovation.* (Working Paper No. 797). Levy Economics Institute of Bard College.

Chakraborty, L. (2016a). *Asia: A survey of gender budgeting experiences* (International Monetary Fund Working Paper 16/150). IMF.

Chakraborty, L. (2016b). *Fiscal consolidation, budget deficits and macroeconomy: monetary-fiscal linkages.* Sage Publications.

Chakraborty, L. (2016c). *Gender budgeting as mechanism design*, NIPFP blog.

Chakraborty, L. (2021). *Indian fiscal federalism at the crossroads: Some reflections*, (Working Paper 937), Levy Economics Institute of Bard College.

Chakraborty, L. (2022). *Union budget 2022: Fiscal-monetary interface and green bonds*, 57(13), Economic and Political Weekly.

Chakraborty, L., & Singh, Y. (2017). *Fiscal policy, as the employer of last resort: The gender differential impacts of MGNREGA in India*, (Working Paper No. 210). National Institute of Public Finance and Policy.

Chakraborty, L. S., & Harikrishnan, S. (2022). *COVID-19 and fiscal-monetary policy coordination: Empirical evidence from India* (Working Paper 1002). Levy Economics Institute of Bard College.

Chakraborty, L., Marian, I., & Yadawendra, S. (2017). *Effectiveness of gender budgeting on gender equality outcomes and fiscal space: Evidence from Asia Pacific*. (GRoW Research Paper WP 2017-09). McGill University.

Chakraborty, P., Chakraborty, L., Karmakar, K., & Kapila, S. M. (2010). *Gender equality and taxation in India: An unequal burden?* In C. Grown, & I. Valodia (Eds.), Taxation and gender equity: A comparative analysis of direct and indirect taxes in developing and developed countries (pp. 94–118). Routledge.

Demery, L. (2000). *Benefit incidence: A practitioner's guide*. Poverty and Social Development Group. The World Bank.

Dollar, D., & Gatti, R. (1999). *Gender inequality, income, and growth: Are good times good for women?* World Bank Policy Research Report on Gender and Development, (Working Paper Series 1). World Bank.

Elson, D. (1999). *Commonwealth gender responsive budget initiative: Background papers*. The Commonwealth Secretariat.

Elson, D. (2000). *Progress of the World's women 2000*. UNIFEM Biennial Report. United Nations Development Fund for Women.

Elson, D. (2006). *Budgeting for women's rights: Monitoring government budgets for compliance with CEDAW*. UNIFEM.

Elson, D., & Cagatay, N. (2000). The social content of macropolicies. *World Development, 28*(7), 1347–1364.

Grown, C., & Valodia, I. (Eds.). (2010). Taxation and gender equity: A comparative analysis of direct and indirect taxes in developing and developed countries. Routledge.

Hurwicz, L. 1952. *A criterion for decision making under uncertainty*. Technical Report, 355. Cowles Commission.

Kabeer, N., & Natali, L. (2013). *Gender equality and economic growth: Is there a winwin?* (IDS Working Paper No. 417). Institute of Development Studies.

Klasen, S. (1999). *Does gender inequality reduce growth and development? Evidence from cross-country regressions*. World Bank Policy Research Report on Gender and Development. World Bank.

Klasen, S. (2002). Low schooling for girls, slower growth for all? Cross-country evidence on the effect of gender inequality in education on economic development. *World Bank Economic Review, 16*(3), 345–373.

Kolovich, L. (Ed.). (2018). *Fiscal policies and gender equality*, IMF.
Lahiri, A., Lekha, S. C., & Bhattacharya, P. N. (2002). *Gender diagnosis and budgeting in India*. National Institute of Public Finance and Policy.
Maskin, E. (2008). *Mechanism design: How to implement social goals*. Les Prix Nobel 2007. 296–307.
North, D. C. (1991). Institutions. *Journal of Economic Perspectives*, 5(1), 97–112.
Palmer. (1995). Public finance from a gender perspective. *World Development*, 23(11), 1981–1986.
Polzer, T., Isabella, M. N., & Johann, S. (2021, September 13). *A review of academic studies on gender budgeting*, IMF Blog.
Sayeh, A., Jiro, H., Carolina, R., & Vincent, T. (2021). *Engendering the recovery: Budgeting with women in mind*, IMF Blog, International Monetary Fund.
Seguino, S. (2008). "*Gender, distribution, and balance of payments constrained growth in developing countries.*" PERI Working Paper 133. Political Economy Research Institute.
Sen, G. (2000). Gender mainstreaming in finance ministries. *World Development* 28/7.
Sharp, R. (2003). *Budgeting for equity: Gender budgeting initiatives within a framework of performance oriented budgeting*. UNIFEM.
Stiglitz, J., & Rasheed, H. (2020, June 8). Which economic stimulus works? *Project Syndicate*.
Stotsky, J. G. (2016). *Gender budgeting: Fiscal context and overview of current outcomes*. (Working Paper 16/149). International Monetary Fund.
Stotsky, J. G. (2021). *Using fiscal policy and public financial management to promote gender equality*. Routledge Studies in Gender and Economics.
Roubini, N. (2022, February 25). *Russia's war and global economy. Project Syndicate*.
United Nations Development Programme (UNDP). (2010). *Power, voice and rights: A turning point for gender equality in Asia and the Pacific*. Macmillan
World Bank. (2011). *Gender equality and development*. World Development Report. World Bank

CHAPTER 2

Macroeconomic Policy Coherence for Gender Equality in Asia-Pacific

Integrating gender budgeting in the rules-based policy space is challenging, especially when the macroeconomic policy framework itself is not flexible to integrate specific policy tools. Macroeconomic policy management is a significant element for delivering the Sustainable Development Goals (SDGs). It has been increasingly recognized as an important core strategy in the implementation of the SDG 2030 Agenda. Against this backdrop of COVID-19 pandemic, fiscal and monetary policy stimulus packages are designed by governments and central banks for economic growth recovery. The livelihood crisis is addressed through specific components in the fiscal stimulus packages including food security measures, strengthening social infrastructure, social protection, and the employment policies (Chakraborty et al., 2021). The liquidity infusion, maintaining status quo policy rates, and other regulatory measures are the major policy measures taken up by the central banks. The lack of proper fiscal and monetary policy coordination has also resulted in suboptimal policy outcomes (Chakraborty, 2021a, 2021b, 2021c, 2021d, 2021e; Chakraborty et al., 2021; Kaur et al., 2021; Stigliz & Rashid, 2020). The lockdown strategy without adequate emphasis to the principle of subsidiary through providing more powers to the lower tiers of government turned out to be partial in tackling the dual crisis of health and macroeconomic crisis. The fiscal space determined the size of the pandemic economic stimulus and given the constraints, the pandemic

© The Author(s), under exclusive license to Springer Nature Singapore Pte Ltd. 2022
L. S. Chakraborty, *Fiscal Policy for Sustainable Development in Asia-Pacific*, https://doi.org/10.1007/978-981-19-3281-6_2

packages have not been enough to tackle the economic recession and livelihood crisis.

This chapter analyses how macroeconomic policymaking—monetary, fiscal, and structural reforms—can be improved so as to contribute to the 2030 Agenda. Specifically, the chapter attempts to identify the significant constraints of the macro policymaking in the region and identify specific tools to understand how macro policies relate to the 2030 Agenda integrating the gender equality concerns. The SDGs were officially adopted by the member nations at the UN Summit in New York in September 2015. The SDGs are more ambitious than expiring MDGs as "leave no one behind" is the strategy adopted by the SDGs, by focusing on five key elements: people, planet, peace, prosperity, and partnership. There are 17 SDGs and 169 targets. Two global meetings need special mention in this context. One is the Addis Ababa Action Agenda on sustainable financing strategy and second the UN Climate Summit in Paris on a global agreement on climate change commitments. The SDGs hold the view that development needs to be economically, socially and environmentally sustainable. The commitment to the SDGs is made by each country at two levels: internal and external. The internal commitment aims to create enabling macroeconomic environment and robust sustainable growth. The external commitment is stability in trade and financial flows, and cooperation among countries to ensure a coherent macroeconomic policy framework.

Specifically, the chapter focusses on the role of fiscal policy, to address the SDGs. The analysis carries out an overview of the focus of fiscal policy in Asia-Pacific and a normative assessment of what fiscal policy "ought to be" (normative) in achieving SDGs using a methodology to reach SDGs. It also analyses how structural and regulatory policies can contribute to achieving the SDG agenda. The role of monetary policy towards the implementation of the 2030 Agenda—incorporating the elements of prices, unemployment, and assets—is discussed and a critical analysis of monetary policy stance in the region is undertaken, conducive or not for SDGs. The empirical evidence suggests that economic growth does not translate into SDG attainment and therefore we need to identify the critical gaps and the complementary fiscal and monetary policies required to improve development outcomes.

Fiscal Policy Stance

SDGs require large public investments to achieve the goals by 2030. To ensure that, the countries require fiscal sustainability. However, a number of countries in the region have huge fiscal deficits, with fiscal consolidation measures on board. Fiscal consolidation is the rules-based policy initiative in the region where the fiscal deficit to GDP ratio is restricted to 3 per cent of GDP. Given the rule-based fiscal dynamics, which has led to the transition in the fiscal policy from discretion to rules, attaining SDGs would be a major challenge. Most countries, including China, Indonesia, the Republic of Korea, and the Russian Federation, had wider fiscal deficits or narrower surpluses and slower economic growth in the period 2014–2016 compared with the period 2011–2013, while India and Pakistan had higher economic growth and smaller fiscal deficits (UNESCAP, 2017). However, Chakraborty et al. (2021) revealed that many countries in the region have a high public debt-GDP ratio during the time of pandemic and a matter of concern if it is unaccompanied by high economic growth. As long as the real rate of interest (r) is below real rate of growth of economy (g), it is plausible to run primary deficits. Indeed the use of public debt needs to be substantiated. If the high public debt is used for public infrastructure investment or for reducing the output gap, high public debt is desirable. In terms of debt sustainability, $r > g$ is the point where debt becomes unsustainable and it can affect a country in meeting SDGs. In Sri Lanka, though debt-GDP ratio is above 100, $r < g$ provides them leverage to engage in human development financing. In the South Asian region, Sri Lanka stands out in human development achievements irrespective of the fact that it is a low-income country.

The impact of deficits on economic growth has been captured in two ways, one through the link between fiscal stance and output gap to arrive at whether fiscal policy is countercyclical (Tanzi, 2016), which is a short-run fiscal consolidation exercise and the other link is through analysing the impact of the deficit on crucial macroeconomic variables including the rate of interest, private corporate investment (Chakraborty, 2016b). It is often debated that rule-based fiscal consolidation measures have provided Asia-Pacific region strong macroeconomic fundamentals. However, this argument is correct only if there is significant macroeconomic channels operating from fiscal deficit to other fundamental variables like rate of interest, private investment, rate of inflation and capital flows. Empirical evidence is mixed, if deficit causes rise in real interest rates and there are strong fiscal-monetary linkages in the region (Chakraborty, 2016a, 2016b). The real interest rates are mostly determined significantly by inflationary expectations, not deficits. This is especially true in the context when Central Banks in the region increasingly moving towards rule-based inflation targeting framework. Financial crowding out through pre-emption of resources for financing deficits and in turn restricts the loanable funds available to private sector. However, empirical evidence revealed that public investment crowds-in private corporate investment (Vinod et al., 2020).

If the impact of deficit is increasingly nil in worsening the macroeconomic fundamentals, the argument that fiscal prudence through deficit control mechanisms is essential for sustainable growth in the region fails. This may be confirmed looking into the patterns of fiscal policy stance in the region, especially during negative shocks like the global financial crisis of 2007/08. It is the fiscal re-dominance that helped the region to cope with the global financial crisis through economic stimulus packages than the fiscal prudence of restrictive public spending.

Enhancing the role of fiscal policy stance for inclusive policies for SDGs may or may not have trade-offs with fiscal sustainability. Over the years, the fiscal policy stance in Asia-Pacific is to sustain economic growth through public infrastructure investment and human capital formation. This leads to the question what "ought to be" the role of the State in the region to maintain and achieve the SDGs—a "security state" or a "development state" (Horst et al., 2017). In the context of G20 countries, it has been revealed that public spending on innovation and human capital formation has more impact on economic growth (Horst et al., 2017). Other studies have concluded that public spending on defence does not ensure peace, security and stability (SIPRI, 2017).

Public spending in Asia-Pacific is lower than in advanced economies. This makes it compelling to analyse whether strict adherence to fiscal rules is for fiscal prudence in revenue/current expenditure or has it eroded the capital formation in the region which in turn has severe long-term growth consequences. If fiscal prudence is achieved through less or no spending on capital formation, the fiscal consolidation may result in stagnation in economic growth. The path of fiscal consolidation may be as important as the target of fiscal consolidation. If the targets are achieved through cuts in capital spending, fiscal responsibility legislation to control the deficit might lead to adverse macroeconomic consequences.

Phasing out revenue deficit (revenue deficit is revenue expenditure minus revenue receipts. It is also referred to as current deficit in fiscal literature) is yet another significant tool of fiscal consolidation. Early warning signals need to be provided to the Asia-Pacific region to design their fiscal consolidation packages judiciously. These policy articulations have direct consequences for achieving SDGs. Fiscal stance and output gap links need to be empirically analysed to understand whether the fiscal policy is countercyclical or pro-cyclical (Chakraborty & Chakraborty, 2006; Chakraborty & Kaur, 2020). Restrictive macroeconomic policies might result in constrained fiscal space to sustainably finance the implementation of the SDGs. Empirical analysis showed that expansion in fiscal space is more likely to be sustainable when public spending finances investment rather than consumption (Roy & Heuty, 2009).

Economic growth and debt sustainability are the two significant priorities of the fiscal policy regime in Asia-Pacific. If the region has to frame the fiscal policy for SDGs, the policies may have to move forward from economic growth paradigms and fiscal rule-based policy prescriptions. Asia-Pacific countries need sustained economic growth to reach advanced economies, but if growth is at the cost of inclusiveness, SDGs cannot be met because the majority of people in the region live in poverty. It is also relevant to analyse the structural transformation, along with the aggregate economic growth. What kind of structural transformation that promotes economic growth and employment is an empirical question, specific to country-contexts. Decent jobs are a matter of urgent concern, especially when informal employment accounts for about 70 per cent of all jobs in Sri Lanka, almost 90 per cent in Bangladesh, India, and Pakistan, and up to 95 per cent in Nepal (ILO, 2015).

There is also a significant empirical link between governance and the ability of the countries to raise tax revenue. The reasons may be corruption in tax collection and low tax morale due to perceived governance deficits. Considering the relationship between governance and social development, it has been shown that the efficiency of the public provisioning of health and education services is affected by governance performance, particularly through corruption and ineffective bureaucracy (ESCAP). Governance is a crucial determinant in reducing the income and development gap in Cambodia, Lao People's Democratic Republic, Myanmar, and Vietnam (CLMV) countries, along with other factors such as the availability and quality of physical capital, the availability of decent, skilled and productive jobs, strong macroeconomic fundamentals, wage and social protection systems, or effectiveness of the fiscal policy. From the SDGs perspective, it has been found that ineffective governance and weak institutions can exacerbate income inequality.

On fiscal policy, the issues are related to what rules governments should follow, e.g. should they have a maximum level of fiscal deficit, debt-to-GDP or tax-to-GDP? The consensus among the macro policymakers was that there is no golden rule. For instance, to analyse fiscal deficit issues, besides quantity, governments should also consider quality. There was no consensus on which "deficit" needed to be targeted to remain fiscally prudent—whether revenue deficit, primary deficit (fiscal deficit minus interest payments), or fiscal deficit. As the revenue generation of various nations is predominantly hydroelectric power generation among the LDCs in the region, it may also be worth exploring the Public Sector Borrowing Requirement (PSBR) to measure the deficits as it includes the intra-public sector budgetary transactions in addition to the governmental budgetary transactions.

In terms of fiscal policy, policy deliberations among countries were about using progressive taxation systems and having social security and safety nets—under several formats. Inequality, as measured by the Gini coefficient, is often a problem. Some countries such as Bhutan have education and healthfully subsidized, which is particularly good because it favours inclusiveness. In Bangladesh, the financing required to achieve the SDGs was estimated at 1 trillion USD. Then it was studied how much could be contributed by the different stakeholders. Once the financing gap was identified, tapping capital markets and local currency bonds is expected. The country's strategy is to create an enabling environment where finance can be mobilized, both in local and international currency, both by national and foreign actors. The Universal Basic Income (UBI) may be another option. However, as the capacity of health and education infrastructure is poor in many countries in the region, the UBI may not be enough to achieve the intended results.

Effective Fiscal Management and Governance

A global governance arrangement and regulatory framework is required to make sure that foreign investment promotes equality and sustainability as well as economic growth across geopolitical entities. A global governance arrangement and regulatory framework is required to make sure that foreign investment promotes equality and sustainability as well as economic growth across geopolitical entities. A transparent and equitable tax system is a prerequisite for adequate revenue mobilization to meet SDGs. The Panama Papers released in April 2016 revealed 214,488 offshore tax havens, created through tax avoidance. Reforms are required to track illicit financial flows and flaws in the global financial architecture.

The introduction of GST in India is expected to bring transparency into the system as tax invoices are required to redeem tax credit and this in turn is expected to prevent tax avoidance, and avoid cascading effects of multiple taxation at various levels of inputs. There is a growing recognition towards domestic resource mobilization and fiscal self-reliance to achieve SDGs. Fiscal consolidation through enhanced tax buoyancy is better than cuts in expenditure. A few countries have introduced innovative taxes, for instance, carbon tax, which could be an additional source of financing SDGs.

Inequalities in Fiscal Policy

Monitoring outcomes of public expenditure is equally significant as designing public expenditure policies. The public expenditure benefit incidence analysis (BIA) across categories of gender, geography, and social groups can capture the distributional impacts of public spending. The public expenditure BIA is based on two factors: unit costs and unit utilized. The unit costs are prepared from budgets, while unit utilized data is collected from sectoral National Sample Surveys. The BIA quintile wise revealed that in India and in the Philippines, the poor (q1) depend on public provisioning of health care and education. It can be technically analysed using concentration curves of BIA, whether the public spending on education and/or health care is pro-poor. The public spending BIA deciphered that the access and utilization of public spending are regressive in the Philippines and India, with gender-differentiated patterns while in Sri Lanka a study showed gender parity in the utilization of public provisioning across sectors. These empirical evidences showed that unless governance and implementation issues are taken care of, a well-designed public spending system can be regressive—and therefore continue making it difficult to attain the SDGs. Inequalities in fiscal policy incidence can be captured through BIA. We will revisit this in Chapter 10.

Higher budgetary allocation per se does not ensure higher spending. There can be budget forecast errors or unspent money which in turn affects the outcomes. Capturing this deviation or errors between budget estimates and actual spending is called "fiscal marksmanship analysis". The analysis can determine whether these deviations or errors are random or happened due to some policymaking bias. Fiscal marksmanship is the accuracy of budgetary forecasting. This can be one important piece of such information the rational agents must consider in forming expectations. Empirical studies have used Theil's inequality coefficient (U) based on mean square prediction error, to estimate the magnitude and sources of budgetary forecast errors. In the context of India, the analysis revealed that neither revenue nor expenditure forecasts uphold rational expectations (Chakraborty & Sinha, 2018). It was also revealed that the capital budget revealed more forecast errors than the revenue budget (Chakraborty & Sinha, 2018; Chakraborty et al., 2020c; Nitin & Roy, 2016). If the proportion of error due to random variation is significantly higher, it reflects that these errors have beyond the control of the forecaster or the macro policymaker. In India, empirical studies showed that errors due to policymaker's bias have been negligible. Fiscal marksmanship is conducted at the aggregate revenue and expenditure categories. From the SDGs perspective, sectoral fiscal marksmanship analysis is highly relevant, and therefore a matter for future macroeconomic policy research in the region.

Linking Resources to Results: Outcome Budgets

Several countries in the region have undertaken fiscal reforms to promote efficient fiscal management and fiscal sustainability. These initiatives include Fiscal Councils, Medium Term Fiscal Framework (MTFF), accrual accounting, and outcome budgets. Fiscal Councils are autonomous public institutions aimed at strengthening commitments to sustainable public finances through various functions, including public assessments of fiscal plans and performance, and the evaluation or provision of macroeconomic and budgetary forecasts. Medium-term Expenditure Framework Statement is a statement presented to the Parliament, which outlines a three-year rolling target for the expenditure indicators with the specification of underlying assumptions and risks involved. Accrual accounting is an accounting method that measures performance regardless of when cash transactions occur. Outcome budgets aim to measure and control the expenses of concerned ministries to introduce effectiveness in the public expenditure. These fiscal reforms aim to improve the performance, efficiency and prioritization of public spending by converging national and line ministry's outcomes with programmes and budgetary resources through integrating planning, budgeting, and auditing. SDGs are integrated in this processes or not in these countries is a matter of concern.

There is a growing recognition that fiscal policy can affect household dynamics, for instance, division of labour by supporting initiatives that reduce the burden of women in unpaid care work. Examples of such government intervention are improved infrastructure in the water sector, rural electrification, sanitation services, and better transport infrastructure. The public infrastructure deficit in rural areas may deepen rural poverty due to the time allocation across gender skewed towards more unpaid work, which is time otherwise available for income earning market economy activities. Public investment in infrastructure, like water and fuel, can also have positive social externalities in terms of educating the girl child and improving the health and nutritional aspects of the household (Chakraborty, 2008). There can be a link between deterioration in infrastructure and rural poverty.

Raghabendra and Duflo (2001) analysed whether feminization of governance alters public expenditure decisions favouring women's preferences and needs. They measured the impact of the feminization of governance at the local level on the outcomes of decentralization with data collected from a survey of all investments in local public goods made by the village councils in one district in West Bengal. They found that women leaders of village councils invest more in infrastructure that is relevant to the needs of rural women (like drinking water, fuel, and roads) and that village women are more likely to participate in the policymaking process if the leader of their village council is a woman (Chakraborty, 2010). Stern (2002) highlighted their inferences that placing women in local level governance can change the expenditure decisions of the local bodies and, in turn, change the types of public-good investments at the local level to correspond more to the revealed preferences (voice) by women.

In terms of fiscal policies to redress poverty, the aspects of time poverty are often surpassed. An individual is time poor if he/she is working long hours and is also monetary poor, or would fall into monetary poverty if he/she were to reduce his/her working hours below a given time poverty line. Time poverty affects income poverty. Fiscal policies designed to redress income poverty can be partial if they do not take into account the aspects of time poverty. This policy discussion has a gender dimension, as women are time poor, and fiscal policies designed for pro-poor measures need to incorporate the time allocation aspects across gender (Chakraborty, 2014a, 2014b, 2016a; Chakraborty et al., 2020a).

Using time use statistics of water revealed that the incidence is significantly higher for girls and women in both rural and urban areas, which, in turn, points to the deficiency in adequate infrastructure in water and sanitation (Chakraborty, 2008). It has significant fiscal policy implications, as easy accessibility to drinking water facilities might lead to an increase in school enrolment, particularly for girls, by reducing the time utilized for fetching water. The time budget statistics enable the identification of the complementary fiscal services required for better gender-sensitive human development.

In fiscal federalism, SDG commitments cannot be confined just to the national governments. There is a growing recognition of the role of intergovernmental fiscal transfers (IGFT) in SDGs to integrate climate change and disaster management. However, there are relatively a few attempts to translate the financial devolution commitments into SDG commitments. This financial devolution refers to intra-country arrangements, not inter-country arrangements. This fiscal devolution refers to the flow of funds from the upper government to lower tiers of government, which is also referred to as Inter-governmental fiscal transfers (IGFT). For instance, the Fourteenth and Fifteenth Finance Commissions in India have incorporated climate change variable as one of the criteria for devolution of funds. This is a radical approach because the criteria of devolution across countries in the region are more or less confined to fiscal and growth variables. Variables relating to natural disasters also form part of fiscal devolution, as an exogenous shock at the subnational government levels, and usually, the disaster management devolution is granted through specific transfers than through unconditional formula-linked fiscal transfers. This opens a significant debate of integrating human development-related variables in fiscal devolution. As another example, Chakraborty (2010) has argued for integrating gender criteria in IGFT.

Normative Framework and Methodology to Analyse the Fiscal Policy for Gender Equality

Sen's Capability Approach may provide an analytical framework to build a normative framework and methodology to analyse the fiscal policy for SDGs. Such frameworks were used by Meghnad Desai in his Discussion paper at the London School of Economics, in integrating poverty and inequality variables in "ought to be" macro policies using Sen's framework and methodology. It is plausible to adopt this normative framework to integrate SDGs into the macro policy framework (Chakraborty, 2020).

In terms of Sen's capability approach, there are three crucial layers, which need interpretation in the context of SDGs: capabilities, functioning, and commodities. Capability Approach has been central to the Human Development Reports series (HDRs) launched by UNDP in 1990s by Sen's close associate, the late Mahbub ul Haq, and has subsequently influenced policy at World Bank during the Wolfensohn era (Gasper, 2002). It provided a channel for an alternative economic development thinking, which goes beyond the undue emphasis on economic growth as in the economic planning of the 1970s and its trickling-down effects. It revealed that GDP (economic growth) was never suited to be a measure of well-being as it conceals extreme deprivation for large parts of the population. The first step of the capability approach is to propose a list of basic capabilities relates to 17 SDGs. Basic capabilities can be a set of capabilities that should have only a few elements and this set is common for all individuals. These capabilities can be the capability to stay alive and live long, the capability to lead a healthy life, the capability to have the knowledge, the capability to have social interaction, etc., which are closely linked to SDGs. The second step would be to gather relevant information on the *functioning of different socio-economic variables*, that are observable data. In this step of listing the functionings, the data needs to be incorporated in terms of SDG targets. The third step is to estimate the optimal *commodity space*, especially the fiscal and monetary policy stance in terms of SDGs, which is necessary to be at the individual's command to match commodity characteristics and capability requirements and then analyse the actual commodity space to identify the gaps.

Monetary Policy Stance

Globally there is a growing recognition about how to address the challenges of existing macroeconomic thinking and policymaking—both fiscal and monetary policies—including the issues related to inflation, unemployment, rising inequality, stagnating productivity, and unresponsiveness of long-term interest rates to rising public debt, among others (Chakraborty et al., 2021).

Blanchard and Summers (2017) highlighted the use of monetary and fiscal policy tools to reduce risks and react to adverse shocks through stabilization measures. They have also argued for active financial regulation and macro-prudential policy measures to reduce inequalities. Bernanke (2017) in a paper titled "Monetary policy in a new era" has highlighted that Central Bankers are looking forward to an era of relative financial and economic stability in which growth and distribution—growth and inequality—the issues that are the "not primarily" the province of Central bankers, but how monetary policy can meet these challenges of growth and rising inequalities. Furman (2017) in his paper titled "Should policymakers care whether inequality is helpful or harmful for growth?" argued that high levels of inequality can make sustained growth impossible or even cause recessions. He argued that exogenously higher levels of inequality result in lower longer-run growth rates and policy coordination is required to address this. This has direct policy inferences for integrating SDGs in macroeconomic policies to reduce widening inequalities. Furman (2017) further argued that equal weight to $1 added to the income of a poor person or a billionaire is misplaced, and most social welfare functions would place more weight on the bottom than on the top. Therefore, the macroeconomic policies—monetary and fiscal policies—that reduce inequality while increasing growth are clearly worth prioritizing.

Against this backdrop, the calibration of regulatory frameworks, both discretion and rules in the financial system, requires reforms. The monetary and financial system are dynamic and adaptive to address the question of inequalities. The distributional effects of many policies are orders of magnitudes larger than the growth effects (Furman, 2017). This section would be focusing on different targets (prices, unemployment, assets) that the Asia-Pacific region has been applying in the monetary policy stance and collating the evidence of these developments in the Central Bank's perspectives of monetary policy targets in the region.

The role of monetary policy is primarily price stability, credit control, financial inclusion, and debt management. In other words, the objectives of central banks are maintenance of price and exchange rate stability and curbing inflationary pressures. The emerging market economies in Asia have increasingly adopted monetary policy strategies to establish price stability, especially after the global financial crisis (Filardo & Genberg, 2010). The countries have adopted inflation targeting approaches to peg their policy rates based on the nominal anchor. Inflation targeting has been accepted by advanced countries as the superior framework of monetary policy (Bernanke et al., 1999).

Most countries follow a specific monetary policy regime, to provide an institutional structure for the monetary policy stance. This regime also decides on the tools of the monetary policy and the decisions to be communicated clearly to the people. The basic monetary regimes include monetary targeting, exchange rate targeting, a regime with inflation targeting, and a regime with an "implicit" nominal anchor. A multiple indicator approach is also followed by many Central Banks. In the monetary targeting regime, the monetary aggregates are targeted. The growth of chosen monetary aggregate—money supply—is closely watched in this regime. This is based on the assumption that in the long term, the rate of change in prices (inflation) is affected by the money supply. The choice of selecting a desirable monetary aggregate is with the specific country. However, over the years, Central Banks have realized that digitization, financial innovation, and financial liberalization have weakened the relationship between monetary aggregates and price changes.

The Central Bank announces an inflation "target" under the inflation targeting regime, and frames policy relates to achieving this target. Inflationary expectations form a crucial determinant of this regime. In many countries, expectations surveys are carried out to arrive at inflationary expectations. This regime requires wider information than just information on monetary aggregates and exchange rates. This regime requires information about employment, labour markets, the output gap (the deviation of actual output from the potential output), nominal and real interest rates, fiscal variables, and the nominal and real exchange rates. Each country articulates their policy rates, inflationary expectations and the "target" of inflation differently.

Exchange rate targeting focusses on nominal exchange rate stability pegging to a currency of an "anchor" country through FOREX interventions or interest rate differentials. This regime thus "imports" price stability from the anchor country. The exchange regime requires a sufficient level of international reserves and a macroeconomic policy which ensures minimum inflation differentials between the country and the anchor country, and a favourable Terms of Trade and competitiveness and political stability. The legal and institutional framework is important for the exchange rate regime to function without uncertainties. The autonomy of monetary policy is constrained to a great extent under the exchange rate regime. A regime with an implicit nominal anchor is targeting a variable without it being announced explicitly by the Central Bank. The credibility of Central Bank is highly significant for arriving at "implicit" nominal anchor, internally by the monetary policymakers. The Central bank internally makes the desirable changes in inflationary expectations to achieve the price stability, without announcing it publically, using explicit targets.

Apart from inflation targeting regime, monetary policy has several other regimes as mentioned above. In most of the Asian countries, an eclectic policy regime is also framed in case of monetary policy. Inflation targeting, is usually misunderstood as just targeting the rate of inflation as an objective of economic policy. In reality, inflation targeting includes five steps. One, the setting a numerical target range for the rate of (price) inflation, usually Central Bank in coordination with the Government. Two, the use of monetary policy as the key policy instrument to achieve the target, with monetary policy pegging the policy rate incorporating inflation expectations. Three, the operation of monetary policy is in the hands of an "independent" Central Bank, unless an agreement between Central Bank and the Government is framed for a Monetary Policy Framework. Four, the monetary policy is only concerned with price stability. Usually, the other plausible effects of monetary policy on other policy objectives including economic growth are ignored. Chakraborty (2021e) narrates the policy uncertainty about interest rates—against the backdrop of a plausible decision by US Fed to raise the interest rates—whether to maintain the status quo to protect growth recovery or to raise the rates to pre-empt a capital flight.

Yet another significant issue is to distinguish between goal independence and operational independence. What independence do central banks seek? In India, Monetary Policy Committee (MPC) was set up in 2016 for operational independence. In the Report of Currency and Finance published by the Reserve Bank of India in 2021, empirical evidence was provided in favour of a new monetary policy framework in providing price stability (RBI, 2021). It is often argued that it is more relevant for the government to set a goal of price stability and pursue the central bank towards this goal by independently setting the operations and instruments. The instrument independence enables the central bank to be forward-looking. Yet another limitation of undertaking monetary policy within committees is that committees can tend to be inertial and maintain the status quo in maintaining policy rates in the monetary policy stance for long. The MPCs may laboriously aggregate individual preferences that tend to be inertial, irrespective of whether is a strong Chairman for MPC or not. This would in turn lead the central banks to overstay their stance. Inflation targeting may not be a sufficient tool to handle balance sheet problems. These imbalances in the balance sheets may not have immediate impacts on inflation, but they have impacts on output and employment. The ultimate form of these balance sheets disorder can be asset price bubbles, which inflation targeting may not address effectively.

Against the backdrop of COVID-19 pandemic, central banks have engaged in emergency bond purchase programmes to provide liquidity (Chakraborty et al., 2021). Flexible inflation targeting is a long-run monetary policy strategy to minimize price instabilities as well as minimize the fluctuations in the output (unemployment). Because the main limitation of "nominal anchor" is that such an inflation target does not leave much room for macroeconomic stabilization in terms of output fluctuations as it is confined only to price stability. The flexible inflation targeting framework provides simultaneously space to a dual mandate to monetary policy—both price stability and macroeconomic activity—to focus on both output (unemployment) and price fluctuations. The flexible inflation targeting accommodates symmetrically both inflation and the output gap. This central bank's function contains forecasts for both inflation and output gap as target variables. However empirical evidence from the region are mixed regarding the impact of monetary policy on economic growth.

STRUCTURAL REFORMS

This section deals with how can structural reforms contribute to achieving the SDG agenda. Structural policies are defined as the macroeconomic policies framed to impact the total factor productivity (TFP) of the country, incorporating the regulatory policies. Total factor productivity can be obtained as the residual from sector-specific estimations of a logarithmic Cobb–Douglas production function, and the coefficients can be estimated using Levinsohn and Petrin (2003). Taking natural logs of Cobb–Douglas production function in a linear function, we obtain where is the physical output of firm i in period t; K_{it}, L_{it}, and M_{it} are inputs of capital, labor, and materials, respectively; and A_{it} is the Hicksian neutral efficiency level of firm i in period t and where β_0 measures the mean efficiency level across firms and over time; ε_{it} is the time- and producer-specific deviation from that mean, which can then be further decomposed into an observable and unobservable component. These structural policies comprise innovation policies, price and energy policies, regulations and labour market policies. Looking into the determinants of TFP, the following variables have been denoted: knowledge and skills; education and research and development activities; exports, imports and FDI and institutional quality, good governance and infrastructure. It has been suggested that Asia-Pacific economies made progress in enhancing the quality of labour forces, with the increase in the average years of schooling of adults, the literacy rate, and the net enrolment rate at the secondary level. Average public spending on research and development activities in the region has increased in terms of GDP, to almost equal to the world average—though slightly below the OECD average. The expansion of trade that has taken place in the Asia-Pacific region over the past 25 years, and the dramatic increase in FDI into the region have contributed to the overall increase in total factor productivity. Poor governance, low institutional quality and inadequate infrastructure can negatively affect TFP growth by increasing the cost of inputs. Countries with lower levels of corruption experience higher TFP growth. Lack of physical infrastructure, in particular, transport infrastructure and trade facilitation systems increases costs of production and reduces TFP.

The structural policies by government for lifeline infrastructure like electricity, gas, mining and communication services are significant for enhancing economic growth. In India, the recent policy reform to absorb the power debt of the DISCOMS (electricity distribution companies) is called UDAY (Ujjwal Discom Reassurance Yojana). UDAY is introduced in a special context where the country has excess power generation, but due to the huge debt of DISCOMs the power is not distributed across Provinces and many poor live without electricity. This policy was introduced to provide electricity to the poor by correcting the financial and operational efficiency parameters of DISCOMs (Kaur & Chakraborty, 2019; Kaur et al., 2021). The procedure consisted of the state governments absorbing the power debt of DISCOMs—by issuing bonds through a tripartite form between the Central government, State government, and the DISCOMs. Though the programme has led to marginal improvements in access for poor to electricity, the subnational public finance of a few States has encountered problems in terms of their deficit going up beyond the fiscal legislations, which hindered these states not to accessing excess borrowing powers in the bond market which otherwise they were entitled to. From the SDG perspective, though this programme is to provide "lifeline infrastructure", it has aggravated the public finance management issues by exploding the debt deficit conundrum in particular states.

Another major structural policy initiative in the region is related to natural resources and extractive industries. Despite having one of the highest reserves of coal, India is also the highest importer of coal. The carbon tax is framed from the production and import of coal, with 500 Rupees per metric ton, to be used as clean energy access (Chakraborty, 2014c; Chakraborty et al., 2016, 2020b). Yet another major initiative is to link the fiscal space derived from mining revenue to the spatial and human development of the region where the revenue is extracted from. These social impact policies relating to extractive industries are rare. As per the recent MMDR policy a fund is created as DMF to link fiscal space to human development. This has positive implications in terms of SDG, as the socio-economic indicators of the mining districts are the worst in the country when compared to non-mining districts. Such policies can be compared to BEE (Black Economic Empowerment) policy of South Africa and Oil-to-Cash policies of Ghana, linking fiscal space to human development in the mining sector.

The financial sector legislation reforms commission (FSLRC) in India has prepared the Indian Financial Code, which is another highlight of the structural policy initiative. The aim of FSLRC is to ensure a sound financial system with less Ponzi finance and in turn, lead to higher economic growth. The labour market reforms are relevant especially when growth is not followed by an increase in jobs. The states like Rajasthan and Maharashtra have begun to loosen rules for hiring of labour. The labour market policies should attempt to avoid both excessive regulation and extreme disregard for labour conditions. Improving skills and Start Ups are other initiatives to improve productivity. The bankruptcy code introduced in India is a structural reform to give a public resolution and restructuring for the firms in loss and for a turnaround.

Mapping of Macro Policies in Asia-Pacific

This section maps macro policies on SDGs in the region and provides examples. However, this mapping is not comprehensive with all 17 SDGs. Widening inequalities within and between countries in wealth, opportunity, and power as well as persistent gender inequalities are confronting the world today and hence formed the framework for the 2030 Agenda for Sustainable Development. The United Nations System Shared Framework for Action 2017 has articulated the need to build upon the lessons of the Millennium Development Goals (MDGs), and move towards the commitments to "leave no one behind" and to reach the furthest behind first. It aims not only to end poverty and hunger, but also "to combat inequalities within and among countries; to build peaceful, just and inclusive societies; [and] to protect human rights and promote gender equality and the empowerment of women and girls" and "to ensure that all human beings can fulfil their potential in dignity and equality and in a healthy environment".

At the national level, governments must attempt to boost investor confidence, strengthening public finances, social inclusion, and environmental regeneration. A global analysis of normative SDG assessments of SDG14 is carried out by IIED showed how fiscal instruments can be designed to provide the necessary incentives for achieving SDG 14 and the goal of leaving no one behind, using of three particular fiscal instruments (taxes, subsidies and conditional transfers) to this sector. Empirical studies have analysed the fiscal policy tools in green economy sector linking to SDG and how to integrate climate change commitments within public policy frameworks (Andersen & Ekins, 2009; Chakraborty, 2021c, 2021d; Heine et al., 2012; Kaur & Chakraborty, 2019). Examples are rare in the region in terms of technical cooperation for SDGs. UNESCAP highlighted one such recent initiative- "Evolution" initiative—launched by Japan to provide developing countries with a one-stop mechanism including technical support, for preparing energy policies. Other examples are the Green Technology Center-Korea (which links the Republic of Korea's public–private cooperative green technology research projects with the demand for green technology from developing countries) and a new centre jointly planned by China's National Energy Administration and the International Energy Agency to enhance partnership in attaining energy data, renewable and clean energy policy technologies.

The fiscal policy in health sector of Pacific Islands analysed by UNESCAP revealed that highly constrained national budgets of Pacific island developing economies are often subject to volatility from a narrow revenue base, dependency on foreign aid and recurring external shocks, such as natural disasters. The Pacific Islands require a better design and implementation of fiscal policy to improve health outcomes while ensuring fiscal sustainability. Public spending on health in most Pacific island developing economies averaged close to 9 per cent in 2014, ranged between almost 5 per cent of GDP in Fiji and Papua New Guinea to about 17 per cent of GDP in Marshall Islands and Tuvalu. This is higher than the case of India where public spending on health by national governments is only around one per cent of GDP.

Identifying Specific Policy Tools

The role of fiscal policy in attaining SDGs may take two routes. One, a route of fiscal policy, acting as "employer of last resort" by providing "participation income" in return to economic activity. Two, fiscal policy acting as a provider of "basic income" to all citizens unconditional and non-targeted. In Asia-Pacific, fiscal policy has acted the role of providing "participation income" through employment programmes rather than "basic income". Globally, "participation income" is attained through a direct employment transfer—a Job Guarantee programme—which is an "employer of last resort" fiscal policy. This policy envisions the government bearing a guarantee to provide paid work opportunities of predictable duration at a predetermined wage for public works. Though many such job guarantee initiatives have been introduced over the years across the countries, the popular and largest in scale are the US New Deal programmes, ex post to 1929 Great Depression; the *Jefes* programme in Argentina and the Expanded Public Works Programme (EPWP 2004–2005) in South Africa, other than the Mahatma Gandhi National Rural Employment Guarantee Act in India, specific to the region. These programmes are targeted at labour-intensive work in the field of environmental interventions and in providing public benefits in asset-creating public works.

A major lacuna of the existing studies on job guarantee programmes is the lack of analysis on the impact of time use patterns and in turn the care economy infrastructure in strengthening the participation of women in wage employment. It is based on the principle of self-selection, and it is a step towards legal enforcement of the right to work, as an aspect of the fundamental right to live with dignity. This programme aims to redress the seasonal, cyclical, and structural unemployment in the country by providing the low-skilled poor a work entitlement thereby ensuring that when all else fails, the government acts as "employer of last resort".

On the other hand, "basic income" is an unconditional cash transfer. It can be universal or targeted, and can involve 2 types of errors: I or II. It is often argued that universal is better than targeted as the latter can encounter exclusion I error (non-targeted getting included) and exclusion II error (needy getting excluded). The fiscal implications of universal basic income is a matter of concern within the constraints of fiscal rules. It is always a dilemma for the government to design "universal basic" income or "participatory" income. If the priority of the government is to design policies to enable people to "participate" in economic activity, then they go for employment-related policies. However, "basic income" has received significance amidst the increasing automation process and lack of job availability.

In addition to these two fiscal policy designs, energy subsidies also form a major policy. The fossil fuel subsidy is increasingly phased out or better targeted in the region. In India, the policy to provide clean fuel at affordable prices to the poor is considered a major public policy in terms of gender equity. As women spend disproportionate hours collecting fuel wood and spend prolonged hours cooking with non-clean fuel with poor ventilation can lead to increase in health risks of respiratory diseases. UNESCAP (2017) pointed out that in Asia energy subsidies (especially on petroleum products and electricity) accounted for about one third of global energy subsidies in 2013. Such subsidies accounted for about 20 per cent of GDP in the Islamic Republic of Iran, followed by the Russian Federation and India (both at about 10 per cent), Indonesia (7 per cent) and China (4 per cent). In the wake of the global oil price decline in 2014, a number of countries, including Indonesia, have aggressively phased out fuel subsidies.

Financial inclusion means that individuals and businesses have access to useful and affordable financial products and services that meet their needs—transactions, payments, savings, credit, and insurance—delivered in a responsible and sustainable way. In India, the first-ever unique identification project, where identities are biometrically scanned, is enabling unbanked individuals to access credit and other banking services through JanDan project. In the Asia-Pacific region, the Philippines has enabling policy environment and business support which helped in implementing affordable and efficient financial services (micro savings and micro insurance) to the poor through technological innovations and mobile banking. In July 2017, the Asian Development Bank (ADB) and Cantilan Bank, in partnership with Oradian, launched a pilot project on cloud-based core banking technology in the southern Philippines to provide digital financial services to poor in hard to reach terrains in Philippines. This digital financial services provide platform for the poor people to save, make a payment, get a small business loan, send a remittance, or buy insurance. TabunganKU (My Savings) and People's Business Credit are the two significant microfinance programmes in Indonesia. The private sector also plays an active role in Indonesia in microfinance programmes. For instance, Bank Rakyat Indonesia, a private bank, has introduced financial inclusion projects to serve unbanked firms and individuals. In Thailand, financial inclusion is prominently pursued by the Government. The Village Fund of Thailand is recognized as one of the largest microfinance institutions in the world, providing subsidized credit to farm households and small firms in rural areas.

To conclude, the inventory analysis of macro policies for SDGs reveals that the countries in the Asia-Pacific region do not have any policy documents relating to macroeconomic policies to attain the SDGs. Broadly, policymakers have articulated a plethora of legislative and regulatory mechanisms to implement SDGs at national and subnational levels. However, the most significant, and often overlooked, are the macro policy tools that they have to complement these broad approaches.

References

Andersen, M. S., & Ekins, P. (Eds.). (2009). *Carbon-energy taxation: Lessons from Europe*. Oxford University Press.

Blanchard, O., & Summers, L. (2017). *Rethinking stabilization policy. Back to the future* (Working Paper). Peterson Institute for International Economics.

Bernanke, B. (2017). *Monetary policy in a new era* (Working Paper). Co-published by Peterson Institute for International Economics and Hutchins Center on Fiscal and Monetary Policy.

Bernanke, B. S., Laubach, T., Mishkin, F. S., & Posen, A. (1999). *Inflation targeting: Lessons from the international experience*. Princeton University Press.

Chakraborty, L. (2008). *Deficient public infrastructure and private costs: Evidence from a time-use survey for the water sector in India* (Working Paper No. 536). Levy Economics Institute.

Chakraborty, L. (2010). *Determining gender equity in fiscal federalism: Analytical issues and empirical evidence from India* (Working Paper No. 590). Levy Economics Institute.

Chakraborty, L. (2014a). *Gender budgeting, as fiscal innovation* (Working Paper 797). The Levy Economics Institute.

Chakraborty, L. (2014b). *Integrating time in public policy: Empirical description of gender-specific outcomes and budgeting* (Working Paper 785). Levy Economics Institute.

Chakraborty, L. (2014c). *Revival of mining sector in India: Analysing legislations and royalty regime* (Working Paper No. 129). National Institute of Public Finance and Policy.

Chakraborty, L. (2016a). *Asia: A survey of gender budgeting experiences* (Working Paper 16/150). International Monetary Fund.

Chakraborty, L. (2016b). *Fiscal consolidation, budget deficits and macroeconomy: Monetary-fiscal linkages*. Sage Publications.

Chakraborty, L. (2020). *Macroeconomic policy coherence for SDG 2030: Evidence from Asia Pacific* (Working Paper 292). National Institute of Public Finance and Policy.

Chakraborty, L. (2021a). Union Budget 2021a–22: The macroeconomic framework. *Economic and Political Weekly, 56*(9).

Chakraborty, L. (2021b). *Fiscal federalism, expenditure assignments and gender equality* (Working Paper 334). National Institute of Public Finance and Policy.

Chakraborty, L. (2021c). Mainstreaming climate change commitments through finance commission's recommendations. *Economic and Political Weekly*, 56(33).

Chakraborty, L. (2021d, October 22). *Greening the monetary policy*. Editorial Column. The Financial Express.

Chakraborty, L. (2021e, October 14). *Why RBI has not been hawkish in its monetary policy?* The Indian Express.

Chakraborty, P., & Chakraborty, L. (2006). *Fiscal stance and output gap: An empirical estimation*, The Policy Innovations, Carnegie Foundation.

Chakraborty, L., & Kaur, A. (2020, December 23). *Why output gap is controversial?* The Financial Express.

Chakraborty, L. S., & Sinha, D. (2018). *Has fiscal rule changed the fiscal marksmanship of union government? Anatomy of budgetary forecast errors in India* (Working Paper 234). National Institute of Public Finance and Policy.

Chakraborty, L., Garg, S., & Singh, G. (2016). *Cashing in on mining: The political economy of mining regulations and fiscal policy practices in India* (Working Paper 161). National Institute of Public Finance and Policy.

Chakraborty, L., Nayyar, V., & Jain, K. (2020a). *The political economy of gender budgeting: Empirical evidence from India* (Working Paper No. 256). National Institute of Public Finance and Policy.

Chakraborty, L. S., Thomas, E., & Gandhi, P. (2020b). *Natural resources revenue buoyancy in India: Empirical evidence from state-specific mining regime* (Working Paper No. 313). National Institute of Public Finance and Policy.

Chakraborty, L. S., Chakraborty, P., & Shrestha, R. (2020c). *Budget credibility of subnational governments: Analyzing the fiscal forecasting errors of 28 states in India* (Working Papers Series WP No. 964). Levy Economics Institute.

Chakraborty, L., Kaur, A., Rangan. D., & Farida Jacob, J. (2021). *Covid 19 and fiscal-monetary policy responses in Asia Pacific*. NIPFP Publications.

Filardo, A., & Hans, G. (2010). *Monetary policy strategies in the Asia and Pacific region: What way forward?* (Working Papers 195/ADBI). Asian Development Bank Institute.

Furman, J. (2017). *Should policymakers care whether inequality is helpful or harmful for growth?* Jason Furman Harvard Kennedy School.

Gasper, D. (2002). Is sen's capability approach an adequate basis for considering human development? *Review of Political Economy, 14*(4), 435–461. https://doi.org/10.1080/0953825022000009898

Heine, D., Norregaard, J. & Parry, I. (2012). *Environmental tax reform: Principles from theory and practice to date* (IMF Working Paper 12/180). International Monetary Fund.

Horst, H., Chakraborty, L. S., & Khurana, S. (2017). *Fiscal policy, economic growth and innovation: An empirical analysis of G20 countries* (Working Paper Archive 883). Levy Economics Institute.

International Labour Organization (ILO). (2015). *Social protection in Asia and the Pacific and the Arab states*. ILO Bangkok.

Kaur, A., & Chakraborty, L. (2019). *UDAY power debt in retrospect and prospects: Analyzing the efficiency parameters* (Working Papers id: 12968), eSocialSciences. https://ideas.repec.org/p/ess/wpaper/id12968.html

Kaur, A., Chakraborty, L., & Rangan, D. (2021). Covid-19 economic stimulus and state-level power sector performance: Analyzing the efficiency parameters. *Economic and Political Weekly, 56*(43).

Levinsohn, J., & Petrin, A. (2003). Estimating production functions using inputs to control for unobservables. *Review of Economic Studies*, 317–341.

Nitin, K., & Roy, R. (2016). Finance commission of India's assessments: A political economy contention between expectations and outcomes, *Applied Journal, 48*(2).

Raghabendra, C., & Duflo, E. (2001). *Women's leadership and policy decisions: Evidence from a nationwide randomized experiment in India* (Working Papers Sereis dp-114). Boston University–Department of Economics.

Reserve Bank of India. (2021). *Report on currency and finance*. Reserve Bank of India.

Roy, R., & Heuty, A. (2009). *Fiscal space: Policy options for financing human development*. Routledge.

SIPRI. (2017). Yearbook trends in world military expenditure. SIPRI.

Stern, N. (2002, January 10). *Public finance and policy for development: Challenges for India*. Silver Jubilee Lecture. National Institute of Public Finance and Policy (NIPFP).

Stiglitz, J., & Rashid, H. (2020, July 31). A global debt crisis is looming: How can we prevent it? *Project Syndicate*.

Tanzi, V. (2016). Review of *fiscal consolidation, budget deficits and macroeconomic* activity. Sage Publications in Blog, National Institute of Public Finance and Policy.

UNESCAP. (2017). *Fiscal policy for better health outcomes in the Pacific*. UNESCAP.

Vinod, H., Karun, H., & Chakraborty, L. (2020). *Encouraging private investment in India?* In H. Vinod, & C. R. Rao (Eds.), Handbook of Statistics (155–183), Vol. 42. Elsevier.

CHAPTER 3

Gender-Budgeting and Gender Equality Outcomes: Evidence from Asia-Pacific

Assessing the impact of fiscal policy—in particular gender budgeting—on women's development in the region is complex. Linking gender budgeting to outcomes requires not only assessing the success of gender budgeting in influencing fiscal policies but also assessing the linkage of fiscal policy to gender equality and women's development (Chakraborty, 2016a; Stotsky, 2020; Stotsky & Zaman, 2016; Stotsky et al., 2019). Since there is a contemporaneous transformation of many socio-economic and policy variables that result in gender-related development, it is a difficult task to establish a link between the fiscal policies specifically and gender-related development (Chakraborty et al., 2018; Lahiri et al., 2002). However, the ability to establish such links would enable us to assess whether government investments, especially in human development and gender budgeting, result in women's development and more gender equality. Two overarching primary motivations for gender budgeting: its perceived positive impacts on economic efficiency, growth, and productivity, and its positive impacts on equity, both in terms of inclusive development and equal realization of human rights. Growth is often cited as an outcome of reducing gender inequality, which serves to close inefficient gender gaps in workforce participation, education, and health (Berik et al., 2009; Dollar & Gatti, 1999; Esteve-Volart, 2004; Hill & King, 1995; Klasen, 1999; Knowles et al., 2002). However, as many scholars

© The Author(s), under exclusive license to Springer Nature Singapore Pte Ltd. 2022
L. S. Chakraborty, *Fiscal Policy for Sustainable Development in Asia-Pacific*, https://doi.org/10.1007/978-981-19-3281-6_3

point out, pinning the direction of causality between growth and reduction of gender inequality is tricky (Cuberes & Teignier, ; Stotsky & Zaman, 2016).

Literature on gender budgeting often posits the advancement of gender equality and women's and girls' development as a motivation for gender budgeting (Sharp & Elson, 2008; Stotsky, 2016). Moreover, governments adopting gender budgeting also highlight the amelioration of gender disparities and the empowerment of women as the key motivation. For example, in Asia, the Indian, South Korean, and Afghan gender-budgeting initiatives all posit women's advancement as the motivator for their programmes (Chakraborty, 2016b; Kolovich & Shibuya, 2016; Stotsky, 2020).

Yet another basic element of gender budgeting is the collection of sex-disaggregated statistics, and several countries have begun their gender-budgeting efforts with a mandate for greater disaggregation of sector-specific statistics (Chakraborty, 2016a; Kolovich & Shubuya, 2016). This sex-disaggregated data can be used to justify the passage of laws addressing gender disparities, such as laws promoting women's health and safety, access to education, equal rights to work, etc.

Using a fixed-effects model of pooled least squares for the early 1990s, Lahiri et al. (2002) find that there is a positive functional relationship between per capita combined expenditure on health and education and the UNDP's Human Development Index and the associated Gender Development Index. This result confirms that public expenditure on human capital formation, despite the constraints of intra-household disparities in resource allocation, especially on human capital formation, leads to better gender development indicators.

Chakraborty (2003) and (2005) examine the link between public expenditure on human development and the Gender Development Index by incorporating economic growth variables. Empirical evidence shows that in a semi-logarithmic framework, regressing proportionate shortfalls of life expectancy against per capita GDP reveals that nearly half of the variations in the life expectancy can be attributed to differences in GNP per head (Anand & Ravallion, 1993). In this context, it is important to note that the substantial impact of higher GDP per head on life expectancy and other social outcomes of better literacy level, low mortality rates among children, and better schooling among children seems to work via factors in which the public policy stance plays a significant part. Chakraborty (2003) and (2005), using fixed effects panel estimation, in the context of Asia-Pacific, find that both economic growth and the public policy stance matter for gender-related development, however, public policy variables (expenditure on human development, especially education and health) were more meaningful than economic growth in determining the outcomes for gender-related development. This reinforces the significance of fiscal policy for human development and gender budgeting. A point to be noted here is that the effectiveness of public expenditure on education and health for women and men are different due to the asymmetric scales of socio-economic development. As noted, the evidence from gender-disaggregated benefit incidence analysis revealed that the effectiveness of education and health spending across gender and regions are different. This strengthens the case for gender budgeting in social sectors like education and health.

As Stotsky and Zaman (2016) have observed, there have been few efforts to assess the results of gender budgeting in a quantitative manner. Yet most other studies evaluating the success of gender budgeting initiatives tend to focus on the success of their *implementation*—that is, whether governments are following the steps of gender budgeting, rather than their *impact* in achieving their goals of equality, growth, inclusive development, and human rights [see, for example, Nakray (2009) and Mushi and Edward (2010)]. Lahiri et al. (2002) using a fixed effects model of pooled least squares for the early 1990s, find that increase in spending on health and education resulted in an increase in Human Development Index (HDI) and GDI for the period between 1993 and 2002. This demonstrates that public expenditure on human capital formation positively impacts gender development indicators. It is important to note that the effectiveness of public expenditures on health and education may vary across regions according to asymmetric scales of socio-economic development (Chakraborty, 2016a, 2016b). Stotsky and Zaman (2016) analysed whether the practice of gender budgeting has yielded greater gender equality in school enrolment (as a proxy for gender equality) and increased spending on social services, education, health, welfare, and infrastructure in Indian states. This chapter seeks to take this literature forward by testing the link between gender budgeting and gender equality outcomes in the context of Asia-Pacific.

Measuring Gender Equality

Globally a data revolution is required to capture the inequalities in gender-sensitive human development, and in turn to construct appropriate measurement indices. This challenge is indeed substantial and methodological. Lately, there are many models that analyse the relationship between gender inequality and economic growth, but the statistics and indices about gender inequalities are not adequate for assessing such empirical links with economic growth (Anand & Sen, 1995; Dijkstra, 2002, 2006; Ferrant, 2009). Beyond measuring aggregate affluence, the United Nations Development Program (UNDP) was the pioneer in constructing gender-related indices. The 1995 *Human Development Report* (HDR) introduced two gender-based indices—the Gender-related Development Index (GDI) and Gender Empowerment Measure (GEM). These were the first composite indices designed to reflect gender disparities in capability deprivation at a global level and were widely used by many researchers across the globe for studying gender disparities between women and men.

In measuring gender-sensitive human development, the economic growth measures used in early empirical literature had constraints in capturing the wider aspects of well-being and the contingent process of development. Noorbakhsh (1998) noted that the criticisms against using economic growth as the proxy for assessing human development can be traced back to the UN *Report* of 1954. Since then, the array of literature in favour of using social indicators to measure human development has resulted in the collation of data on a spectrum of socio-economic indicators across countries, which has inevitably resulted in attempts to construct composite indices of human development and gender inequality (Adelman & Morris, 1967; Hicks & Streeten, 1979; Morris, 1979; UNDP, 1995; UNRISD, 1972). To analyse the link between fiscal policy and gender equality, the measurement issues relate to the latter are crucial. GDP is no longer a proxy for human development.

The Human Development Index (HDI) is a gender-neutral index of the basic capabilities in three dimensions of human development: the geometric mean of selected dimensions of health, education, and income. The process of enlarging people's choices and raising the level of well-being is defined as human development. Conceptually, these choices can be infinite. These choices can vary intertemporally and spatially. From the infinite set of choices, UNDP had selected three dimensions as the most critical and socially valuable: the ability to lead a long and healthy life; the choice to acquire knowledge and be educated; and access to resources needed for a decent level of living (UNDP Human Development Reports, various years).

The Gender Development Index (GDI) was constructed in 1995 by the UNDP to measure gender development. The GDI used the same variables as HDI, but adjusted for the degree of disparity in achievement across genders. The average value of each of the component variables is substituted by "equally distributed equivalent achievements." The equally distributed equivalent achievement (X_{ede}) for a variable is taken as the level of achievement that, if attained equally by women and men, would be judged to be exactly as valuable socially as the actually observed disparate achievements. Lahiri et al. (2002) noted that taking an additively separable, symmetric, and constant elasticity marginal valuation function with an elasticity of 2, the equally distributed equivalent achievement X_{ede} for any variable X turns out to be as follows:

$$X_{ede} = [n_f(1/X_f) + n_m(1/X_m)]^{-1}$$

where X_f and X_m are the values of the variable for females and males, and n_f and n_m are the population shares of females and males. X_{ede} is a "gender-equity-sensitive indicator" (GESI). Thus, for this chosen value of 2 for constant elasticity marginal valuation function, GDI is computed as follows:

$$\text{GDI} = \{L_{ede} + (2/3 \times A_{ede} + 1/3 \times E_{ede}) + Y_{ede}\}/3$$

The Inequality Adjusted Human Development Index (IHDI) adjusts the HDI for inequality in each dimension across the entire population. Like HDI, it is calculated using the geometric mean but using inequality-adjusted dimension indices. The IHDI takes into account achievements in terms of health, education, and income by discounting each dimension's average value according to its level of inequality. Under perfect equality, HDI will equal IHDI. In cases of inequality, IHDI will fall below HDI. The difference between IHDI and HDI is the loss of human development due to inequality. IHDI is calculated for 145 countries by the UNDP. Life expectancy is distributed across a group of subjects who have shared a particular event distribution presented over different age intervals, whereas years of schooling and income are distributed across individuals.

The inequality measure, A, is defined as $1 - \frac{g}{\mu}$ where g is the geometric mean and μ is the arithmetic mean of the distribution. Symbolically,

$$A_x = 1 - \frac{\sqrt[n]{X_1 \ldots \ldots X_n}}{\overline{X}}$$

Owing to the conceptual and methodological problems identified by researchers in the calculation of these indices, the 2010 HDR introduced a new measure of gender inequality, the Gender Inequality Index (GII). This index was designed to capture women's disadvantages in three dimensions—reproductive health, empowerment, and economic activity. It reflects the loss in achievement due to inequality between men and women. An index of 0 implies that both the genders fare equally in all three select dimensions, whereas an index of 1 implies complete inequality.

Gender Inequality Index (GII), which replaced the GDI in 2010, reflects gender-based disadvantage in mainly three dimensions: reproductive health, proxied by maternal mortality ratio (MMR) and adolescent fertility rate (AFR); empowerment, as proxied by the share of parliamentary seats held across gender (PR) and attainment of secondary education (SE); and economic activity is proxied by the labour market participation rate (LFPR), which measures the participation of men and women in the market economy. The maternal mortality rate is defined as the number of female deaths per 100,000 live births annually, from any cause related to, or aggravated by, pregnancy or its management. AFR is the number of births per 1000 women aged 15–19.

GII reflects the loss in development due to inequality across genders. An index of 0 implies women and men fare equally whereas an index of 1 implies that one of the two genders fares as poorly as is possible. The first step in the calculation of GII involves treating zeros and extreme values (i.e. the outliers). GII is calculated by taking the geometric mean across the dimensions; because the geometric mean cannot be calculated for zero values, a minimum of 0.1 per cent is set for all the components. The maximum value for the maternal mortality rate is taken as 1000 deaths per 100,000 births and the minimum value is 10 per 100,000 births. A higher maternal mortality rate suggests poor maternal health. After treating zeros, if any, we aggregate across dimensions within each gender group using geometric means. As the reproductive health variables are used, the aggregation formula for men and women is different.

$$Gf = \sqrt[3]{\left(\sqrt{\left(\frac{10}{MMR} \cdot \frac{1}{AFR}\right)} \cdot \sqrt{(PRf.SEf)}.LFRPf\right)}$$

The rescaling by 0.1 is required to take into account the truncation of the maternal mortality ratio minimum at 10.

For males, the formula is as follows:

$$Gm = \sqrt[3]{\left(1 \cdot \sqrt{(PRm.SEm)}.LFRPm\right)}$$

Once the geometric mean of the three dimensions that determine the inequality index is taken, the next step is to aggregate across gender using the harmonic mean. The argument for using the harmonic mean is that it captures the inequality between women and men and further adjusts for the association between dimensions, but this method is open to criticism (Hawken & Munck, 2013).

The Harmonic Mean (HARM) index is as follows:

$$HARM(Gf, Gm) = \left(\frac{(Gf)^{-1} + (Gm)^{-1}}{2}\right)^{-1}$$

Before calculating the final index, a composite index is calculated using the geometric means of the arithmetic means; this step is to give equal weights to both genders. We then aggregate it across the various dimensions, i.e. health, empowerment, and economic activity.

The composite index is as follows:

$$G(\overline{f,m}) = \sqrt[3]{\left(\overline{Health}.\overline{Empowerment}.\overline{LFPR}\right)}$$

Where

$$\overline{Health} = \frac{\left(\sqrt{\left(\frac{10}{MMR} \cdot \frac{1}{AFR}\right)} + 1\right)}{2}$$

$$\overline{Empowerment} = \frac{\left(\sqrt{(PRf.SEf)} + \sqrt{(PRm.SEm)}\right)}{2}$$

$$\overline{LFPR} = \frac{(LFPRf + LFPRm)}{2}$$

Symbolically, the GII is as follows:

$$GII = 1 - \frac{HARM(Gf, Gm)}{G(\bar{f}, \bar{m})}$$

The higher the value of GII, the higher the gender gap and the loss in the potential for human development. Hence in order to utilize all our resources fully, we need to bridge this gender gap.

Hawken and Munck (2013) pointed out data availability was not seen as a constraint for the construction of GII and that new data can be generated to measure certain indicators that are considered central to an index's overarching concept. However, Permanyer (2013) points out, that an increase in MMR and AFR systematically represents an increase in gender inequality levels while, on the other hand, decreases in women's education or labour force participation rates (LFPR) do not necessarily represent a worse state of affairs as long as men's education and LFPR decrease by the same amount. Also, the corresponding value of MMR and AFR for men is taken as 1, which is far from realistic and leads to overestimation of the gap between women's and men's health standards.

Yet another problem with using indicators like reproductive health is that it penalizes low-income countries, as health standards are usually low in developing countries. While the proponents of the index might rightly argue that it makes sense to penalize those countries with bad reproductive health conditions for women, it is fair to say that a country's performance in those areas is influenced by a myriad of factors other than gender-related issues (Permanyer, 2013). This calls for variables that are broader and capture the health standards of both the sexes equally.

The third sub-indicator of the GII is LFPR, which measures the involvement of men and women in paid work. We know that housework, childcare, and care of elderly relatives represent women's unpaid work—which is an indispensable financial benefit to the entire economy (Bartuskova & Kubelkova, 2014)—yet it fails to capture the care economy where women are typically overrepresented. Owing to the importance of unpaid work and the differences in the representation of genders in Systems in National Accounts (SNA) and non-SNA activities, it is desirable to incorporate unpaid work into the gender inequality index.

Aggarwal and Chakraborty (2015) highlight the shortcomings of GDI and GII as none of the measures address the statistical invisibility of the care economy.

Interpreting Data

Asian countries encompass a range of levels of development and show differing degrees of gender inequality, with most falling into the middle or lower-income categories. Asian countries have generally been making progress in addressing gender inequality and women's advancement, even though gender inequality remains high. Figure 3.1 shows gender inequality in secondary education, where we can see that the trend is towards greater equality. Figure 3.2 shows gender inequality in under 5 mortality, where boys have a natural disadvantage. The high female to

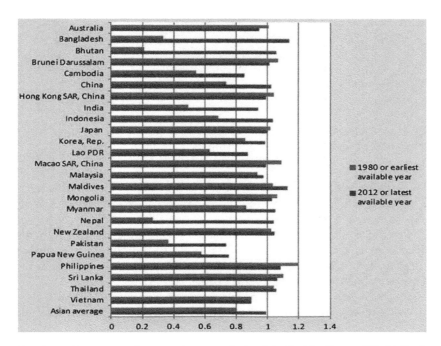

Fig. 3.1 Gross secondary enrolment ratio in Asia-Pacific (*Source* World Bank, World Development Indicators database; and authors' estimates)

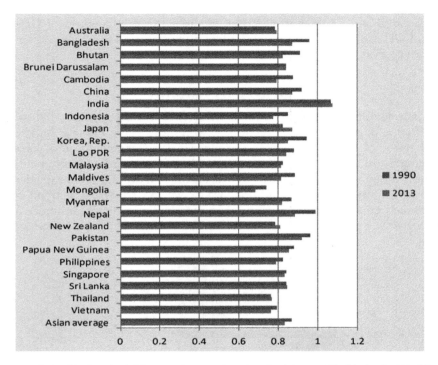

Fig. 3.2 Under 5 child mortality in Asia-Pacific (*Source* World Bank, World Development Indicators database; and authors' estimates)

male ratio in India is notable, which skews the natural advantage of girls in survival and missing women estimates (Anderson & Ray, 2010; Klasen, 1994; Klasen & Wink, 2003).

Figure 3.3 shows maternal mortality, a key indicator of women's advancement, and the almost universal trend in the region of declining mortality, even while maternal mortality remains high in many countries (Thaddeus & Maine, 1994; van den Broek & Falconer, 2011).

Figure 3.4 shows gender gaps in labour force participation rates, ages 15–64 (female to male ratio), where the trend is towards equality, though notably, a number of countries show a declining ratio (Fig. 3.5).

While individual indicators are illustrative of developments in key variables, gender equality indices provide a useful summary of an aggregation of indicators. Figure 3.6 presents a summary of the Gender Development

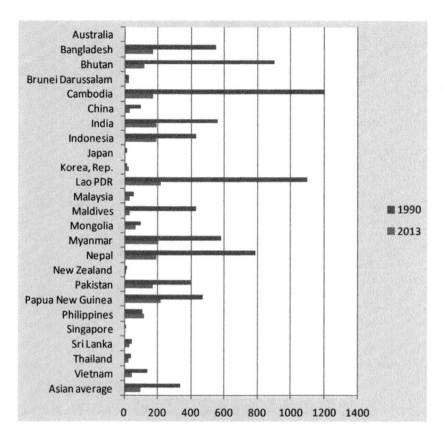

Fig. 3.3 Maternal mortality ratio in Asia-Pacific (*Source* World Bank, World Development Indicators database; and authors' estimates)

Index (GDI) across the region for the latest year for which data are available. This index generally ranges from 0 to 1, where higher numbers represent more equality. The range of results suggests that the region as a whole has made progress in recent decades. Advanced countries in the region and some of the developing countries are doing better overall, while the south Asian countries clearly tend to lag.

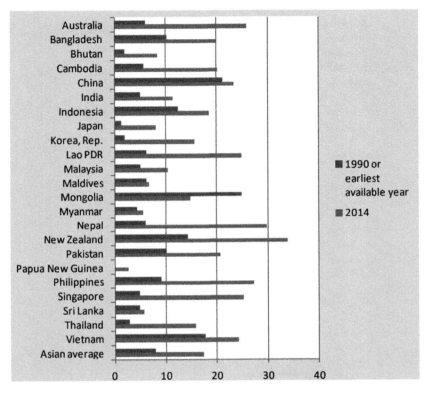

Fig. 3.4 Labour force participation rate in Asia-Pacific (*Source* World Bank, World Development Indicators database; and authors' estimates)

The Empirical Investigation

Gender equality (GE) is captured in the models by Gender Development Index (GDI) and Gender Inequality Index (GII). Under the GDI, the average value of each of the component variables in the index—education, health, and income—is substituted with "equally distributed equivalent achievements" (Lahiri et al., 2002). The equally distributed equivalent achievement (X_{ede}) represents the level of achievement that would, if attained equally by women and men, be considered exactly as valuable to society as the actually observed disparate achievements. The

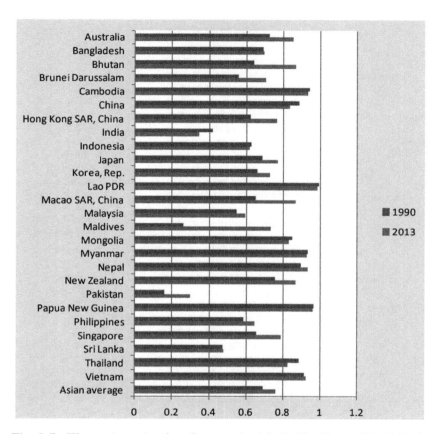

Fig. 3.5 Women in national parliaments in Asia-Pacific (*Source* World Bank, World Development Indicators database; and authors' estimates)

GII is a measure of disparities between the genders across three dimensions: (i) reproductive health, represented by the maternal mortality ratio (MMR) and the adolescent fertility rate (AFR); (ii) women's empowerment, represented by the proportion of parliamentary seats held by each sex (PR) and the sexes' rates of attainment of secondary education (SE); and (iii) economic activity, represented by the labour force participation rate (LFPR) of men and women in the market economy. The GII shows the loss in development resulting from gender inequality, where a score of **0** represents complete equality and a score of **1** implies complete

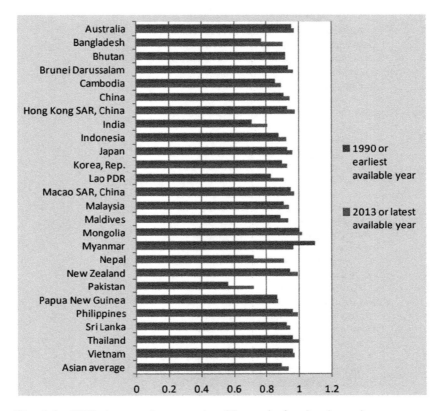

Fig. 3.6 GDI, time consistent version (*Source* Authors' estimates)

inequality. The model we consider for analysis is $\mathbf{GE}_{it} = a + b_1\mathbf{GB}_{it} + b_2 X_{it} + \mu_{it}$, where we test whether gender budgeting (GB) is a significant determinant of gender equality (GE) in the Asia-Pacific region, along with control variables (X). The control variables we use in our models are the log of public spending on health and education, GDP per capita, and female labour force participation.

The dynamic panel estimates in Table 3.1 show that gender budgeting is significantly and positively related to the GDI in the Asia-Pacific countries. In the dynamic panel model, public spending on health and education, as well as growth, are found to be insignificant in determining the GDI. The results also show that the GII is significantly determined

Table 3.1 Determinants of GDI, GII, and sectoral spending: panel estimates

Variables	Model (1) GDI	Model (2) GII	Model (3) (Health)	Model (4) (Education)
Lagged GDI	0.7711*	0.7167*	–	–
	(10.5700)	(0.0571)		
Log of GDP per capita	0.0001	0.0000	0.0001*	0.0020*
	(0.8300)	(0.0000)	(0.0000)	(0.0010)
Female labour force participation rate	0.0019	–0.0041*	–	–
	(1.6200)	(0.0017)		
Log of public spending on education	0.0004	0.0031	–	–
	(0.2800)	(0.0022)		
Log of public spending on education (lag)	–	–	–	0.7065
				(0.5473)
Log of public spending on health	–0.0011	–0.0045*	–	0.8933
	(–0.7400)	(0.0024)		(0.5774)
Log of public spending on health (lag)	–	–	0.6795*	–
			(0.0447)	
Gender budgeting in call circular regime	0.0024*	–0.0035*	–0.0068	0.1982
	(3.1100)	(0.0008)	(0.0167)	(0.3511)
Female literacy rate				–0.1893*
				(0.0991)
Maternal mortality rate	–	–	0.0017*	–
			(0.0007)	
Constant	–1.8669*	2.9819*	6.3525	–172.6384
	(–3.1300)	(0.6693)	(14.4790)	(297.4006)

* 1 % level of significance
Note The figures in the brackets refer to standard errors
Source UN Human Development Reports, IMF Gender Database, and World Development Indicators (various years, basic data)

by gender-budgeting initiatives, public spending on health, and female labour force participation. Spending on education and economic growth variables are found to be insignificant in reducing the GII. The estimates showed that public health spending in the Asia-Pacific region and GII are inversely related. Also, an increase in female labour force participation can reduce the GII in the region.

Against a backdrop of fiscal consolidation and rule-based fiscal policy, countries in the Asia-Pacific region are increasingly adhering to a 3 per cent ratio of fiscal deficit to GDP. In India, the Fiscal Responsibility and Management Act has recommended that national and subnational governments adhere to a debt–GDP ratio of 60 per cent. In determining education and health sector expenditure, could gender budgeting be a determinant? To analyse this, we have examined sectoral patterns in public spending in education and health, and examined whether gender budgeting has any impact on public spending on these sectors. The dynamic panel estimates in Table 3.1 reveal that gender budgeting is found to be insignificant in increasing fiscal spending on health (Model 3). We used the MMR to proxy the gender-related health indicator, which was found to be significant in determining fiscal spending on health. Public spending on health does increase with an increase in economic growth. The dynamic panel estimates, following the methodology of Arenallo and Bond (1991), show that gender budgeting does not have an impact on education spending **(Model 4)**. Moreover, the impact of gender budgeting on aggregate expenditure has not been attempted, as the sectoral inferences are insignificant. Overall GDP and the sectoral outcome indicators are found to be the determinants of sectoral spending.

The Significance to Go Beyond Models

The empirical evidence reveals that gender-budgeting efforts have a more significant impact on gender-equality-sensitive indices as compared to economic growth. Public policy variables, like public spending on health and education, were also found to be relevant for the progress of gender equality in the region. The analysis showed the impact of gender budgeting on increasing fiscal spending in health and education, using the MMR as a proxy for health and the gender disparity ratio in education as a proxy variable for education outcomes. The implications of gender budgeting in these areas were insignificant. This has public policy implications, against the backdrop of fiscal rules, as the countries in the Asia-Pacific region have not yet incorporated gender budgeting as a priority in their spending decisions. The limited purpose of the chapter is to analyse the growth versus public spending variables on gender equality outcomes. The results need to be read with caution as the variables relate to intra-household variables and gender-specific behaviour variables are not included in the models in analyzing the gender equality outcomes. As Nelson (2017) pointed out, the gender differences in behaviour are socially constructed than naturally, which in turn affects the education, leadership, and employment outcomes. As Christine Lagarde (former Managing Director of IMF) asked, if Lehman Brothers (the first bank to fail in the USA) had been Lehman Sisters would there have been a crisis? This remark was made partly in jest (Perrons, 2018), but nonetheless, it implied that rather than there being any problems with the financial system of neoliberalism, the crisis was due to the overexuberance of the testosterone-driven macho men of Wall Street whose risky behaviour might have been curbed by the presence of more "naturally" risk-averse women (Prugl, 2012). This view suggests the limitations of existing empirical research and the requirement to unpack the models in behavioural economics because the findings are more nuanced and complex. This is beyond the scope of this book, however, that sets the agenda for further research in empirical gender economics.

REFERENCES

Adelman, I., & Morris, C. T. (1967). *Society, politics and economic development*. John Hopkins University Press.

Aggarwal, B., & Chakraborty, L. (2015). *Towards 2030 UN agenda on sustainable development goals: Technical challenges in measuring gender inequality in Asia Pacific* (Working Paper No. 157). Levy Economics Institute.

Anand, S., & Ravallion, M. (1993). Human development in poor countries: On the role of private incomes and public services. *Journal of Economic Perspectives, 7*, 133–150.

Anand, S., & Sen, A. (1995). *Gender inequality in human development: Theories and measurement (Occasional Paper 19)*. United Nations Development Programme, Human Development Report Office.

Anderson, S., & Ray, D. (2010). Missing women: Age and disease. *Review of Economic Studies, 77*, 1262–1300.

Arenello, & Bond, S. (1991). Some tests of specification for panel data: Monte Carlo evidence and an application to employment equations. *The Review of Economic Studies, 58(2),* 277–297.

Bartuskova, L., & Kubelkova, K. (2014). Main challenges in measuring gender inequality. *Proceedings of FIKUSZ, 14,* 19–28.

Berik, G., van der Meulen Rodgers, Y., & Seguino, S. (2009). Feminist economics of inequality, development, and growth. *Feminist Economics, 15,* 1–33.

Chakraborty. (2003). *Public expenditure and human development: An empirical investigation*. Presented in World Institute for Development Economics Research Conference on Inequality, Poverty and Human Well-Being.

Chakraborty. (2005). Public policy stance and human development: An empirical analysis. In B. B. Bhattacharyya, & Arup Mitra (Eds.), *Macroeconomics and Welfare*. Academic Publishers.

Chakraborty, L. (2016a). *Asia: A survey of gender budgeting experiences* (Working Paper 16/150). International Monetary Fund.

Chakraborty, L. (2016b). *Fiscal consolidation, budget deficits and macroeconomy: Monetary-fiscal linkages*. Sage Publications.

Cuberes, D., & Teignier, M. (2012). *Gender gaps in the labor market and aggregate productivity* (Sheffield Economic Research Paper (SERP) Number 2012017).

Cuberes, D., & Teignier, M. (2014). Gender inequality and economic growth: A critical review. *Journal of International Development, 26*, 260–276.

Chakraborty, L., Ingrams, M., & Singh, Y. (2018). *Fiscal policy effectiveness and inequality: Efficacy of gender budgeting in Asia Pacific* (Working Paper No. 224). National Institute of Public Finance and Policy.

Dijkstra, A. G. (2002). Revisiting UNDP's GDI and GEM: Toward an alternative. *Social Indicators Research, 57*, 301–338.

Dijkstra, A. G. (2006). Towards a fresh start in measuring gender equality: A contribution to the debate. *Journal of Human Development, 7*, 275–283.

Dollar, D., & Gatti, R. (1999). *Gender inequality, income, and growth: Are good times good for women?* (Working Paper Series 1). World Bank Policy Research Report on Gender and Development, World Bank.

Esteve-Volart, B. (2004). *Gender discrimination and growth: Theory and evidence from India* (Development Economics Papers 42), The Suntory and Toyota International Centres for Economics and Related Disciplines, London School of Economics.

Ferrant, G. (2009). *A new way to measure gender inequalities in developing countries: The gender inequalities index (GII)* (CEAFE Papers). http://www.tn.auf.org/CEAFE/Papiers_CEAFE10/MacroI/Ferrant.pdf

Hawken, A., & Munck, G. L. (2013). Cross-national indices with gender-differentiated data: What do they measure? How valid are they? *Social Indicators Research, 111*(3), 801–838.

Hicks, N., & Streeten, P. (1979). Indicators of development: The search for a basic needs yardstick. *World Development, 7*, 567–580.

Hill, M. A., & King, E. (1995). Women's education and economic wellbeing. *Feminist Economics, 1*(2), 21–46.

Klasen, S. (1994). Missing women reconsidered. *World Development, 22*, 1061–1071.

Klasen, S. (1999). *Does gender inequality reduce growth and development? Evidence from cross-country regressions*. Policy Research Report on Gender and Development. World Bank.

Klasen, S., & Wink, C. (2003). Missing women: Revisiting the debate. *Feminist Economics, 9*, 263–299.

Kolovich, L., & Shibuya, S. 2016. Middle east and central Asia: A survey of gender budgeting efforts (IMF Working Papers 16/151). IMF.

Knowles, S., Lorgelly, P., & Owen, P. D. (2002). Are educational gender gaps a brake on economic development? Some cross-country empirical evidence. *Oxford Economic Papers, 54*(1), 118–149.

Lahiri, A., Chakraborty L., & Bhattacharyya, P. N. (2002). Gender budgeting in India. *Follow the Money Series*. UNIFEM.

Morris, M. D. (1979). *Measuring the condition of the world's poor: The physical quality of life index*. Pergamon.

Mushi, V., & Edward, M. (2010). Challenges and successes of gender budgeting initiatives: A case study of Tanzania. *Accountancy and Business Review Journal, 7*(2), 19–24.

Nakray, K. (2009). Gender budgeting: Does it really work? Some experience from India. *Policy and Politics, 37*(2), 307–310.

Nelson, J. A. (2017). *Gender and risk-taking: Economics*. Routledge.

Noorbakhsh, F. (1998). A modified human development index. *World Development, 26*(3), 517–528.

Permanyer, I. (2013). A critical assessment of the UNDP's gender inequality index. *Feminist Economics, 19*(2), 1–32.

Perrons, D. (2018, July). Review of gender and risk-taking: Economics, evidence, and why the answer matters. *Gender and Development, 26*(2).

Prugl, E. (2012). "If Lehman brothers had been Lehman sisters...": Gender and myth in the aftermath of the financial crisis. *International Political Sociology, 6*(1), 21–35.

Sharp, R., & Elson, D. (2008). *Improving budgets: A framework for assessing gender responsive budget initiatives*. Hawke Research Institute for Sustainable Societies, University of South Australia.

Stotsky, J. G. (2016). *Gender budgeting: Fiscal context and overview of current outcomes* (IMF Working Paper 16/149). International Monetary Fund.

Stotsky, J. (2020). *Using fiscal policy and public financial management to promote gender equality international perspectives*. Routledge.

Stotsky, J., & Zaman, A. (2016). *The influence of gender budgeting in Indian states on gender inequality and fiscal spending* (International Monetary Fund Working Paper 16/227).

Stotsky, J., Chakraborty, L., & Gandhi, P. (2019). *Impact of intergovernmental fiscal transfers on gender equality in India: An empirical analysis* (Working Paper). National Institute of Public Finance and Policy.

Thaddeus, S., & Maine, S. (1994, April). Too far to walk: Maternal mortality in context. *Social Science and Medicine, 38*(8), 1091–1110.

United Nations Development Programme (UNDP). (1995). *Human development report*. UNDP.

United Nations Research Institute for Social Development (UNRISD). (1972). *Contents and measurement of socio-economic development*. Praeger Publishers.

Van den Broek, N. R., & Falconer, A. D. (2011). Maternal mortality and millennium development goal 5. *British Medical Bulletin, 99, 25–38.* (Working Paper No. 273).

CHAPTER 4

Gender Budgeting and the Efficacy of Measuring Unpaid Care Economy

Gender budgeting is a tool of accountability that provides thrust to the unpaid care economy, which is otherwise statistically invisible. It is not just confined to specifically targeted programmes for women in the existing budget. Measuring the unpaid care economy is a unique contribution to the economic literature and policy discourses as it captures the roles and well-being of children, women, and men, especially poor women and mothers, in ways that extend beyond the scope of standard economic indicators (Grown et al., 2010). In the theory of the allocation of time, the allocation and efficiency of nonmarket working time may be more important to economic growth than market working time. Yet, the attention paid by economists to the market economy skews any paid to the other; nonmarket work continues to remain statistically invisible. Time-use data is used to capture the chronology of time, in which the time is dichotomized into market time and nonmarket time. The impact of the crisis on unpaid care economy work has been conducted against the backdrop of the global financial crisis (Bahçe-Kaya & Memiş, 2013; Berik & Ebru, 2013; Floro & Hitomi, 2011; Yamamoto, 2017) and recently ex post to COVID-19 pandemic outbreak (Andrew et al., 2020; Chakraborty et al., 2021; Deshpande, 2020; İlkkaracan & Emel, 2021).

© The Author(s), under exclusive license to Springer Nature Singapore Pte Ltd. 2022
L. S. Chakraborty, *Fiscal Policy for Sustainable Development in Asia-Pacific*, https://doi.org/10.1007/978-981-19-3281-6_4

Against the backdrop of COVID-19 pandemic, the time-use surveys are becoming more relevant to capture the fragility of work–life balance of employed women and the plausible window of opportunity created by men's increased participation in unpaid work (Andrew et al, 2020; İlkkaracan & Emel, 2021). In the context of Turkey, during the COVID-19 pandemic, women's unpaid work time almost doubled, while men's quadrupled. İlkkaracan and Emel (2021) highlighted the need for work–life balance policies and for investment in social care economy infrastructure in times of covid19. In India, Deshpande (2020) has analysed the first-order effects of lockdown on gender gaps in time allocation and in turn labour market outcomes. Chakraborty (2021) has analysed the gender components of economic stimulus packages—both fiscal and monetary policies—of selected countries in the Asia–Pacific region and identified that care economy infrastructure has not been given adequate emphasis in the stimulus packages in the region. The data from rapid gender assessment surveys investigating the socioeconomic consequences of COVID-19 on women's and men's lives, reveals that the impact of the pandemic goes far beyond health consequences (Seck et al., 2021); and given the labour markets in turmoil, work from home with young children out of school and intensified care needs of elderly and ill family members, there is a significant increase in the demand for unpaid domestic and care work during the COVID-19 pandemic. The study noted that with the market economy being closed, women are disproportionately bearing the burden of unpaid care and domestic work triggered by the lockdowns, and they are losing their livelihoods faster than men, and women are disproportionately affected by mental health issues (Seck et al., 2021). Craig and Brendan (2021) report early results on how the pandemic affected paid work, domestic work, and caring responsibilities. Their findings revealed that women shouldered most of the extra unpaid workload, but men's childcare time increased more in relative terms, so average gender gaps narrowed. These inferences reflect a need for sustained policy attention to the care economy to narrow rather than widen gender disparity during the time of pandemic. Gender budgeting is a promising fiscal framework to incorporate these significant concerns related to the unpaid care economy.

Statistical Invisibility of Unpaid Care Economy

In theory, the nonmarket time aggregates leisure and work at home. The justification for aggregating leisure and unpaid work at home rests on two assumptions: (a) the two elements react similarly to changes in the socio-economic environment and, therefore, nothing is gained by studying them separately; and (b) the two elements satisfy the conditions of a composite input—that is, the relative price is constant and there is no interest in investigating the composition of the aggregate since it has no bearing on production and the price of the output (Gronau, 1977). However, the time-use survey findings did reveal that these two assumptions are wrong, as unpaid work at home and leisure are not affected in the same way by changes in socioeconomic variables and the composition of the aggregate affects many facets of the intra-household behaviour. The findings from time-use survey—tricotomising the allocation of time into work in market, work at home, and leisure—can provide insights to integrate the nonmarket work into economic modelling and, in turn, in macroeconomic policymaking. This is particularly relevant when public investment policy can redress intra-household inequalities in terms of household division of labour by supporting initiatives that reduce the time allocation of women in unpaid work. Examples of such public policy interventions are improved infrastructure in the water sector, rural electrification, roads, sanitation services, and better transport infrastructure.

Despite the growing recognition of implications of time-budget statistics for macroeconomic policymaking, there have been relatively few examples of empirical literature on the topic. Bredie and Beeharry (1998) revealed that easy accessibility to drinking water facilities might lead to an increase in school enrollment, particularly for girls; in Madagascar, 83 per cent of the girls who did not go to school spent their time collecting water, while only 58 per cent of the girls who attended school spent time collecting water. Khandker (1988) showed that it was not the patriarchy per se that restricts women's time from market work in Bangladesh, but rather economic factors like low wages and low education. In the context of Pakistan, Ilahi and Franque (2000) indicated that worsening water-gathering infrastructure caused an increase in the total work burden of women. Empirical evidence suggests that women workers in Thailand experience a higher incidence of work intensity and hence lower quality of life compared with men (Floro & Anant, 2010). Using time-use data, analysis of "time poverty" (defined as lack of enough time for rest and leisure after accounting for the time that has to be spent working, whether in the labour market, doing domestic work, or performing other activities such as fetching water and wood) and found that women are more likely to be "time poor" than men (Bardasi & Quentin, 2010; Gammage, 2010). Motiram and Lars (2010) use the Indian Time Use Survey (ITUS, 1999) to analyse gender inequalities in the allocation of household tasks among girls and boys and their parents, finds more mixed evidence regarding gender favoritism in human capital investment. Liu Lan and Xiao-yuan Dong, Xiaoying Deng, 2010 unveil striking differences in labour market outcomes between caring for parents and caring for parents-in-law: caring for parents does not affect the caregiver's employment status and work hours, whereas caring for parents-in-law has a statistically significant, sizable, negative effect on the caregiver's probability of employment and hours of paid work. John (2020) analysed the link between women's paid work participation and intimate partner violence and found that in Nepal, the evidence refutes the economic bargaining models which contend that women's paid work reduces violence experienced due to increased bargaining power. The study found that in a traditional setting, working women are more likely to experience increased violence as they transgress traditional gender roles and the underlying gender hierarchies.

Nonmarket work remains significantly invisible in national accounts. A recognized shortcoming of the present system of national accounting (SNA) is the omission of nonmarket production from national accounts (Chakraborty, 2014; Mullan, 2010). The attempt of the United Nations Statistical Division in extending the production boundary of the Systems of National Accounts (SNA) in 1993 has led to the inclusion of nonmarket work into the national accounting system as satellite accounts (Box 4.1). Based on SNA 1993, the TUS classified the activities into SNA activities (that get included in GDP calculations), non-SNA activities (that do not get included in GDP but should be included in the satellite accounts), and residual activities.

In the Time Use Survey conducted in India by the National Statistical Organisation, the International Classification of Activities for Time Use Statistics 2016 (3-digit code) (ICATUS) was used to record the activities of the household members. The classification of activities in System of National Accounts (SNA) Production, non-SNA, and other remaining activities is given in the Box 4.2.

Box 4.1: Time-Use Survey classification of activities in SNA and Non-SNA, India 2020

- SNA production
- Employment in corporations, government and non-profit institutions
- Production of goods for own final use
- Employment in household enterprises to produce goods
- Employment in household enterprises to provide services
- Ancillary activities and breaks related to employment
- Training and studies in relation to employment
- Employment-related travel
- Unpaid trainee work and related activities
- Unpaid direct volunteering for other households for production of goods or for production of goods/services for market/non-market units
- Unpaid community- and organization-based volunteering for production of goods or for production of goods/services for market/non-market units
- Other unpaid work activities (other than those which are already covered in SNA or covered in non-SNA production)
- Non-SNA production
- Unpaid domestic services for household members
- Unpaid caregiving services for household members
- Unpaid direct volunteering for other households for production of services for the Households
- Unpaid community- and organization-based volunteering for production of services for the Households
- Other residual activities
- Seeking employment
- Setting up a business
- Commuting
- Learning
- Socializing and communication, community participation and religious practice
- Culture, leisure, mass-media and sports practices
- Self-care and maintenance

Source Government of India (2020), Time Use Survey 2020, National Statistical Office

Box 4.2: Systems of National Accounts 1993

The 1993 System of National Accounts (SNA) limits economic production of households for their own consumption to the production of *goods* alone and excludes the own-account production of personal and domestic services (except for the services produced by employing paid domestic staff, the own-account production of housing services produced by employing paid domestic staff, and the own-account production of housing services by owner-occupants). This allows the SNA to avoid valuing activities such as eating, drinking, and sleeping, which are difficult for a person to obtain from another person. But, in the process, activities such as fetching water from the river or the well, collecting fuel wood, washing clothes, house cleaning, and preparation and serving of meals, as well as care, training, and instruction of children and care of sick, infirm, or old people also gets excluded from the definition of economic activity. These services are mostly performed by women, but can also be procured from other units. While these activities are excluded partly because of the inadequate price systems for valuing these services, this exclusion principle leads to the economic invisibility and a statistical underestimation of women's work. It is interesting to recall in this context the famous economist Pigou's comment that if a housemaid employed by a bachelor were to marry him, national income would fall, since her previously paid work would now be performed unpaid

SNA 1993 suggests development of estimates for the value of household production of services for own use in satellite accounts of an alternative concept of gross domestic product (GDP). Estimation of the "unpaid" work of women in the care sector can suggest a quantification of the contribution of women to the economy. The quantification can also be useful for two more reasons. First,

> it would provide a fuller understanding of how resources and time are allocated in the economy. Second, it would indicate the extent to which economic development and the associated feminization of labor—through the substitution of own-account production of services by purchases from the market (for example, households using self-service laundry services instead of washing at home)—would give a fillip to the growth rate of GDP as it is measured. Monitoring such estimates over time can also help in understanding the effect of policies on these own-account production of services, which are critical for welfare
> *Source* Systems of National Accounts, UNSD (1993), Lahiri et al. (2002), Chakraborty (2014).

The latest Time Use Survey (TUS) of India was conducted from January to December 2019, for each member of age 6 years and above of the selected 1,38,799 households (rural: 82,897 and urban: 55,902). The Time Use Survey covered 4,47,250 persons of age 6 years and above, with 2,73,195 in rural India and 1,74,055 in urban India. The TUS 2020 noted that the survey covered the whole of the Indian Union except the villages in the Andaman and Nicobar Islands which are difficult to access. The first large-scale survey time-use survey conducted in India from July 1998 to June 1999 covered 18,591 households in India, covering all members of the household aged six years and above, for only six selected States.

The Time Use Survey gives a better understanding of how time is allocated across gender in the economy and provides some insights into the extent of statistical invisibility of women's work in India. The time allocation of different activities under the unpaid care economy sector is highlighted in the analysis in this section. The estimates of latest Time Use Survey are used for the analysis, however, the State-level estimates of the first Time Use Survey are selectively used for valuation of care economy as per cent of Gross State Domestic Product due to required data availability for the valuation.

The time-use data is generated usually on the basis of the time-diary method, confined to a probability sample of all types of days (weekdays and weekends). Time diary is a retrospective method in which the respondents are asked to keep an account of a recent twenty-four hours chronology of the use of time and researchers code the responses to a standard list of activities. Time-use diaries are preferred over the other methods, for they tend to be more comprehensive, they enable respondents to report activities on their own terms, and they have some form of a built-in check that increases the reliability of the data (Juster & Stanford, 1985).

The time-diary method has certain deficiencies. The significant one is the presence of multitasking or omission of overlapping activities. This results from the imposition of a rigid constraint of time use, namely, no person has either more or less time available than twenty-four hours per day (time constraint), and the set of activities capable of being measured, described, and analysed must add up to a fixed number of hours or days (Floro, 1995). Theoretically, it can be solved by defining the new activity as a joint activity, but the codes for possible diary activities would explode in number. The practical way of solving this problem is to indicate one activity as primary and the other as "secondary". Yet another way to conceptualize secondary activities is to argue that there is only one activity at any given time, but there are frequent switches between activities and if the time grid were fine enough, the issue of secondary activities would effectively disappear. Finally, it seems plausible that the issue of multiple or joint activities is the key source of the major failure of alternative recall methods. Recall accuracy falls when the respondents make primitive attempts to respond to questions about hours of an activity in the last week or month by engaging in a kind of *temporal double counting*—adding in periods when the activity was secondary to periods when it was central (Juster & Stanford, 1985).

Time-Use Pattern Across Gender and Geography in India

The estimates of time use per day in different activities are presented in this section for the Indian context, considering the participants in different activities and also presented considering all persons irrespective of their participation in activities to understand the distribution of total time of 1440 minutes available for each person in a day in different activities (Government of India, Time Use Survey, 2020). The participation rate in a day in any activity is defined in the Time Use Survey as the percentage of persons performing that activity during the 24 hours of the reference period. The average time (in minutes) spent in a day per person in SNA production, non-SNA productions, and residual other activities in India is given in Table 4.1. In rural India, women spent 286 minutes (around 5 hours) while men spent only 40 minutes a day. In urban India, men spent only half an hour in the care economy, while women spent 270 minutes a day (Table 4.1).

The percentage share of SNA production, non-SNA production, and residual other activities of the total time in a day per person based on India is given in Table 4.2. The estimates reveal that 19.9 per cent of time spent by women in the care economy in rural India is compared to

Table 4.1 Time allocation in SNA and Non-SNA, India 2020

Description of the activity (all India)	Male	Female	Person
Rural			
SNA production	262	87	176
Non-SNA production	40	286	161
SNA and non-SNA production	301	373	337
Residual other activities	1139	1067	1103
Total	1440	1440	1440
Urban			
SNA production	288	63	179
Non-SNA production	33	270	148
SNA and non-SNA production	321	333	327
Residual other activities	1119	1107	1113
Total	1440	1440	1440
Aggregate			
SNA production	269	80	177
Non-SNA production	38	281	157
SNA and non-SNA production	307	361	334
Residual other activities	1133	1079	1106
Total	1440	1440	1440

Note (i) The estimates have been calculated considering all the activities in a time slot
(ii) Figures may not add up to 1440 due to rounding
Source Government of India (2020), Time Use Survey 2020, National Statistical Office

Table 4.2 Distribution (%) of time use into SNA and Non-SNA, India 2020

Description of the activity (all India)	Male	Female	Person
	Rural		
SNA production	18.2	6.0	12.2
Non-SNA production	2.8	19.9	11.2
SNA and non-SNA production	20.9	25.9	23.4
Residual other activities	79.1	74.1	76.6
all	100.0	100.0	100.0
	Urban		
SNA production	20.0	4.4	12.4
Non-SNA production	2.3	18.8	10.3
SNA and non-SNA production	22.3	23.1	22.7
Residual other activities	77.7	76.9	77.3
all	100.0	100.0	100.0
	Aggregate		
SNA production	18.7	5.6	12.3
Non-SNA production	2.6	19.5	10.9
SNA and non-SNA production	21.3	25.1	23.2
Residual other activities	78.7	74.9	76.8
all	100.0	100.0	100.0

Note (i) The estimates have been calculated considering all the activities in a time slot
(ii) Figures may not add up to 100 due to rounding
Source Government of India (2020), Time Use Survey 2020, National Statistical Office

2.8 per cent by men. In urban India, it is slightly reduced to 18.8 per cent by women and 2.3 per cent by men (Table 4.2).

The average time (in minutes) spent in a day per person of different age groups in SNA production, non-SNA production, and residual other activities reveal that in rural India, women even in the age group 60 years and above spent around 217 minutes a day in unpaid care economy sector while men spent 52 minutes a day. In urban India, women and men in the age group, 60 years and above spent 204 minutes and 48 minutes, respectively, a day. The estimates of other age groups suggest that women spent around 5 hours a day in the care economy (Table 4.3).

The percentage share of unpaid activities, paid activities, and residual other activities of the total time in day per person of different age groups

Table 4.3 Age-disaggregated time allocation in SNA and Non-SNA in India, 2020

Description of the activity (all India)	Age group (time in minutes)								
	15–29 Years Male	15–59 Years Female	60 Years + Person	15–29 Years Male	15–59 Years Female	60 Years + Person	15–29 Years Male	15–59 Years Female	60 Years + Person
Rural									
SNA production	244	62	151	327	104	215	222	80	154
Non-SNA production	35	332	186	44	345	196	52	217	132
SNA and non-SNA production	280	393	337	372	448	411	275	297	285
Residual other activities	1160	1047	1103	1068	992	1029	1165	1143	1155
All	1440	1440	1440	1440	1440	1440	1440	1440	1440
Urban									
SNA production	255	58	161	356	77	220	161	33	98
Non-SNA production	28	265	142	35	318	173	48	204	125
SNA and non-SNA production	284	323	303	391	395	393	209	237	223
Residual other activities	1156	1117	1137	1049	1045	1047	1231	1203	1217
All	1440	1440	1440	1440	1440	1440	1440	1440	1440

(continued)

Table 4.3 (continued)

Description of the activity (all India)	Age group (time in minutes)								
	15–29 Years Male	15–59 Years Female	60 Years + Person	15–29 Years Male	15–59 Years Female	60 Years + Person	15–29 Years Male	15–59 Years Female	60 Years + Person
	Aggregate								
SNA production	248	60	155	337	95	217	204	65	136
Non-SNA production	33	312	172	41	337	189	51	213	130
SNA and non-SNA production	281	373	327	378	432	405	255	279	267
Residual other activities	1159	1067	1113	1062	1008	1035	1185	1161	1173
All	1440	1440	1440	1440	1440	1440	1440	1440	1440

Note (i) The estimates have been calculated considering all the activities in a time slot
(ii) Figures may not add up to 100 due to rounding
Source Government of India (2020), Time Use Survey 2020, National Statistical Office

reveal that women in the age group 60 years spent 15.1 per cent and 15–29 years age group spent 23.1 per cent in care economy in rural India, when compared to men of same age groups, respectively, 3.6 per cent and 2.4 per cent of entire day (Table 4.4). The pattern is the same for urban India as well.

The average time (in minutes) spent in a day per participant in different activities reveals that women in rural India spent 301 minutes on an average in unpaid domestic services including household chores while men spent only 98 minutes. In urban India, time allocation in household chores by men and women respectively was 97 and 299 minutes. In addition to household chores, women spent 132 minutes on the unpaid caregiving services within the household compared to 77 minutes by men in rural India. In urban India, the time allocation by men and women in unpaid care services was, respectively, 75 and 138 minutes, as per the time-use statistics 2020 (Table 4.5).

The average time (in minutes) spent in a day per participant of different levels of education reveals that despite the levels of education, the time spent in care economy by men and women in unpaid household services and unpaid caregiving services remained almost unchanged. The time spent by women on household chores was around 5 hours across categories of education (Table 4.6).

The geographically disaggregated average time (in minutes) spent in a day per participant in different activities reveals that in rural and urban India women spent around 300 minutes on unpaid domestic services for household members as compared to around 98 minutes by men (Table 4.7). In caregiving services for household members, men spent little more than an hour while women spent more than two hours in rural and urban India.

The percentage share of total time in different activities in a day per person reveals that in rural India, women spent 17.2 per cent of total time on unpaid domestic services and 2.6 per cent on unpaid caregiving services for household members; while these figures are, respectively, 1.9 per cent and 0.8 per cent for men (Table 4.8). In urban India, these

Table 4.4 Age-disaggregated distribution (%) of time allocation in SNA and Non-SNA, India 2020

Age group	15–29 Years Male	15–59 Years Female	60 Years + Person	15–29 Years Male	15–59 Years Female	60 Years + Person	15–29 Years Male	15–59 Years Female	60 Years + Person
Description of the activity (all India)	Rural								
SNA production	16.9	4.3	10.5	22.7	7.2	14.9	15.4	5.6	10.7
Non-SNA production	2.4	23.1	12.9	3.1	24	13.6	3.6	15.1	9.2
SNA and non-SNA production	19.4	27.3	23.4	25.8	31.1	28.5	19.1	20.6	19.8
Residual other activities	80.6	72.7	76.6	74.2	68.9	71.5	80.9	79.4	80.2
All	100	100	100	100	100	100	100	100	100
	Urban								
SNA production	17.7	4	11.2	24.7	5.3	15.3	11.2	2.3	6.8
Non-SNA production	1.9	18.4	9.9	2.4	22.1	12	3.3	14.2	8.7
SNA and non-SNA production	19.7	22.4	21	27.2	27.4	27.3	14.5	16.5	15.5
Residual other activities	80.3	77.6	79	72.8	72.6	72.7	85.5	83.5	84.5
All	100	100	100	100	100	100	100	100	100

Age group	15–29 Years Male	15–59 Years Female	60 Years + Person	15–29 Years Male	15–59 Years Female	60 Years + Person	15–29 Years Male	15–59 Years Female	60 Years + Person
	Aggregate								
SNA production	17.2	4.2	10.8	23.4	6.6	15.1	14.2	4.5	9.4
Non-SNA production	2.3	21.7	11.9	2.8	23.4	13.1	3.5	14.8	9
SNA and non-SNA production	19.5	25.9	22.7	26.3	30	28.1	17.7	19.4	18.5
Residual other activities	80.5	74.1	77.3	73.8	70	71.9	82.3	80.6	81.5
All	100	100	100	100	100	100	100	100	100

Note (i) The estimates have been calculated considering all the activities in a time slot
(ii) Figures may not add up to 100 due to rounding
Source Government of India (2020), Time Use Survey 2020, National Statistical Office

Table 4.5 Time allocation of men and women in a day in different activities in India, 2020

Description of the activity (time given in minutes)	Rural			Urban			Aggregate		
	Male	Female	Person	Male	Female	Person	Male	Female	Person
Employment and related Activities	434	317	404	514	375	485	459	333	429
Production of goods for own final use	203	123	158	134	64	85	198	116	151
Unpaid domestic services for household members	98	301	249	94	293	247	97	299	248
Unpaid caregiving services for household members	77	132	113	75	138	116	76	134	114
Unpaid volunteer, trainee and other unpaid work	99	98	98	111	101	106	102	99	101
Learning	422	422	422	435	425	430	426	423	424
Socializing and communication, community participation and religious practice	151	139	145	138	138	138	147	139	143
Culture, leisure, mass-media and sports practices	162	157	159	171	181	176	164	165	165
Self-care and maintenance	737	724	731	711	720	715	729	723	726

Note (i) The estimates have been calculated considering all the activities in a time slot
(ii) Figures may not add up to 100 due to rounding
Source Government of India (2020), Time Use Survey 2020, National Statistical Office

Table 4.6 Time allocation by men and women of different levels of education in India, 2020

Description of the activity	Literate and level of education						Literate and level of education				
	Not Literate	Below primary	Primary	Upper primary/ middle	Secondary and above	All	Not Literate	Below primary	Primary	Upper primary/ middle	Secondary and above	All
	Male						Female					
Employment and related activities	447	430	449	464	471	459	342	303	315	305	349	333
Production of goods for own final use	217	196	197	198	184	198	140	107	108	98	89	116
Unpaid domestic services for household	108	93	95	94	95	97	296	301	304	308	295	299
Unpaid caregiving services for household	77	84	75	73	76	76	126	126	131	131	146	134
Unpaid volunteer, trainee and other unpaid	92	87	94	102	111	102	103	90	98	91	102	99

(continued)

Table 4.6 (continued)

Description of the activity	Literate and level of education (Male)						Literate and level of education (Female)					
	Not Literate	Below primary	Primary	Upper primary/ middle	Secondary and above	All	Not Literate	Below primary	Primary	Upper primary/ middle	Secondary and above	All
Learning	366	416	438	450	417	426	355	411	440	453	410	423
Socializing and communication, community	169	125	140	142	149	147	159	122	130	131	132	139
Culture, leisure, mass-media and sports	150	190	166	156	164	164	159	186	165	157	165	165
Self-care and maintenance	751	760	734	723	710	729	738	749	721	713	702	723

Note (i) The estimates have been calculated considering all the activities in a time slot
(ii) Figures may not add up to 100 due to rounding
Source Government of India (2020), Time Use Survey 2020, National Statistical Office

Table 4.7 Time allocation in different activities by geography, 2020

Description of the activity	Rural			Urban			Aggregate		
	Male	Female	Person	Male	Female	Person	Male	Female	Person
Employment and related Activities	434	317	404	514	375	485	459	333	429
Production of goods for own final use	203	123	158	134	64	85	198	116	151
Unpaid domestic services for household members	98	301	249	94	293	247	97	299	248
Unpaid caregiving services for household members	77	132	113	75	138	116	76	134	114
Unpaid volunteer, trainee and other unpaid work	99	98	98	111	101	106	102	99	101
Learning	422	422	422	435	425	430	426	423	424
Socializing and communication, community participation, and religious practice	151	139	145	138	138	138	147	139	143
Culture, leisure, mass-media, and sports practices	162	157	159	171	181	176	164	165	165
Self-care and maintenance	737	724	731	711	720	715	729	723	726

Note (i) The estimates have been calculated considering all the activities in a time slot
(ii) Figures may not add up to 100 due to rounding
Source Government of India (2020), Time Use Survey 2020, National Statistical Office

Table 4.8 Distribution (%) of time, by geography and gender, in India, 2020

Description of the activity (all India)	Rural			Urban			Aggregate		
	Male	Female	Person	Male	Female	Person	Male	Female	Person
Employment and related Activities	16.9	4.2	10.6	21.3	4.3	13.1	18.3	4.2	11.4
Production of goods for own final use	2.7	2.2	2.4	0.3	0.3	0.3	1.9	1.6	1.8
Unpaid domestic services for household members	1.9	17.2	9.4	1.5	16.1	8.6	1.7	16.9	9.2
Unpaid caregiving services for household members	0.8	2.6	1.7	0.7	2.5	1.6	0.8	2.6	1.7
Unpaid volunteer, trainee, and other unpaid work	0.2	0.1	0.1	0.2	0.1	0.1	0.2	0.1	0.1
Learning	7.1	5.7	6.4	7	6.1	6.6	7.1	5.8	6.5
Socializing & communication, community participation, and religious practice	9.6	8.8	9.2	8.7	8.8	8.8	9.3	8.8	9
Culture, leisure, mass-media, and sports practices	9.7	9	9.4	10.9	11.7	11.3	10.1	9.8	9.9
Self-care and maintenance	51.2	50.3	50.8	49.4	50	49.7	50.6	50.2	50.4
Total	100	100	100	100	100	100	100	100	100

Note (i) The estimates have been calculated considering all the activities in a time slot
(ii) Figures may not add up to 100 due to rounding
Source Government of India (2020), Time Use Survey 2020, National Statistical Office

estimates are 16.9 per cent and 2.6 per cent for women; and 1.7 per cent and 0.8 per cent for men.

The percentage of persons participating in different activities as per the usual principal activity status revealed that labour market participation has not reduced the percentage of women participating in unpaid domestic chores in the care economy. Around 93 per cent of women workers (as per broad usual principal status) spent time in unpaid domestic services for household members as compared to 17.8 per cent of men (Table 4.9).

Valuation of Unpaid Care Economy: An Illustration

The valuation of the care economy for six selected States in India is attempted, using the estimates of first time-use survey. The first time-use survey found that, in the production of own-account services that qualify for inclusion in the satellite accounts as per SNA 1993, on average, a female spent 34.6 hours per week compared to 3.6 hours by a male (Table 4.10). In these activities, females in Gujarat scored the most time spent (39.08 hours per week), followed by Madhya Pradesh (35.79 hours) and Orissa (35.70 hours).

Time-use data of combined states suggest that women spent 50.52 per cent of their time on unpaid work while men spent only 33.15 per cent (Table 4.11). The interstate differences revealed that per cent of time spent by females in unpaid activities was highest in Haryana (85.99 per cent), followed by Meghalaya (76.39 per cent) and Orissa (69.44 per cent); the lowest time spent was in Tamil Nadu (32.45 per cent).

Imputing value to labour time spent on unpaid work, the contribution of nonmarket work was estimated across six states of India. District-wise data on wage rates for agricultural labour and wage rates for urban, unskilled manual labour have been used for valuing unpaid work in rural and urban areas, respectively. With this methodology, projecting the TUS results by age and district of the population, the valuation of time spent on unpaid activities by females in Meghalaya and Madhya Pradesh indicates that the value of unpaid activities could be as much as 38–41 per cent of

Table 4.9 Percentage of men and women participating in different activities (usual principal activity status)

Description of the activity (all India)	Broad usual principal activity status				
	Worker	Unemployed	Labour force	Not in labour force	All
	Male				
Employment and related activities	84.9	21.3	82.7	6.3	57.3
Production of goods for own final use	18.8	12	18.6	5.6	14.3
Unpaid domestic services for household members	31	33.9	31.1	16.1	26.1
Unpaid caregiving services for household members	17.8	9.7	17.5	7	14
Unpaid volunteer, trainee, and other unpaid work	3.2	3.9	3.2	1.6	2.7
Learning	1.2	22.5	1.9	67.8	23.9
Socializing and communication, community participation, and religious practice	94.4	96.1	94.5	85.2	91.4
Culture, leisure, mass-media, and sports practices	85.2	95.1	85.5	94.6	88.5
Self-care and maintenance	100	100	100	100	100
	Female				
Employment and related activities	73	12.9	70.9	5.5	18.4
Production of goods for own final use	27.9	14.8	27.4	18.2	20

(continued)

Table 4.9 (continued)

Description of the activity (all India)	Broad usual principal activity status				
	Worker	Unemployed	Labour force	Not in labour force	All
Unpaid domestic services for household members	93	85.6	92.8	78.4	81.2
Unpaid caregiving services for household members	24	18.3	23.8	28.5	27.6
Unpaid volunteer, trainee and other unpaid work	2.8	3.2	2.9	1.8	2
Learning	1.7	34	2.9	24	19.8
Socializing and communication, community participation, and religious practice	90.9	94.9	91.1	91.3	91.3
Culture, leisure, mass-media and sports practices	79.9	92.5	80.4	86.5	85.3
Self-care and maintenance	100	100	100	100	100

Note (i) The estimates have been calculated considering all the activities in a time slot
(ii) Figures may not add up to 100 due to rounding
Source Government of India (2020), Time Use Survey 2020, National Statistical Office

the relevant State Domestic Product (SDP). For example, the total value of such activities by females was Rs. 29,034 crore in Madhya Pradesh, relative to SDP of Rs. 70,832 crore (Table 4.12).

Compared to females, the valuation of unpaid activities by males was limited to only about 2 per cent of SDP in Gujarat and Haryana. The unpaid work, as a proportion of SDP, is as high as 49.93 per cent in Meghalaya and 47.30 per cent in Madhya Pradesh.

Table 4.10 Time allocation by women and men, selected states of India (weekly average time in hours)

States	Female				Male				Total		
	SNA	Ext-SNA	Residual Non-SNA		SNA	Ext-SNA	Residual Non-SNA		SNA	Ext-SNA	Residual Non-SNA
Haryana	21.26	31.06	115.67		37.7	1.99	128.23		30.19	15.24	122.52
Madhya Pradesh	19.85	35.79	112.38		42.1	4.43	121.47		31.54	19.22	117.19
Gujarat	17.6	39.08	111.36		43.6	3.19	121.12		31.24	20.27	116.44
Orissa	17.07	35.7	115.2		40.1	4.47	123.45		28.69	19.91	119.36
Tamil Nadu	18.97	30.46	118.61		42.5	3.19	122.27		30.68	16.87	120.45
Meghalaya	26.34	34.52	107.15		45.9	7.16	114.78		35.88	21.28	110.84
Combined States	18.72	34.63	114.58		42	3.65	122.42		30.75	18.69	118.62

Table 4.11 Distribution (%) of time use in SNA and Non-SNA: Selected states in India

States	Male			Female			Total		
	Paid	Unpaid	% of time use on unpaid activities	Paid	Unpaid	% of time use on unpaid activities	Paid	Unpaid	% of time use on unpaid activities
Haryana	33.09	18.12	35.38	4.13	25.34	85.99	20.6	21.37	51.58
Madhya Pradesh	29.41	23.34	44.25	14.3	15.75	52.4	22.99	20.12	46.67
Gujarat	44.37	14.17	24.21	17.2	13.87	44.67	33.26	14.05	29.7
Orissa	31.25	22.42	41.77	8	18.18	69.44	20.55	20.47	49.9
Tamil Nadu	41.42	13.36	24.39	21.8	10.32	32.45	32.74	12.04	26.89
Meghalaya	17.34	35.39	67.12	7.83	25.34	76.39	12.65	30.44	70.64
Combined States	36.54	18.12	33.15	14.9	15.18	50.52	27.16	16.85	38.29

Table 4.12 Valuation of unpaid care economy: Selected states of India

States	Value of nonmarket work (Rs. Crores)			SDP (Rs. cr.)	"Nonmarket Work" as a % of State Domestic Product		
	Male	Female	Total	1997–98	Male	Female	Total
Haryana	928.74	10,209.30	11,138.04	37,427	2.48	27.28	29.76
Madhya Pradesh	4466.03	29,034.09	33,500.12	70,832	6.31	40.99	47.3
Gujarat	2209.55	22,577.63	24,787.18	86,609	2.55	26.07	28.62
Orissa	1463.78	11,343.88	12,807.65	32,669	4.48	34.72	39.2
Tamil Nadu	3073.37	19,922.04	22,995.40	87,394	3.52	22.8	26.31
Meghalaya	260.45	862.97	1123.42	2250	11.58	38.35	49.93

Source Pande (2000)

GENDER BUDGETING: THE LINK BETWEEN PUBLIC INVESTMENT AND TIME ALLOCATION

The valuation of unpaid care economy has significant policy implications, in terms of gender budgeting. It is often argued that mainstream public expenditure, such as infrastructure, is non-rival in nature and therefore applying a gender lens to these expenditures may not be feasible. This argument is refuted by the time-use statistics. The time-use data revealed that this argument is often flawed, as there is an intrinsic gender dimension to the non-rival expenditure. The time allocation in activities like fetching of water and fuel has significant gender differentials, therefore infrastructure investment with gender-sensitive water and energy policies can really benefit women. The gender-disaggregated statistics of time use in the water sector across the six selected states in India from the first time-use survey clearly revealed that women spent more time in fetching water than men, except in Gujarat (Table 4.13).

Apart from the time allocation in the activity, it is to be noted that the travel time for fetching water, fuel, etc. is also equally time-consuming. The time-use data also revealed the gender differentials in travel time. There is thus a clear link between access to water and time allocation of women, who have a primary responsibility to ensure drinking water to their households, which suggests that changes in the availability of water infrastructure can lessen their burden in fetching the water, as well as release their time locked up in nonmarket work for the income-earning economic activities. In other words, investment in water infrastructure

Table 4.13 Time-use pattern by men and women in water sector (weekly average time in hours)

States	Rural			Urban			Total		
	Male	Female	Total	Male	Female	Total	Male	Female	Total
Haryana	3.2	5.54	5.38	3.08	4.79	4.71	3.19	5.48	5.33
Madhya Pradesh	3.21	5.4	5.03	1.21	2.96	2.76	3.11	5.22	4.88
Gujarat	14	0	14	0	0	0	14	0	14
Orissa	5.96	8.02	7.83	0	5.21	5.21	5.96	7.94	7.76
Tamil Nadu	3.85	4.79	4.69	2.56	4.62	4.26	3.33	4.74	4.57
Meghalaya	4.69	5.21	5.04	9.54	7.08	8.31	5.34	5.34	5.34
Combined States	3.83	5.11	4.97	3.02	4.63	4.35	3.61	5.02	4.85

Source Chakraborty (2014)

can help women in reallocating their labour time and reduce the stress related to walking long distances to fetch water.

In the next section, an illustrative empirical investigation of this hypothesis is undertaken using the data from the Time-use Survey for variables on time and finance accounts of selected states of India for the variable related to public infrastructure.

Ideally, the empirical analysis requires comprehensive time-use data, either in terms of longitudinal surveys or across considerable cross-section units. However, within the data constraints of limited cross-section units of time-use data collected in rural and urban regions of selected states of India, an illustrative analysis is undertaken to examine the link between infrastructure and time allocation. The hypothesis under investigation is whether better access to water infrastructure can help women to spend more time on market-oriented activities. The theoretical framework is given in Box 4.3.

Box 4.3: The link between time allocation and public investment

The link between infrastructure investment and time allocation is interpreted in Becker-Gronau models of time allocation. This framework is derived by refuting the assumption of *labor force exogeneity* in the treatment of the nonmarket economy, which is intrinsic to the neoclassical labor supply models of consumption and leisure.

In other words, the model has incorporated the intra-household gender asymmetries in the allocation of time, as well as the choices and constraints regarding labor-force participation in the market and nonmarket economy. The improvised model recognizes the dynamic interaction between the dual sets of economic activity—that is, the statistically invisible nonmarket economy and market economy

The model assumes that the household's utility function depends on the commodities consumed (z_i) and the leisure of its members (t_i^1):

$$u_i = u_i(z_i, t_1^1, t_2^1) \tag{4.1}$$

Consumption is generated through a household production function:

$$z_i = z_i(W_i, x_i, t_1^e, t_2^e) \tag{4.2}$$

where W_i is the amount of water used by the household, x_i is a monetized input, and t_i^e denotes the time allocated to nonmarket work (e-SNA) by family members; $i = 1, 2$

The water production function, in turn, is generated by:

$$W_i = f(t_i^w, \Omega_i) \tag{4.3}$$

where t_i^w is time allocated to fetch water and parameter Ω_i captures the access to water infrastructure

The household agents maximize their welfare subject to budget and time constraints given by:
max

$$u_i = u_i(z_i, t_i^1) \tag{4.4}$$

subject to

$$t_i^w + t_i^m + t_i^e + t_i^1 \geq T_0 \tag{4.5}$$

and

$$x_i = w_1 t_1^m + w_2 t_2^m + v_i \quad (4.6)$$

where t_1^m is the market time, T_0 is total time endowment, w_i is the market wage rate, and
v_i is the unearned income

Combining Eqs. (4.5) and (4.6), the full income constraint is obtained as follows:

$$x_i + w_i\left(t_i^w + t_i^e + t_i^1\right) = w_i T_0 + v_i \quad (4.7)$$

Solving for the first order conditions, a set of selected determinants of optimum time and commodity demand functions are derived as follows:

$$t^m = t^m(w, v, \Omega) \quad (4.8)$$

and

$$x^* = x(w, v, \Omega) \quad (4.9)$$

For econometric estimation, a reduced system of time equation is specified as follows:

$$t^m = t^m(w, v, \Omega) + \mu_i \quad (4.10)$$

Source Chakraborty (2008).

The model specification is proposed as follows:

$$t_i^m = \alpha + \beta infra_i + \gamma infrasq_i + \lambda t_i^0 + \delta t_i^c + dummy + u_i;$$

where $t_i{}^m$ is time allocation in SNA activity (otherwise referred as market time). The variable infra$_i$ denotes allocation and access to water infrastructure. The financial input variable of allocation is proxied by the log of public investment in infrastructure across cross-section units, while access to infrastructure or the distance variable is captured through the time-use budget of travel (*ttimi*). The squared term of infrastructure reflects the plausible quadratic relationship between access to infrastructure and market time—that is, market time falls with fetching distance but at a decreasing rate. The variable t_i^o denotes the opportunity cost of time, which is captured through market wage rate. Wage rates for agricultural labour and wage rates for urban, unskilled manual labour have been used for proxying the t_i^o in rural and urban areas, respectively. The unearned income is proxied by the spouse's wage in selected models. As variables of opportunity cost of time and unearned income reported multicollinearity problems, estimations are done in separate models. The models are controlled for the nonmonetized work done in the *care economy* (t_i^c). A dummy is defined as takes the value of one if the unit of analysis is rural and a value of zero otherwise. The parameters β and γ measure the effect of infrastructure on time variables; μ_i is a random error term. The econometric results are given in Table 4.14.

Table 4.14 Econometric Link between Infrastructure and Time Allocation

Dependent Variable↓	Female		Male	
	Model 1	Model 2	Model 3	Model 4
A	149.454	−21.126	174.714	101.721
	(2.468)*	(−0.489)	(4.882)*	−5.988
Log (public infrastraucture)$_i$	−27.466		−18.719	–
	(−1.947)*		(−2.241)*	
log (public infrastructuresquared)$_i$	1.539		1.112	–
	−1.859		(2.262)*	
ttimi (travel time)$_i$	–	−1.707	–	−0.0009
		(−0.821)		(−0.002)
ttimsqi (travel time squared)$_i$	–	0.132	–	0.0003
		−0.579		−0.024
tio (male wage)	–	8.177	−12.81	−14.056
		−1.024	(−4.459)*	(−3.673)
tio (female wage)	0.597	–	–	–
	−0.157			
tic (non-monetized care economy)	−0.588	0.032	−1.419	−1.363
	(−2.298)*	−0.072	(−3.663)*	(−2.601)
Dummy	12.699	16.308	−0.081	0.712
	(7.631)*	(4.669)*	(−0.079)	−0.463
R^2	0.94	0.91	0.88	0.77
DW	1.85	2.15	2.05	1.95

Source (Basic Data), Finance Accounts of selected six States and Time-use Survey (2000)

The results, though tentative due to data constraints, suggest that there is a quadratic relationship between access to infrastructure and market work; market time decreases with travel time to fetch water, but at a decreasing rate. The estimated coefficients suggest that the relationship between infrastructure access and time allocation in SNA activity is negative, which supports the hypothesis that better public infrastructure may release women's time to more market-oriented work. The financial input proxy for infrastructure also shows an initially decreasing and then increasing link with SNA activity, which needs a careful interpretation. The results indicate that higher infrastructural investment per se does not release the time of women towards SNA activity. This points to the fact that higher budgetary allocation for infrastructure per se does not mean higher spending. Gender-budgeting studies showed that there is a significant deviation between what is budgeted and what is actually spent (Lahiri et al., 2002). The lag in the implementation of infrastructural projects may be a reason for the concave relationship. The results of linear models are not reported, as the quadratic models turned out to be the better fits.

Theoretically, a positive relationship between wages and market work is expected, which explains that as opportunity cost of time rises, women may allocate more time to market work. However, results revealed that wage is not a significant determinant of women's time in SNA activity. The labour-supply models predict an inverse relationship between unearned income and SNA activity. However, the estimated coefficient of spouse's wage is not found significant in determining women's time allocation in SNA activity. The model is controlled for the nonmonetized work in the care economy, inclusive of child care, care for sick, and elderly care. The results showed that there is an inverse relationship between the work in the care economy and market economy, however, it was significant only for the models with financial input variable.

Broadly, the estimates suggest that there can be a link between deterioration in infrastructure and rural poverty, as worsening water infrastructure could lock in the time of women in unpaid work that would otherwise be available for income-generating SNA activity. Time poverty affects income poverty; however, the aspects of *time poverty* are often overlooked when framing macro policies. The point to be noted here is that even with the unit-record data, the analysis of the poverty-related aspects of time allocation and its implications for public investment may be severely restricted, as time-use data across income quintiles or monthly per capita consumer expenditure (mpce) quintiles is not available for India. To conclude, the chapter provides new evidence on the link between public infrastructure and time allocation related to the water sector in India. The estimated coefficients suggest that worsening public infrastructure affects market work with evident gender differentials. The results, though tentative, indicate that access to public infrastructure can lead to substitution effects in time allocation between unpaid work and market work, which has implications for reducing the poverty in the household. In addition to the link between public investment and time allocation, the time-use surveys can also be used to understand the other aspects of macro-fiscal policies including the policies relate to work–life balance, care provider's perspectives and the dual work burden of women (Amarante & Cecilia, 2018; Antonopolos & Indira, 2004; Arora & Codrina, 2017; Craig & Brendan, 2021; Floro & Hitomi, 2011; İlkkaracan & Emel, 2021; İlkkaracan et al., 2020; Qi & Xiao-yuang, 2018; Seymour et al., 2020; Stevano et al., 2019). The broad conclusion is that fiscal policies designed to redress income poverty can be partial if they do not take into account aspects of *time poverty*.

References

Amarante, V., & Cecilia, R. (2018). Unfolding patterns of unpaid household work in Latin America. *Feminist Economics, 24*(1), 1–34.

Andrew, A., Sarah, C., Dias, M., Christine, F., Lucy, K., Sonya, K., ... Almudena, S. (2020). *How are mothers and fathers balancing work and family under lockdown?* Institute for Fiscal Studies.

Antonopolos, R., & Indira, H. (2004). *Unpaid work and the economy gender, time use and poverty in developing countries*. Palgrave Macmillan.

Arora, D., & Codrina, R. (2017). A gendered model of the peasant household: Time poverty and farm production in rural Mozambique. *Feminist Economics, 23*(2), 93–119.

Bahçe-Kaya, S., & Memiş, E. (2013). Estimating the impact of the 2008–09 economic crisis on work time in Turkey. *Feminist Economics, 19*(3), 181–207.

Bardasi, E., & Quentin, W. (2010). Working long hours and having no choice: Time poverty in Guinea. *Feminist Economics, 16*(3), 45–78.

Berik, G., & Ebru, K. (2013). Time allocation of married mothers and fathers in hard times: The 2007–09 US recession. *Feminist Economics, 19*(3), 208–237. https://doi.org/10.1080/13545701.2013.798425

Bredie, J., & Beeharry, G. (1998). *School enrolment decline in Sub-Saharan Africa* (World Bank Discussion Paper No. 395).

Chakraborty, L. (2008). *Deficient public infrastructure and private costs: Evidence from a time use survey for the water sector in India* (Working Paper No. 536). New York: Levy Economics Institute.

Chakraborty, L. (2014). *Integrating time in public policy: Empirical description of gender-specific outcomes and budgeting* (Working Paper No. 785). Levy Economics Institute (New York: Levy Economics Institute).

Chakraborty, L. (2021). *Gender analysis of Covid19 economic stimulus packages in Asia Pacific.* UN Women.

Chakraborty, L., Amandeep, K., Divy, R., & Jannet, F. J. (2021). *Covid19 and fiscal-monetary policy responses in Asia Pacific.* NIPFP Publications.

Craig, L., & Brendan, C. (2021). Working and caring at home: Gender differences in the effects of covid-19 on paid and unpaid labor in Australia. *Feminist Economics, 27*(1–2), 310–326.

Deshpande, A. (2020). The Covid-19 pandemic and lockdown: First order effects on gender gaps in employment and domestic time use in India. *Global Labor Organization, Essen, Germany* (Discussion Paper, No. 607).

Floro, M. S., & Anant, P. (2010). Gender work intensity and well-being of Thai home-based workers. *Feminist Economics, 16*(3), 5–44.

Floro, M. S., & Hitomi, K. (2011). Gender and work in South Africa: What can time-use data reveal? *Feminist Economics, 17*(4), 33–66.

Floro, M. S. (1995). Women's well-being, poverty, and work intensity. *Feminist Economics, 1*(3), 1–25.

Gammage, S. (2010). Time pressed and time poor: Unpaid household work in Guatemala. *Feminist Economics, 16*(3), 79–112.

Government of India. (2020). *Time Use Survey 2020.* National Statistical Organisation.

Gronau, R. (1977). Leisure, home production, and work—The theory of allocation of time revisited. *Journal of Political Economy, 85,* 1099–1123.

Grown, C., Maria, F., & Diane, E. (2010). Unpaid work, time use, poverty and public policy, (Guest Editorial Note). *Feminist Economics, 16*(3), 5–44.

Ilahi, N., & Franque, G. (2000). Public infrastructure and private costs: Water supply and time allocation of women in rural Pakistan. *Economic Development and Cultural Change, 49*(1), 45–76.

İlkkaracan, İ, & Emel, M. (2021). Transformations in the gender gaps in paid and unpaid work during the covid-19 pandemic: Findings from Turkey. *Feminist Economics, 27*(1–2), 288–309.

İlkkaracan, İ., Kijong, K., Masterson, T., Emel, M., & Ajit, Z. (2020). *The impact of investing in social care on employment generation, time- and income-poverty and gender aps: A macro-micro policy simulation for Turkey.* (CWE-GAM Working Paper). Care Work and the Economy-Gender and Macromodeling.

John, N. A. (2020). Exploring the linkages between women's paid and unpaid work and their experiences of intimate partner and non-partner violence in Nepal. *Feminist Economics, 26*(4), 89–113.

Juster, F., & Stanford, F. (1985). *Time goods and well-being*. Institute for Social Research, University of Michigan.

Khandker, S. (1988). Determinants of women's time allocation in rural Bangladesh. *Economic Development and Cultural Change, 37*(1), 111–126.

Lahiri, A., Chakraborty, L., & Bhattacharyaa, P. N. (2002). *Gender budgeting in India, follow the money series*. UNIFEM.

Motiram, S., & Lars, O. (2010). Gender inequalities in tasks and instruction opportunities within Indian families. *Feminist Economics, 16*(3), 141–167.

Mullan, K. (2010). Valuing parental childcare in the United Kingdom. *Feminist Economics, 16*(3), 113–139.

Pande. (2000). *Women's contribution to economy, project paper on gender budgeting*. (Unpublished). National Institute of Public Finance and Policy.

Qi, L., & Xiao-yuan, D. (2018). Gender, low-paid status, and time poverty in urban China. *Feminist Economics, 24*(2), 171–193.

Seck, P. A., Encarnacion, J. O., Cecilia, T., & Sara, D.-V. (2021). Gendered impacts of COVID-19 in Asia and the Pacific: Early evidence on deepening socioeconomic inequalities in paid and unpaid work. *Feminist Economics, 27*(1–2), 117–132.

Seymour, G., Hazel, M., & Agnes, Q. (2020). Measuring time use in developing country agriculture: Evidence from Bangladesh and Uganda. *Feminist Economics, 26*(3), 169–199.

Stevano, S., Suneetha, K., Deborah, J., Malapit, H., Elizabeth, H., & Kalamatianou., S. (2019). Time-use analytics: An improved way of understanding gendered agriculture-nutrition pathways. *Feminist Economics, 25*(3), 1–22.

UNSD. (1993). *Systems of national accounts*. United Nations Statistical Division.

Yamamoto, Y. (2017). *Time use and care economy in macroeconomic policy, lecture delivered to UNESCAP officials, in gender and macroeconomic policy training programme*. UN Centre.

CHAPTER 5

Determining Gender Equality in Fiscal Federalism: Evidence from India

Fiscal federalism is, inherently, neither good nor bad for gender equality (Chakraborty, 2010a, 2010b; Forster, 2018; Vickers, 2011, 2013). The impact of fiscal federalism on gender-related outcome depends on the interface between institutions and intergovernmental transfer design. Political will, institutional capacity, and commitment towards gender equality are also other significant determinants. Although fiscal federalism is a vast literature, the interface of fiscal federalism with gender equality is scarcely analyzed. Despite the growing recognition of fiscal federalism in gender development in the policy realms, there have been relatively few attempts on the topic. This chapter aims to take on this rare range of significant debate, focusing on the plausibility of incorporating gender into the fiscal transfers. It is particularly relevant in this context that India is the first country to institutionalize gender budgeting *within* its Ministry of Finance, adhering to the budgetary accounting framework and analyzing the possibilities of changes in the budgetary classification to integrate gender budgeting in the mainstream budgets.

To be upfront and brief, amidst the plethora of criteria for fiscal devolution, the right thing to do—even from the gender perspective—appears to be to first make fiscal transfers on a per capita basis, which would be much more even and fiscally equalizing, and then make suitable adjustments for backwardness. It goes without saying that weightage to genuine backwardness, in addition to population, is more redistributive than weightage

© The Author(s), under exclusive license to Springer Nature
Singapore Pte Ltd. 2022
L. S. Chakraborty, *Fiscal Policy for Sustainable Development in Asia-Pacific*, https://doi.org/10.1007/978-981-19-3281-6_5

to population alone. Given the magnitude of *missing women* in India and the disturbing practices of gender discrimination that exist *even before birth*, a criterion needs to be incorporated in the unconditional fiscal transfers to penalize the states with an adverse juvenile sex ratio.

Amartya Sen set off an impassioned debate when he claimed that millions of women were "missing" in China and India, referring to the number of females who have died as a result of foeticide and unequal access to household resources, nutrition, health care, and access to property rights (Bhalotra et al., 2019; Klasen, 1994, 2008; Klasen & Wink, 2003; Kynch & Sen, 1983). To quote Klasen and Wink (2003) "Missing women refers to the deviation of the actual sex ratio from the expected sex ratio. It is far from a minor issue, but ranks among the worst human catastrophes of the twentieth century as it is larger than the combined casualties of all famines in the twentieth century and it also exceeds the combined death toll of both world wars and the casualties of major epidemics such as the 1918–1920 global influenza epidemic or the currently ongoing AIDS pandemic". It is critical to assess the role of public policy, within fiscal federalism, in addressing gender inequality (Chakraborty, 2010b). The nature of gender-related concerns varies across this very diverse region, and ranges from a focus on addressing the burden of the unpaid care economy to redressing female deprivation in education and health. Gender budgeting is ideally an approach to fiscal policies and administration that translates gender commitments into fiscal commitments through identified processes, resources, and institutional mechanisms, and can work on both the spending and revenue sides of the budget.

Theoretical and Empirical Literature

The theoretical literature on intergovernmental transfers largely deals with the conceptual elements and design of intergovernmental fiscal transfers (IGFT) in a context of competitive federalism (Boadway & Shah, 2007; Bird & Smart, 2002; De Mello, 2000; Hinojosa et al., 2010; Musgrave, 1997; Smart, 1996). The relative effectiveness of intergovernmental transfers on fiscal spending—flypaper effects—is analyzed but without a gender perspective (Stotsky et al., 2019). Habibi et al. (2003) in the context of Argentina analyze the impact of fiscal transfers on human development and found a positive relationship between the two. Lü (2011) analyses the effect of intergovernmental fiscal transfers on education spending in the context of China for the period 1994–2000 and could not find strong effects. Litschig and Morrison (2013) analyze the link between fiscal transfers and local public expenditure in Brazil for the education sector. Their results reveal that there is a positive and significant relationship between transfers and local education spending, and between per capita spending and education outcomes.

In India, Chakraborty L. (2016a, 2016b, 2020a, 2020b, 2020c, 2021), Chakraborty and Chakraborty (2016), Chakraborty P. (2021), Isaac and Chakraborty (2008), Rao (2018), and Rao and Singh (2007) examine fiscal federal relations and the subnational state finances in the context of India. Only a few of the existing studies on IGFT in India have incorporated gender equity concerns. Chakraborty (2010a, 2010b) and Anand and Chakraborty (2016) examine how integrating gender criteria/principles in the IGFT formula can improve horizontal equalization across jurisdictions. Chakraborty et al. (2018) look at how conditional transfers can alter gender equality outcomes.

Within the intergovernmental transfer framework, the impact of gender budgeting on gender outcomes is a new area of empirical research. Stotsky and Zaman (2016) analyze the impact of gender budgeting on gender equality outcomes in the context of India and found that gender budgeting has a positive effect on gender equality in education at the primary and secondary levels. Chakraborty et al. (2017) analyze the effectiveness of gender budgeting on sectoral gender outcomes in the context of the Asia Pacific region. They find that gender budgeting has a positive and significant effect on education and health outcomes, but there is no impact on labour force participation rates. This reinforces the view that care economy policies to augur the female work force participation have been meagre in the region.

One shortcoming of this existing research on the gender budgeting research in the Indian context is that this study does not incorporate IGFT on gender equality outcomes. The integration of IGFT into a model examining the determinants of gender equality outcomes and fiscal spending, controlling for gender budgeting, is the main innovation here and provides a more realistic view of subnational decision-making in India. In addition, the feminization of governance at the third tier could change the types of public expenditure at the local level to correspond more to the revealed preferences ("voice") by women. An MIT study by Raghabendra Chattopadhyay and Esther Duflo (2001) has measured the impact of the feminization of governance at the local level on the outcomes of decentralization with data collected from a survey of all investments in local public goods made by the village councils in one district in West Bengal. They found that women leaders of village councils invest more in infrastructure that is relevant to the needs of rural women (like drinking water, fuel, and roads) and that village women are more likely to participate in the policymaking process if the leader of their village council is a woman. Thus, placing women in a leadership position in governance at the local level can change the expenditure decisions of the local bodies and, in turn, change the types of public-good investments at the local level to correspond more to the revealed preferences (voice) by women (Stern, 2002). The study, however, has confronted a few criticisms. Bardhan and Mookherjee (2000) noted that without direct evidence on the nature of women's preferences relative to men's, and since women's reservation in the leadership positions in local government was not linked to the distribution of women in the village, this study does not quite address how local democracy affects the underrepresented groups in the village to implement their desired outcomes.

There is a growing recognition that fiscal policy can redress intra-household inequalities in terms of household division of labour by supporting initiatives that reduce the time allocation of women in unpaid work. Examples of such government intervention are improved infrastructure in water sector, rural electrification, sanitation services, and better transport infrastructure. As analyzed in Chapter 4, the public infrastructure deficit in rural areas may deepen rural poverty due to the time allocation across gender skewed towards more unpaid work, which is time otherwise available for income-earning market economy activities. Public investment in infrastructure, like water and fuel, can also have positive social externalities in terms of educating the girl child and improving the health and nutritional aspects of the household. There can be a link between deterioration in infrastructure and rural poverty. In terms of fiscal policies to redress poverty, the aspects of *time poverty* are often surpassed. Time poverty affects income poverty. Fiscal policies designed to redress income poverty can be partial if they do not take into account the aspects of time poverty. This policy discussion has gender dimension, as women are time poor and fiscal policies designed for pro-poor measures need to incorporate the time allocation aspects across gender. Using time-use statistics of water revealed that the incidence is significantly higher for girls and women in both rural and urban areas, which, in turn, points to the deficiency in adequate infrastructure in water and sanitation (Chakraborty, 2008, 2009). It has significant fiscal policy implications, as easy accessibility to drinking water facilities might lead to an increase in school enrolment, particularly for girls, by reducing the time utilized for fetching water. In other words, time budget statistics enable the identification of the *complementary fiscal services* required for better gender-sensitive human development.

Fiscal Federalism in India: Institutional Details

There is a growing recognition that something fundamental is happening in Indian fiscal federalism ex post institutional changes such as the abolition of the Planning Commission, the creation of the National Institution for Transforming India (NITI) Aayog, the constitutional amendment to introduce the Goods and Services Tax (GST), the establishment of the GST Council, and the historically high tax devolution to the states based on the 14th Finance Commission's recommendations. Recently, policymakers and experts have raised a few issues, including: whether or not to make Finance Commissions "permanent" or to abolish them by making the tax devolution share constant through a constitutional amendment; the need for an institution to redress spatial inequalities in order to fill the vacuum created by abolishing the Planning Commission; and making the case for Article 282 of the constitution to be circumscribed. The debates are also focused on whether there is a need to establish a link between the GST Council and Finance Commissions, and if India should devise a mechanism of transfer that is predominantly based on sharing of grants for equalization of services rather than tax sharing. Creating a plausible framework for debt-deficit dynamics while keeping the fiscal autonomy of states intact and ensuring output gap reduction and public investment at the subnational level without creating disequilibrium were also other matters of concern. These debates are significant, especially when a group of states came together for the first time ever to question the terms of reference of the 15th Finance Commission amid growing tensions in the federal-state relations in India.

The historically high 42 per cent devolution of the central government's divisible tax pool to the states, as recommended by the 14th FC, was hailed by governments and scholars in India and abroad alike. The same magnitude is retained in the Fifteenth Finance Commission. However, if we look at the aggregate transfers to the states as a percentage of gross revenue of the central government, it has remained constant over the years (Chakraborty, P., 2021). A concern whether the labyrinth of "entitlement-based central legislations" (for instance, the Mahatma Gandhi National Rural Employment Guarantee Act of 2005, the Right of Children to Free and Compulsory Education Act of 2009, and the National Food Security Act of 2013) conflict with the 7th schedule of the constitution (based on Article 246) was one of the highlights of the contemporary federalism debates (Singh, 2019). The 7th schedule of the constitution clearly lays down the subjects for the union list (expenditure functions assigned to the federal government), the concurrent list (shared functions between federal and state governments), and the state list (functions exclusively assigned to the state governments), with the expectation that each will respect the territorial limits of the other. Over the years, there has been a transgression of the central government into state subjects through centrally sponsored schemes (CSS) and the enlargement of the concurrent list (Reddy & Reddy, 2019, 76) on the grounds that such spending will better serve national priorities. It was cautioned that through this process, the fiscal autonomy of the Indian states was severely circumscribed. This intergovernmental fiscal transfer (IGFT) outside the purview of the Finance Commissions is the most sensitive part of the federal-state fiscal relations in India, as the states feel that these transfers are large, discretionary, arbitrary, and regressive (Reddy & Reddy, 2019, 77). Have things changed after the 14th FC award? The answer is mixed. The share of general-purpose transfers that are unconditional has increased from 51.41 per cent of the total to around 60 per cent of the total, with a corresponding decline in specific-purpose or conditional transfers (Chakraborty et al., 2018).

Article 282 of the constitution says: "The Union or a State may make any grants for any public purpose, notwithstanding that the purpose is not one with respect to which Parliament or the Legislature of the State, as the case may be, may make laws". Though Article 282 embodies merely a residuary power, it has been misused totally outside the frames of constitution. How to resolve this contradiction, which creates a dichotomy in the functions of the FCs, requires wider debate (Singh, 2019). With the 42 per cent tax devolution and the rationalization of CSS—mostly conditional grants—prior to the abolition of the Planning Commission, there is a "triumph of experience over expectations" (Reddy & Reddy, 2019, p. 74).

The need for an institutional mechanism, such as a "fiscal council", to enforce fiscal rules and keep a check on the central government's fiscal consolidation was highlighted. Singh (2019) emphasized that there is a need for a consolidated fiscal roadmap for both the central government and the states, with the same rules of the game for both. Another concern is that there is no constitutional check over borrowings for the central government, only for state government liabilities, as Article 293 (3) provides a constitutional check over state borrowings.

Is there a need for an institution to redress spatial inequalities in order to fill the vacuum created by abolishing the Planning Commission? One aspect that did not receive adequate recognition in the context of "what holds India together" is the role of the Finance Commissions. Reddy and Reddy (2019) rightly highlights the significance of the existing institutional mechanisms, such as a Finance Commission, for providing "predictability in the federal fiscal relations", along with a smooth transition of political regimes through peaceful elections, state reorganization mechanisms, and the other institutions of economic management. Reddy and Reddy (2019) sheds light on these aspects of "asymmetric" and "cooperative" federalism in India. The effectiveness of fiscal federalism in creating "convergence" is an empirical question and such empirical questions have gained significance globally. In India, has the "equality of processes" in fiscal federalism resulted inequality of outcomes? Has this goal of economic convergence been achieved, with poor states catching up in growth with the richer Indian states? Existing empirical evidence is mixed. There is convergence in social sector outcomes, such as in education and health, but there is no economic convergence.

Reddy and Reddy (2019) has effectively analyzed how the formation of states, economic convergence, and efficiency-equity principles have intertemporally influenced the thought processes of various Finance Commissions. One such crucial empirical question is about an economy's reliance on history. When the global recession gripped the schools of thought in economics, macroeconomists started realizing financial economics' reliance on history. However, we still do not well understand the significance of the impact of this hysteresis on macroeconomic stability, growth, and development in the evolution of fiscal federal design.

There is a debate about the significance of conditional versus unconditional fiscal transfers. Some economists believe in a quick economic rebound to global goals and economic convergence through designing a plethora of conditional transfers, while some others raise concerns over transfers that are broadly of a one-size-fits-all design. Reddy and Reddy (2019) highlighted the lack of capacity to implement such one-size-fits-all transfers and suggested unconditionality in fiscal transfers. They highlight these questions and remain stoic about them, leaving a cue that researchers need to examine them empirically through the progressivity analysis of tax transfers versus grants.

On public debt, it is contextual to recall the extensive recourse to seigniorage financing—the automatic monetization—since 1957 by providing net RBI credit to the government to finance deficits, and the subsequent shift in the financing pattern from money financing to bond financing since 1990s after to the economic reforms. At the state level, fiscal rules determine a state's access to debt, subject to the approval of the central government. It is interesting to recall the changing perceptions on public debt in macroeconomic debates globally. The recent Fiscal Responsibility and Budget Management/rule-based fiscal policy in India stipulates a 60 per cent threshold for public debt as part of fiscal consolidation. An empirical question one could pose here is whether a state's access to public debt, though not good, can be so bad? Of course the answer is: It is context specific. So what could be the plausible analytical framework to be considered when a Finance Commission takes steps towards public debt management? Oliver Blanchard at the American Economic Association (AEA) meetings in Atlanta in January 2019 had put it up front that "public debt has no fiscal costs if the real rate of interest is not greater than the real rate of growth of the economy" (Blanchard, 2019). He also highlighted that high public debt is not catastrophic if more debt can be justified by clear benefits, like public investment or output gap reduction. He also highlighted the hysteresis effects (the persistent impact of short-run fluctuations on the long-term potential output) and suggested that a temporary fiscal expansion during a contraction could reduce debt over a longer horizon.

There is an increasing recognition of the fact that public investment has suffered from fiscal consolidation across advanced and emerging economies (Blanchard, 2019). This is particularly important when public investment is one of the crucial determinants in strengthening private corporate investment in the context of emerging economies (Chakraborty, 2016a, 2016b; Vinod et al., 2020). Blanchard (2019) mentioned that if we are worried about a bad equilibrium, it is better to have a contingent fiscal rule (which may not need to be used) rather than steady fiscal consolidation. Similarly, Reddy and Reddy (2019) noted that a uniform and rigid fiscal rule not only undermines the fiscal autonomy of the states, but would also result in public (developmental) expenditure compression to comply with the numerical thresholds. This is refreshing, especially in the context when the path towards fiscal consolidation is equally important as the debt-target thresholds, because fiscal consolidation through strengthening tax buoyancy rather than public expenditure compression can be less detrimental to economic growth.

However the output gap can be a difficult notion for Finance Commissions. Extreme precaution is required when we measure deficits. It may be incorrect to think that cyclically adjusted fiscal deficit instead of fiscal deficit is what the Finance Commissions need to focus on. The empirical literature notes that we do not know whether disruptions or downturns permanently depress the level of output and employment or whether the economy can bounce back to its initial upward trend after a decline (as in the notion of a business cycle). In emerging economies there could be a drop from the trend growth rather than a deviation from the trend, illustrating that the "cycle is the trend" (Aguiar & Gopinath, 2007). The cyclicality of deficits can be challenging, as they cannot assume that an upturn in the business cycle can eliminate the cyclical part of a deficit. Such elimination cannot happen if the economic growth cycle does not return to its prior trend growth path and therefore the buoyancy of revenue receipts could remain below their prior potential level.

Reddy and Reddy (2019) gives importance to fiscal decentralization. When it comes to the local government (the third tier), the real issue is unfunded mandates. To analyze this empirically, we need reliable data for the third tier. In India, general government data is a challenge. IMF government finance statistics give cross-country data on the general government (inclusive of national, state, and local governments). The role of the State Finance Commissions (SFCs) also needs to be emphasized given their significance in providing a steady flow of funds to the local governments. There is an increasing concern about the arbitrariness and ad-hocism of fiscal transfers at the third tier. The cross-country experiences of federalism, realizing how different Indian fiscal federalism is from other countries' models. In other federations, IGFTs are predominantly grants, not tax transfers, so such fiscal equalization models may be of different relevance to India.

Fiscal Federalism Arrangements and Gender Equality

In India, the Finance Commission, erstwhile Planning Commission and line ministries of the Union government are responsible for IGFT. India has had 15 Finance Commissions since independence. The duties mandated for the Finance Commission are as follows:

(a) the distribution between the Union and the States of the net proceeds of taxes which are to be, or maybe, divided between them and the allocation between the States of the respective shares of such proceeds;
(b) the principles which should govern the grants in aid of the revenues of the States out of the Consolidated Fund of India; and
(c) any other matter referred to the Commission by the President in the interests of sound finance.

The Finance Commission's recommendations in India are so far conclusively accepted by the National Parliament. After the Parliament accepts the recommendations, the Finance Commission awards to the states, as per their formula, becomes mandatory and these transfers are also therefore referred to as "statutory fiscal transfers". These statutory transfers are unconditional grants or "general purpose transfers". Until recently, a substantial flow of transfers in the form of intergovernmental "grants" has been transferred through the erstwhile Planning Commission of India. The Planning Commission was abolished in 2014. In place of the Planning Commission, the National Institute for Transforming India (NITI) Aayog has been constituted as a think tank to foster cooperative federalism in the country, with no role for intergovernmental fiscal transfers to the states of India. The non-statutory transfers are channelled through the line ministries mostly as conditional grants or tied grants for specific purposes. These conditional grants are also referred to as "centrally sponsored schemes".

Ensuring gender equality in fiscal policies, not only helps to access equitable share of benefits and costs across gender, but also helps in ensuring equity in empowering them. Strengthening of "agency" in women helps in providing greater opportunities and access to paid work, enhances productivity and economically empowers women. Empowerment improves entitlements and thus, enhances economic, social, and political status of the disadvantaged and gives them a greater role in the design most important way in which this can be accomplished is through ensuring gender equity in human development.

Anand and Chakraborty (2018) showed that integrating a gender variable as one of the criteria for intergovernmental fiscal transfers has four advantages. One, it incentivizes states to improve gender inequality. Two, it makes the fund transfer more progressive, Three, it also benefits the poorer states, as the correlation between the gender inequalities and poverty is high. Finally, it makes the per capita income across states, post devolution, more equitable, and increases progressivity in the intergovernmental fiscal transfers.

While social values and ethics reflected in the demographic performance of a state cannot be changed by fiscal fiats alone, a proactive approach by a high constitutional body like the Finance Commission (FC) has always been called for (Chakraborty, 2020a, 2020b, 2020c). This is especially when these prejudices—reflected in the demographic patterns—are blatantly oppressive.

For instance, 15th Finance Commission's decision to give 12.5 per cent weightage to "demographic performance" is laudable. The Commission has decided to use total fertility rate (TFR)—instead of other plausible indicators like the female population of the states or the sex ratio of 0–6 age group—as an indicator of "demographic performance". It was noted that the reduction of TFR—the average number of children that would be born to a woman over her lifetime—also reflects better performance in maternal and child health as well as education, and it reflects the quality of human capital.

Given the disturbing demographics, there has been a growing recognition over the years to the plausibility of incorporating gender into tax transfer formula in India. With the monotonous decline in the 0–6 sex ratio in India, it was believed that there can be no valid objection to using FC transfers for gender equity. Chakraborty (2010a, 2010b) suggested was to use a simple method for introducing some weight in favour of the female population of the states in the fiscal devolution formula. Chakraborty (2020a, 2020b, 2020c) argued that the message would be even stronger and more appropriate if the number of girls in the 0–6 age cohort—is adopted as the basis for determining the states' relative shares of the amount to be disbursed by applying the allotted weight. The demographic pattern of 0–6 age group can also capture the gender discrimination "even before birth". It remains an empirical question whether incorporating TFR or a sex ratio (0–6) makes FC transfers more progressive/equitable (Anand & Chakraborty, 2016). This progressivity analysis is significant to know whether TFR is a better criterion than the other in capturing the "demographic performance".

In addition to incorporating gender criteria in tax transfer formula, specific-purpose transfers can also strengthen the gender budgeting initiatives at the subnational levels, including the third tier. For instance, in India, with the advent of fiscal decentralization aftermath 73rd and 74th Constitutional Amendments and the feminization of local governance in India (33 per cent reservation for women), the imperative for gender equity will be even stronger if the specific-purpose transfers can facilitate integrating the revealed preferences ("voice") of women in local level public expenditure decisions. Ethiopia, too, is in the process of integrating gender in IGFT. In Ethiopia, the process has been initiated by the House of Federations (Senate) and the Terms of Reference (TOR) was moved in Parliament for public hearing. Subsequently, a majority was secured in the Senate for gender-integrated TOR and the country is waiting for the "proclamation" by the Senate to make it a reality in their forthcoming Fiscal Commission. NIPFP has worked in close association with the House of Federation (Senate), the Government of Ethiopia, and the Forum of Federation in this process of integrating gender in fiscal transfers in Ethiopia (Chakraborty, 2020a, 2020b, 2020c).

The Empirical Models and Results

The data are obtained from the IMF Database on gender created in 2016, as part of IMF initiative on gender budgeting, the State Finance Accounts (for budgeted unconditional transfers), federal government ministry web sites (for budgeted conditional transfers), and the Ministry of Women and Child Development (MWCD) gender budgeting information. The descriptive statistics of the variables are given in Table 5.1. The data cover the period 1991–2015. During this period, 16 of the states adopted gender budgeting and 13 did not. We do not include Union Territories because they have limited fiscal autonomy.

The effects of intergovernmental transfers on gender outcomes across the states of India, controlling for whether states have gender budgeting initiatives in place, is analyzed (first model). The flypaper effects, whether fiscal transfers have more impact on subnational spending than own

Table 5.1 Descriptive statistics

Variable (all log terms unless otherwise noted)	N	Mean	Median	Std. Dev	Min	Max
Real per capita income (in millions)	364	64,713.8	56,485.64	37,163.6	13,025.8	257,354
Real per capita income	364	10.94	10.94	0.53	9.47	12.46
Population	364	2.78	3.33	1.62	−0.6	5.35
Real per capita aggregate transfer	364	6.21	5.97	1	4.05	8.47
Real per capita unconditional transfers	364	5.28	5.32	0.65	3.54	7.12
Real per capita conditional transfers	364	5.5	4.99	1.34	3.13	8.25
Real per capita Total public expenditure	364	9.51	9.45	0.68	8.04	11.36
Real per capita education expenditure	364	7.66	7.6	0.62	6.38	9.44
Real per capita health expenditure	364	6.36	6.25	0.73	4.85	8.33
Real per capita infrastructure expenditure	364	7.49	7.37	0.81	5.68	9.84
Real per capita own revenue	364	6.1	6.04	0.83	4.06	8.47

Sources IMF database, Finance Accounts of state governments, and federal government ministry websites, as in Stotsky et al. (2019)

revenues, is also tested (second model). Prima facie, we assume that if the impact of intergovernmental fiscal transfers is significantly more than that of own revenue, there is a flypaper effect. The flypaper effects of ecological fiscal transfers are attempted in the context of India and found a significant link (Chakraborty, 2021; Kaur et al., 2021). Gender budgeting initiatives are difficult to quantify (Stotsky et al., 2019). The specifically targeted allocations for gender development are broadly less than one percent of the entire budget and that is not the entire spending on gender equality. The remaining 99 per cent of the budget often has intrinsic gender-related objectives. Unless we try to quantify this spending as well, using the specifically targeted public spending on gender equality represents only a partial measure. The public spending on gender as a proxy for gender budgeting initiatives is avoided for this reason.

Another dimension of effectiveness of gender budgeting in any state is whether it is made mandatory through legal procedures or not. However, in India (unlike in some countries or subnational entities, where gender budgeting is mandatory), gender budgeting was not made mandatory through law (Stotsky et al., 2019). A third dimension is to categorize the states as per the phase of gender budgeting—whether a state is in an early phase of model building, or second phase of developing gender budgeting statements using matrices and institutionalizing it in the Finance Ministry, or third phase of capacity building of sectoral ministries in integrating gender budgeting and/or in a final phase of designing accountability mechanisms of gender budgeting to understand its impacts (Chakraborty et al., 2021). These four phases are unclear in the state context and therefore an attempt to establish in which phase the different states were, as a measure of gender budgeting in our econometric models, is not undertaken (Stotsky et al., 2019).

Given the data limitations, following Stotsky and Zaman (2016), the states are categorized into gender budgeting and non-gender budgeting states based on the announcement by the government to initiate gender budgeting in any state. We measure the effect of gender budgeting through the use of a dummy variable, where the variable takes a value of 1, if the state has a gender budgeting effort in place and 0, if the state does not. The gender budgeting regime dummies are also matched to the year of implementation of gender budgeting. The year of implementation is used as a regime changing dummy because gender budgeting has not been rolled back in any of the states of India where it has been initiated (Stotsky et al., 2019). Stotsky et al. (2019) estimate the following equations to measure the impact of intergovernmental fiscal transfers and gender budgeting on gender equality outcomes and the fiscal stance respectively.

$$\text{Gender Inequality}_{it} = \beta_1 \text{Gender Budgeting}_{it} + \beta_2 \text{Fiscal Transfers}_{it} + \delta X_{it} + \eta_i + \nu_t + \varepsilon_{it}$$

$$\text{State Public Expenditure}_{it} = \beta_1 \text{Gender Budgeting}_{it} + \beta_2 \text{Fiscal Transfers}_{it} + \beta_3 \text{Own Revenue}_{it} + \delta X_{it} + \eta_i + \nu_t + \varepsilon_{it}$$

The social and cultural variables like religion are excluded in the models because the unit of analysis is the Indian States in which religion is non-homogenous. The fiscal transfers are included not as direct benefit transfers (DBT) to households or individuals, but intergovernmental fiscal transfers from higher government to subnational governments (Stotsky et al., 2019). The political economy variables are not included in the model because intergovernmental fiscal transfers are broadly based on formula or criteria (including population, per capita income, climate change related variables, fiscal discipline), and the discretionary elements arising from political affiliation of national and subnational governments do not appear to be significant variables in determining the IGFT mechanism in India (Stotsky et al., 2019). The ethno-fragmentation of the population of the subnational governments in deciding the quantum of transfers is also beyond the scope of the study, for the same reasons. As noted in Stotsky and Zaman (2016), ideally, the other variables for gender inequality in education beyond the gender parity in enrolment index. However, the database unfortunately does not provide any other gender outcome variables for states of India across time in education. Stotsky et al. (2019) use the following variables as determinants: real income per capita and per capita intergovernmental transfers from the Union government, which is disaggregated in the models into conditional and unconditional fiscal transfers, both measured in the natural log of real per capita amounts; population, measured in millions; and agriculture GDP, manufacturing GDP, and services GDP, all measured as a ratio of subnational GDP. Population is used to control for economies of scale in provision of public services and might also have an effect of gender inequality through indirect means (for instance, states with larger populations might be more exposed to outside influences) (Stotsky & Zaman, 2016). The structural transformation of the economy is captured through the share of the state economy in various types of economic activity. This can affect gender equality outcomes by influencing how women participate in economic activity. In India, "participation income" (income received by participating in economic activity) is more consequential than universal "basic income" (the income transferred to individuals through public policies, irrespective of their participation in economic activity). Public spending on health and education can reflect the revealed preferences of the state incorporating the median voter's utilities (assuming that there is a "Wicksellian connection", meaning there is a link between one unit of tax paid and one unit of utils derived by citizens).

The generalized method of moments (GMM) approaches—using the Arellano and Bond methodology—is used to account for a lagged dependent variable and to address the potential endogeneity of the independent variables. The lagged dependent variable captured in the GMM models can better measure the dynamic process by which gender equality indicators and spending measures evolve over time. The unconditional transfers have a positive and significant effect on gender parity in education in the upper secondary levels. Gender budgeting has a positive and significant impact on gender parity in education at the upper primary school and lower secondary school levels. The conditional transfers are not significant (Table 5.2). The results also suggest that economic growth per se is insufficient, given the weak impact of real income changes, and therefore that the government needs to take specific and focused public policy planning and budgeting measures to ensure gender equality outcomes in India.

The second part of the empirical work examines the effect of IGFT, own revenues, and gender budgeting on fiscal spending. We also examine flypaper effects—whether money sticks where it hits or whether the impact of IGFT is more than own revenue on fiscal spending at the subnational levels. In this analysis, the dependent variable is the log per capita fiscal spending variables. The independent variables are the same as before. Table 5.3 presents results for the GMM estimations of flypaper effects. The own revenue per capita is found to have a significant positive effect on fiscal spending, except in the education sector. The conditional IGFT is positive and significant in determining state infrastructure spending. The unconditional IGFT is not significant in determining state spending, except for a negative impact in the health sector (Stotsky et al., 2019). The IGFT has "substitution effects" with subnational public spending only in the health sector. Gender budgeting has a significant impact on spending at the aggregate level, and only in the education sector. Income is significant, except in health. These results show some variation with the fixed effects. The most consistent finding is the positive effect of gender budgeting on education spending, consistent with the earlier findings of a positive effect of gender budgeting on enrolment parity.

Overall, these results suggest that conditional fiscal transfers and gender budgeting exert some positive effect on fiscal spending. These empirical findings are consistent with the underlying policy formulations

Table 5.2 Impact of intergovernmental fiscal transfers on gender equality, with lagged gender budgeting dependent variable: GMM estimates

Variables	Gender equality index lower primary school (female to male ratio)	Gender equality index upper primary school (female to male ratio)	Gender equality index lower secondary school (female to male ratio)	Gender equality index upper secondary school (female to male ratio)
L_1	−0.2722 (0.122)	0.3058* (0.137)	−0.297* (0.257)	−0.258 (0.0217)
Real per capita unconditional transfers (log terms)	0.0157 (0.0150)	0.005 (0.0176)	0.074 (0.047)	0.127** (0.041)
Real per capita conditional transfers (log terms)	0.0088 (0.1156)	−0.0079 (0.0140)	−0.037 (0.035)	−0.012 (0.033)
Real income per capita (log terms)	0.0029 (0.0225)	0.0609** (0.0275)	0.1996 (0.1217)	−0.0133 (0.098)
Population (log terms)	0.074 (0.057)	0.0675 (0.067)	0.622 (0.442)	1.211** (0.515)
Agriculture GSDP (% of State GSDP)	−0.305 (0.475)	0.2602 (0.558)	0.370 (1.011)	0.304 (0.992)
Manuf. GSDP (% of State GSDP)	−0.306 (0.475)	0.2588 (0.558)	0.369 (1.011)	0.304 (0.992)
Services GSDP (% of State GSDP)	−0.306 (0.475)	0.2598 (0.5579)	0.374 (1.012)	0.303 (0.992)
Gender budgeting	0.009 (0.102)	0.0218** (0.012)	0.0399** (0.0206)	0.028 (0.0198)
Constant	30.92 (47.51)	−26.148 (55.78)	−38.65 (101.14)	−33.09 (99.22)

* 1 % level of significance
Sources IMF database, Finance Accounts of state governments, and federal government ministry websites, as in Stotsky et al. (2019)

of tied central transfers with a matching component of fiscal spending by the subnational governments.

To conclude, using panel estimations, we found that unconditional transfers have a significant and positive impact on gender parity outcomes, measured as enrolment parity, in the education sector at primary

Table 5.3 Impact of IGFT and gender budgeting on fiscal spending, with lagged de-pendent variable—GMM estimates

Variables	Total public expenditure	Education expenditure	Health expenditure	Infrastructure expenditure
L_1	0.129*	0.486***	0.575***	0.364***
	(0.056)	(0.055)	(0.0628)	(0.062)
Real per capita own revenue (log terms)	0.242***	−0.015	0.1639*	0.167**
	(0.034)	(0.049)	(0.064)	(0.022)
Real per capita unconditional transfers (log terms)	−0.036	−0.0601	−0.168**	0.0436
	(0.036)	(0.046)	(0.064)	(0.068)
Real per capita conditional transfers (log terms)	0.0297	−0.036	0.001	0.144**
	(0.024)	(0.0328)	(0.047)	(0.055)
Gender budgeting	0.0578**	0.0296**	−0.065	−0.023
	(0.0219)	(0.0286)	(0.042)	(0.0472)
Real per capita income (log terms)	0.5859***	0.691***	0.594	0.393***
	(0.053)	(0.724)	(0.101)	(0.111)
Population (log terms)	0.045	−0.087	−0.208	−1.247***
	(0.124)	(0.185)	(0.240)	(0.238)
Agriculture GSDP (% of State GSDP)	1.001	0.236	1.174	1.119
	(0.944)	(1.296)	(1.799)	(1.956)
Industries GSDP (% of State GSDP)	0.995	0.235	1.174	1.122
	(0.944)	(1.296)	(1.799)	(1.955)
Services GSDP (% of State GSDP)	1.006	0.241	1.174	1.126
	(0.944)	(1.296)	(1.799)	(1.955)
Constant	−99.978	−26.63	−120.699	−110.448
	(94.43)	(129.59)	(179.87)	(195.548)

* 1 % level of significance
Sources IMF database, Finance Accounts of state governments, and federal government ministry websites, as in Stotsky et al. (2019)

and secondary levels, in comparison to conditional transfers. Gender budgeting is an effective policy tool for promoting gender equality outcomes in education at the state level. Fiscal spending is influenced both by own revenue and IGFT. Own revenue exerts a positive and significant effect on spending, as theory would suggest. Conditional or tied transfers also have a positive effect, in some models. This result likely reflects the design of tied transfers in India within a "co-operative federalism" framework. States must provide a matching component to a tied grant from the Union government in certain sectors. Unconditional fiscal transfers are generally found ineffective in determining fiscal spending, an interesting finding, because these transfers should function like own revenues. This result may reflect a discrepancy between budgeted and actual spending, which requires more detailed data investigation. As an exception, however, in the health sector, a "substitution effect" is noted in the GMM model, meaning fiscal transfers in health are negatively related to state-level public spending on health. Gender budgeting as a policy tool is found to have mixed effects in determining state-level fiscal spending at aggregate and disaggregate sectoral levels.

The unconditional fiscal transfers seem to have a direct effect on gender equality outcomes measured by parity in enrolment compared to conditional transfers and therefore integrating gender criteria in intergovernmental formula-linked fiscal devolution would have positive effects on gender equality, even though the exact mechanism is unclear. Income gains are not sufficient to generate equality of outcomes. Gender budgeting has also been found to have been useful in promoting gender equality. However, given the exact mechanism of influence, further investigation with more detailed fiscal and demographic data and at a finer level for transfer programs is called for.

References

Aguiar, M., & Gopinath, G. (2007). Emerging market business cycles: The cycle is the trend. *Journal of Political Economy, 115*, 69–102.

Anand, A., & Chakraborty, L. (2016). *Engendering' intergovernmental transfers: Is there a case for gender-sensitive horizontal fiscal equalization?* (Working Paper 874). The Levy Economics Institute of Bard College.

Bardhan, P., & Dilip, M. (2000). *Decentralizing anti-poverty program delivery in developing countries* (Working Paper C98-104.1). Center for International and Development Economics Research (CIDER), University of California.

Bhalotra, S., Abhishek, C., Dilip, M., & Francisco, J. P. (2019). Property rights and gender bias: Evidence from land reform in West Bengal. *American Economic Journal: Applied Economics, 11*, 205–237.

Bird, R., & Smart, M. (2002). Intergovernmental fiscal transfers: International lessons for developing countries. *World Development, 30*(6).

Blanchard, O. (2019). Public debt and low interest rate. Presidential address, delivered at the American Economic Association Meetings, Atlanta (January 6).

Boadway, R., & Shah, A. (2007). Intergovernmental fiscal transfers: Principles and practice public sector governance and accountability (Working Paper Series). The World Bank.

Chakraborty, L. (2008). *Analysis of Kerala state budget 2007–08 through a gender lens*. Centre for Development Studies.

Chakraborty, L. (2009). *Fiscal decentralization and gender budgeting in Mexico: An empirical analysis*. Regional Development Studies, Vol. 12. United Nations Center for Regional Development.

Chakraborty, L. (2010a). Determining gender equity in fiscal federalism: Analytical issues and empirical evidence from India (Working Paper No. 590). Levy Economics Institute.

Chakraborty, L. (2010b). *Gender-sensitive fiscal policies: Experience of ex-post and ex-ante gender budgets in Asia-Pacific*. UNDP.

Chakraborty, L. (2016a). *Asia: A survey of gender budgeting experiences* (Working Paper 16/150). International Monetary Fund.

Chakraborty, L. (2016b). *Fiscal consolidation, budget deficits and macroeconomy: Monetary-fiscal linkages*. Sage Publications.

Chakraborty, L. (2020a). *Macroeconomic policy coherence for SDG 2030: Evidence from Asia Pacific* (Working Paper no. 292). National Institute of Public Finance and Policy.

Chakraborty, L. (2020b). *Fiscal prudence for what? Analysing the state finances of Karnataka* (Working Paper no. 293). National Institute of Public Finance and Policy.

Chakraborty, L. (2020c). *Fiscal consolidation ex-post the escape clause: A call for excessive deficit procedure* (Working Paper no. 299). National Institute of Public Finance and Policy.

Chakraborty, L. (2021). *Macroeconomic Framework of Union Budget 2021a–22: Reconsidering the fiscal rules* (Working Paper No. 328). National Institute of Public Finance and Policy.

Chakraborty, L., Ingrams, M., & Singh, Y. (2017). *Effectiveness of gender budgeting on gender equality outcomes and fiscal space: Evidence from Asia Pacific (GRoW Research Paper WP 2017–09)*. McGill University.

Chakraborty, L., Ingrams, M., & Singh, Y. (2018). *Fiscal policy effectiveness and inequality: Efficacy of gender budgeting in Asia Pacific* (Working Paper no. 224). National Institute of Public Finance and Policy.

Chakraborty, P. (2021). COVID-19 context and the fifteenth finance commission: Balancing fiscal need and macroeconomic stability. *Economic and Political Weekly*, 33(14).

Chakraborty, P. & Chakraborty, L. (2016). Beyond fiscal prudence and consolidation. *Economic and Political Weekly*, 51(16).

Chattopadhyay, R. & Duflo, E. (2001) *Women as policy makers: Evidence from a randomized policy experiment in India* (Working Paper No. 01-35). MIT Department of Economics.

De Mello, Jr., L. R. (2000). Fiscal decentralization and intergovernmental fiscal relations: A cross-country analysis. *World Development, 28*(2).

Forster, C. (2018). *Gender equality and federalism*. 50 Shades of Federalism.

Habibi, N., et al. (2003). Decentralization and human development in Argentina. *Journal of Human Development, 4*(1).

Hinojosa, L., Bebbington, A., Barrientos, A., & Addison, T. (2010). *Social policy and state revenues in mineral-rich contexts*. Social Policy and Development Programme Paper 44. United Nations Research Institute for Social Development (UNRISD).

Isaac, T. & Chakraborty, P. (2008). Intergovernmental transfers: Disquieting trends and the thirteenth finance commission. *Economic and Political Weekly, 43*(25).

Kaur, A., Mohanty, R., Chakraborty, L., & Rangan, D. (2021), Ecological fiscal transfers: Any evidence for flypaper effects?. Paper presented at the International Institute of Public Finance Conference, University of Iceland, August 18, 2021.

Klasen, S. (1994). Missing women reconsidered. *World Development, 22*, 1061–1071.

Klasen, S. (2008). Missing women: Some recent controversies on levels and trends in gender bias in mortality. Ibero America Institute Discussion Paper No. 168.

Klasen, S., & Claudia, W. (2003). Missing women: Revisiting the debate. *Feminist Economics, 9*, 263–299.

Kynch, J., & Sen, A. (1983). Women: Well being and survival. *Cambridge Journal of Economics, 7*(3/4), 363–380.

Litschig, S. & Morrison, K. M. (2013). The impact of intergovernmental transfers on education outcomes and poverty reduction. *American Economic Journal: Applied Economics, 5*(4).

Lu, X. (2011). Do intergovernmental transfers enhance local education spending in China?. APSA 2011 Annual Meeting Paper.

Musgrave, R. A. (1997). Devolution, grants and fiscal competition. *Journal of Economic Perspectives, 11*, 4.

Rao, M. G. (2018). Public finance in India: Some reflections. *Decision: Official Journal of the Indian Institute of Management Calcutta*, Springer; Indian Institute of Management Calcutta, *45*(2).

Rao, M. G. & Singh, N. (2007). The political economy of India's fiscal federal system and its reform. *Publius: The Journal of Federalism, 37*(1). Oxford University Press. Winter.

Reddy, Y. V., & Reddy, G. R. (2019). *Indian fiscal federalism*. Oxford University Press.

Singh, N. K. (2019). Indian fiscal federalism. Panel on "Indian Fiscal Federalism," at the book launch by Y. V. Reddy and G. R. Reddy, India International Centre, New Delhi, March 28.

Smart, M. (1996). *Taxation incentives and deadweight loss in a system of intergovernmental transfers* (Working Paper number ut-ecipa-msmart-96-03). Department of Economics and Institute for Policy Analysis, University of Toronto (July 22, 1996).

Stern, N. (2002). *Public finance and policy for development: Challenges for India*. Silver Jubilee Lecture at the National Institute of Public Finance and Policy (NIPFP), New Delhi (January 10).

Stotsky, J., Chakraborty, L., & Gandhi, P. (2019). *Impact of intergovernmental fiscal transfers on gender equality in India: An empirical analysis* (Working Paper). National Institute of Public Finance and Policy.

Stotsky, J., & Zaman, A. (2016). The influence of gender budgeting in Indian states on gender inequality and fiscal spending (Working Paper 16/227). International Monetary Fund.

Vinod, H., Karun, H., & Chakraborty, L. (2020). Encouraging private corporate investment. In H. Vinod & C. R. Rao (Eds.), *Handbook of statistics*. Elsevier.

Vickers, J. (2011). Gendering federalism: Institutions of decentralization and power-sharing. In M. L. Krook, & F. Mackay (Eds.) *Gender, politics and institutions. Gender and politics series*. Palgrave Macmillan.

Vickers, J. (2013). Is federalism gendered? Incorporating gender into studies of federalism. *Publius: The Journal of Federalism, 43*(1), 1–23.

CHAPTER 6

Fiscal Decentralization and Ex Ante Gender Budgeting: Case Studies of Selected Countries Including India

Federations are seen as an "indestructible union of indestructible states". A federal political order is here taken to be "the genus of political organization that is marked by the combination of shared rule and self-rule". Fiscal federalism is the assignment of revenue and expenditure across various tiers of government and the design of intergovernmental fiscal transfers to correct the vertical and horizontal imbalances (Chakraborty, 2020a; Reddy & Reddy, 2019). In countries with very large heterogeneous populations, the central government cannot make efficient fiscal decisions for each and every local government (Bahl, 2008). There is greater potential for fiscal equalization under fiscal federalism (Bahl, 2008; Blöchliger, 2014). With greater fiscal decentralization, variations in fiscal capacities across local jurisdictions can be adjusted to provide an adequate level of public services provisioning without levying unduly high tax rates. This necessitates some form of fiscal equalization to ensure interjurisdictionally adequate finances to meet their public expenditure needs (Bahl, 2008).

The principle of subsidiarity states that fiscal federalism is good for efficiency and equity in the economy based on the rationale that local governments, which are closer to citizens, are more efficient in the provisioning of public services than the higher levels of government (Oates, 2001). This rationale holds good in terms of gender development, as local governments have better information on gender differentials regarding

© The Author(s), under exclusive license to Springer Nature Singapore Pte Ltd. 2022
L. S. Chakraborty, *Fiscal Policy for Sustainable Development in Asia-Pacific*, https://doi.org/10.1007/978-981-19-3281-6_6

needs and preferences. There can be hardly two opinions on the fact that the new-found policy space of feminization of local governance in India, coupled with fiscal devolution to the third tier, may provide an impetus to adopt the *gender lens* more effectively in formulating gender-sensitive fiscal policies. It could be based on dual conjectures. Firstly, greater fiscal autonomy at the local level, with effective feminization of governance, can make a transition in the budgetary decisions by incorporating gender concerns. Secondly, it helps to identify spatial gender needs, which is a step ahead from existing homogeneous *one-size-fits-all* gender budgeting policies. This chapter provides case studies of local level ex ante gender budgeting experiences.

Gender budgeting, as mentioned earlier in the book, is an ex ante and ex post process. An ex-post gender budgeting is an application of gender lens to existing budgetary framework to understand the intensity of gender allocations in the budget and also to analyze the benefit incidence of public expenditure, with a thrust on care economy. At the decentralized levels of government, gender budgeting can be an ex-ante process through the identification of gender needs and incorporate them in budget. Bird and Vaillancourt (2006) explained the three different approaches within fiscal federalism: deconcentration, delegation, and devolution. Deconcentration occurs not through the transfer of any powers or authority to the local or regional offices, but when the central government delegates public service responsibilities to regional or local offices of the central government. In unitary countries, fiscal decentralization occurs in the form of deconcentration as there is no autonomous local governments to deliver services. Deconcentration also exists in fiscal federalism where the federal government is interested in making sure particular services are being delivered across the country (Escolano et al., 2012).

Devolution involves the transfer of expenditure functions and finance to locally elected governments. This form of fiscal decentralization is concerned with "who has done at what level" in the sense who collects what taxes and who undertakes expenditure functions. It is also to deal with vertical and horizontal fiscal imbalance, which results from the devolution of expenditure functions and finance (Escolano et al., 2012).

Fiscal Decentralization and Gender Frameworks

The theoretical underpinnings of the rationale of incorporating gender into intergovernmental fiscal transfers are accountability ("voice" and "exit"), information symmetry, transparency, and appropriate size of government at the local level for effective service delivery. The degree of accountability ("voice") in integrating gender in an intergovernmental fiscal setup is based on dual conjecture—first, the accountability of the subnational government to the higher tier of government and second, to the electorate. The former limits the latter, especially in cases where financial decisions are centralized, but the provision of public goods is decentralized. The separation of finance from the functional assignment can lead to inefficiencies, the most oft-cited problem being unfunded mandates. On the other hand, the real autonomy in the decision making of the Elected Women Representatives (EWR) plays a crucial role in integrating gender-specific needs in the fiscal policies and their accountability to the electorate gets constrained if the flow of funds is through deconcentrated intermediate levels with accountability to the central government. However, fiscal policy in a federal setting promotes government accountability, particularly in geographically or demographically large nations (Stern, 2002). Participatory local governments are generally better informed about the needs and preferences of the local population than the central government is and is the entry point of integrating gender concerns. It helps to improve efficiency in resource allocation, minimize transaction costs in designing and implementing the development policies, and ensure better incentive mechanisms and accountability. In fiscal federal setup, monitoring and control of governance by local communities is easier in principle. At the subnational level, elected governments can be expected to be generally more accountable and responsive to the gender concerns, and more effective in involving the women in the sociopolitical development processes. Decisions at the subnational level give more responsibility, ownership, and, thus, incentives to local agents and local information can often identify cheaper and more appropriate ways of providing public goods (Bardhan & Mookherjee, 1999; Stern, 2002).

Another risk of incorporating gender in the intergovernmental fiscal transfer mechanism is the dominance of elite groups within the jurisdiction and their influence in control over financial resources and in the public expenditure decisions related to the provisioning of public goods and governance. There is growing evidence that power at the local level is more concentrated, more elitist, and applied more ruthlessly against the poor than at the centre (Griffith, 1981). This is referred to as *elite capture* in the theoretical literature. In such a setting, the voice of women elected as representatives may get neutralized by political pressure groups. In addition, if the women in governance are comparatively less empowered, with minimum/no education and basic capabilities, their ad hoc decisions on the systems of public goods and services will not have any major impact on poor and needy women. The benefits of decentralized socioeconomic programmes would be captured by the local elite and, in turn, result in underinvestment in public goods and services for poor women. This is particularly true in the context of heterogeneous communities and underdeveloped rural economies (Bardhan, 1999; Galasso & Ravallion, 2000).

The aberrations in voice may induce the possibility of greater corruption at local levels of government than at the national levels; in turn, corruption deepens capability deprivation. There is empirical evidence indicating that decentralization increases corruption and reduces accountability (Rose-Ackerman, 1997; Tanzi & Davoodi, 2000), however, empirical evidence favours the hypothesis that the participation of women in governance structure lessens the possibilities of corruption (Swamy et al., 2001). The gender differences in the incidence of corruption may range from personality traits (honesty, law-abiding), to the degree of access to networks of corruption, or to lack of proper knowledge of how to engage in corrupt practices. It may also be the case that voice may be a "proxy voice" if the elected women are not empowered and their male relatives operate the local bodies. However, effective participation of female representatives at the local level can change the priorities in budgeting, bring accountability, and ensure quality and efficiency of public goods and services.

The axiom of "exit", which provides yet another mechanism for accountability, refers to the mobility of population. Theoretically, citizens who are dissatisfied with the public provisioning of services by one local government can "vote with their feet" by moving to another jurisdiction that better meets their preferences (Tiebout hypothesis). In practice, there are many constraints on interjurisditional mobility, especially in case of women. In spite of these constraints, there are evidences of interjurisditional labour mobility by women for wage employment. This reveals that factors beyond local service provision in physical and social infrastructure often influence citizen's decision about where to locate. Interjurisdictional labour mobility may be an instrument of local accountability when citizens reveal their preferences by strengthening exit.

A centrally determined *one-size-fits-all* gender policy cannot be a solution to redress gender inequities in a country with a vast population and heterogeneity across jurisdictions. Given the heterogeneity in the efficiency of public service provisioning across jurisdictions, it may be timely to consider the scope of asymmetric federalism in the context of incorporating gender into fiscal policies. Asymmetric federalism refers to federalism based on unequal powers and relationships in political, administrative, and fiscal arrangement spheres between the units constituting a federation. Asymmetry in the arrangements in a federation can be viewed both vertically (between central and states) and horizontally (among the states). If federations are seen as an "indestructible union of indestructible states", and the central government and states are seen to exist on the basis of equality, neither has the power to make inroads into the defined authority and functions of the other unilaterally (Rao & Singh, 2004).

One way of looking at this is the process of accreditation where the subnational governments who pass minimum standards in service and product delivery, as well as specific attributes of governance, could be given greater autonomy in functions and finance. This requires benchmarking the governance of subnational governments, which may catalyze horizontal competition among the states. It can ensure gains in efficiency and increase productivity through the "Salmon mechanism", in which intergovernmental competition is activated by benchmarking the performances of other governments in terms of levels and qualities of services, levels of taxes, or more general economic and social indicators (Salmon, 1987, as cited by Breton and Fraschini [2004] and Rao [2006]). The voters and opposition parties compare the supply performance of their governments with the benchmark performance and influence supply decisions (Breton, 1996; Salmon, 1987). This gender-sensitive benchmarking of local governance can empower women to compare the relative performance of their governments in terms of the tightness of "Wicksellian connections" and influence supply decisions of their jurisdictions to design and implement appropriate policies and programmes to ensure gender equity. A Wicksellian connection is a link between the quantity of a particular good or service supplied by centres of power and the tax price that citizens pay for that good or service. Knut Wicksell (1896) and Erik Lindahl (1919) showed that if decisions regarding public expenditures and their financing were taken simultaneously and under a rule of (quasi) unanimity, a perfectly tight nexus between the two variables would emerge. Breton (1996) argued that competition between centres of power, if it was perfect and not distorted by informational problems, would also generate completely tight Wicksellian connections. In the real world, competition is, of course, never perfect and informational problems abound; as a consequence, Wicksellian connections are less than perfectly tight. Still, as long as some competition exists, there will be Wicksellian connections (Breton & Fraschini, 2004).

Intergovernmental competition and the mechanism of exercising choice by the citizen-voters, either through the exit or by voice, helps to reveal preferences of public services. The theoretical literature elaborated that competition results in innovations in the provision of public services and, in respect of public goods, it helps to identify the beneficiaries and impose user charges on them. However, the efficiency in the service delivery and welfare gains accrued and the enhancement of accountability depends on the nature of intergovernmental competition and political *institutions* (Breton, 1996).

Information symmetry is one of the important factors in holding subnational governments accountable. When policymakers are in close proximity to the people they serve, the information they receive tends to be more accurate regarding the needs and demands of citizens across gender as they participate effectively and exercise their voice in terms of revealing preferences. The higher the information symmetry, the higher the accountability and transparency of the local government. Information symmetry can reduce the transaction costs on both the provider's and the citizen's side.

The size of the lowest tier of the government varies significantly across countries. It is often argued that the smaller the size of the local government, the higher the inefficiency in public service delivery. It is often because of a lack of capacity to manage all the functions assigned to them. On the other hand, the smaller the size of local governments, the greater the participation and accountability become. The real challenge at this point is a judicious structure of local government that is not only politically acceptable, but also can provide efficient delivery of public services. The appropriate scale for key services should be an important element in the governance structure at the local level.

There is no direct attempt so far to incorporate gender concerns in the intergovernmental fiscal relations in India. Given the asymmetries in the assignment of functions and finance, a significant prerequisite of integrating gender into intergovernmental transfers is to lessen the *unfunded mandates*. However, it is also important to gender sensitise the transfer system, as a major share of local government revenue is fiscal transfers.

The point to be noted here is that it would be ideal to incorporate gender in specific-purpose transfers (conditional) rather than in general-purpose transfers (unconditional). The objective of the general-purpose transfer system is to offset the fiscal disabilities and it is desirable to keep the transfer system formula-based, simple, equitable, and without perverse incentives. Any attempt to include a gender component in general-purpose transfers may make it complex and create incentives against undertaking measures to improve gender equity. On the other hand, the objective of specific-purpose transfers is ensuring minimum standards in access to specified services, such as basic education, healthcare, water supply, sanitation, and anti-poverty interventions.

Ideally the transfer system for gender equity should have a judicious mix of both general-purpose and specific-purpose transfers. The objective of the general-purpose transfers is to enable all subnational jurisdictions to provide normatively determined standards of public services. On the other hand, it is important to design specific transfers to implement direct programmes that would enhance the capabilities and entitlements of women, which, in turn, would help them to release the time locked up in the unpaid activities of the care economy and enable them to participate in paid work in the market economy. Despite the enormous literature on federalism in constitutional design, and the growing attention to gender equality in constitutional design, there has been remarkably little attention paid to the interaction between the two. Ryan (2017) argues that political participation by women is central to the development and argues for the recognition of opportunities for women in leadership, political participation, and the strengthening of democracy at the level of subnational governments. Ryan (2017) presents a cross-country analysis of increasing political participation by women in formal political structures and processes in the subnational governance.

The rationale of fiscal federalism is based on the following conjectures: (Chakraborty, 2010)

- Provide greater fiscal autonomy at the local level, with transition in the budgetary decisions and intergovernmental fiscal transfers by incorporating gender concerns.
- Helps to identify special gender needs, unlike *one-size-fits-all* gender budgeting policies.
- It is also significant for the redistribution objectives between regions, which helps cement a diverse nation.

The fiscal decentralization of gender policies holds good, as local governments have better information on gender differentials regarding needs and preferences. Decisions at the subnational level give more responsibility, ownership, and, thus, incentives to local agents and local information can often identify cheaper and more appropriate ways of providing public goods (Bardhan & Mookherjee, 1999; Stern, 2002). The genesis of these debates on how to translate gender commitments into fiscal commitments can be traced to "gender budgeting" experiments—the analysis of the budgets through a "gender lens"—as a tool of accountability (Chakraborty, 2020b, 2020c, 2020d; Kolovich, 2018). Gender perspectives engage many types of issues: political reforms to increase women's representation, extending universal rights and social citizenship benefits to women, and establishing gender rights (Vickers, 2013). In the multi-level fiscal federalism in India, the political economy process of gender in fiscal mechanisms may pass through four distinct phases—innovative knowledge networking, building institutional structures, reinforcing state capacity, and strengthening the accountability mechanisms, at national and subnational levels (Chakraborty et al., 2020; Vickers, 2013).

The analytical matrices for categorizing public expenditure through a gender lens were identified as follows: (Chakraborty, 2014)

1. Specifically, targeted expenditure to women and girls;
2. Pro-women allocations, which are the composite expenditure schemes with a significant women's component; and
3. Residual public expenditures that have gender–differential impacts.

However, these analyses more often get confined to the top level of the government. Identifying the gender issues in fiscal federalism requires acknowledgement of intergovernmental fiscal transfer mechanism. Intergovernmental fiscal transfers are used as a tool for addressing the horizontal and vertical imbalances in fiscal federalism, and incorporating gender as criteria of these transfers can increase the progressivity of the transfers (Anand & Chakraborty, 2016). The revenues of subnational government are twofold. One is intergovernmental fiscal transfers. Two, the own revenue handles of the subnational governments. These own revenue policies and intergovernmental transfers are not gender-neutral.

Third Tier Institutional Details: Fiscal Devolution Through a Gender Lens

India is the largest democratic federal polity in the world. Out of over a quarter-million local governments, only around 3000 are in the urban areas. Structurally, decentralization in India would seem to have been carried to the smallest unit of habitation viz., villages, but their resources and functions are limited. While substantial resources are raised or are devolved further to the second level viz., the states, the third tier suffer acutely from inadequacy of resources.

Although constitutional amendments provide an illustrative list of functions that are considered appropriate for local governments, they remain largely unfunded mandates (Box 6.1). The amendments also made it mandatory to appoint a state finance commission once in every five years to make recommendations regarding the fiscal transfers from the state to the local bodies; progress in terms of functions and finance to local bodies has been tardy. The degree of decentralization in any country is difficult to quantify. Fiscal decentralization can broadly be captured by the share of subnational expenditure in total expenditure and/or local government expenditure as a percentage of the GDP of the country. However, these indices do not capture enough of the governance structure to understand the degree of power in terms of decision-making vested with the local government over expenditure functions. Lack of data on these components of governance structure limits the empirical analysis to a great extent.

Box 6.1: 73rd and 74th Constitutional Amendments

The 73rd and 74th Constitutional Amendments, regarding the local self-governments in India were passed by Parliament in December, 1992. The 73rd Constitutional Amendment Act, 1992 came into force on April 24, 1993 and 74th Amendment Act, 1992 on June 1, 1993, thereby the Local bodies—"Panchayats" and "Municipalities" came under Part IX and IXA of the Constitution of India.

The Salient Features of the 73rd and 74th Constitution Amendment Acts.

The Panchayats and Municipalities will be local self-governments, with Grama Sabha (villages) and Ward Committees (Municipalities) as the basic units of democracy. All adult members are registered as voters. Except in the States where population is below 20 lakhs, there will be three-tier system of panchayats at village, intermediate block/taluk/mandal, and district levels (Article 243B). The seats at all levels to be filled by direct elections [Article 243C (2)]. The seats reserved for Scheduled Castes (SCs) and Scheduled Tribes (STs) and chairpersons of the Panchayats at all levels also shall be reserved for SCs and STs in proportion to their population. One-third of the total number of seats to be reserved for women. One-third of the seats reserved for SCs and STs also reserved for women. One-third offices of chairpersons at all levels reserved for women (Article 243D). Uniform five year term and elections to constitute new bodies to be completed before the expiry of the term. In the event of dissolution, elections compulsorily within six months (Article 243E).

Independent Election Commission is constituted in each State for superintendence, direction, and control of the electoral rolls (Article 243K). Panchayats have to prepare plans for economic development and social justice in respect of subjects as devolved by law to the various levels of Panchayats including the subjects as illustrated in Eleventh Schedule (Article 243G).

The 74th Amendment provides for a District Planning Committee to consolidate the plans prepared by Panchayats and Municipalities (Article 243ZD). The funds constitute the budgetary allocation from State Governments, share of revenue of certain taxes, collection and retention of the revenue it raises, Central

> Government programmes and grants, Union Finance Commission grants (Article 243H). State Finance Commissions determine the financial devolution principles for panchayats and municipalities (Article 243I).
> *Source* www.india.gov.in.

The available estimates showed that the local government expenditure as a percentage of GDP constituted 2.20 percent, while in terms of revenue mobilization, local government revenue constituted 0.54 percent of GDP. Specifically, over a quarter-million rural local bodies in India mobilize only 0.04 percent of GDP. The expenditure of local government constituted 7.90 percent of the total, but their revenues accounted for only 2.73 percent of the total. The available estimates on the fiscal autonomy ratio of local governments (the ratio of own revenue to total expenditure) was as low as 27 percent in India. In the case of low-income states, it was even lower at 13.03 percent (Rao et al., 2004).

Given that a major part of the subnational government revenue accrues from fiscal transfers, the attempt of gender budgeting at the local level in India does not go far enough unless the institutional mechanisms of fiscal decentralization and degree of fiscal autonomy are varied. There is a lack of transparency and accountability in the system because of the extensive use of inadequate revenue assignments, lack of sufficient decentralization to local bodies, and a poorly designed intergovernmental transfer system. However, as local governments depend heavily on transfers from the higher level of government, could engendering the criteria of fiscal devolution be a plausible policy step?

Chakraborty et al. (2018) analyze the fiscal transfer architecture in India, incorporating the various components and channels of transfers. In India, IGFT can be broadly categorized into conditional and unconditional transfers. The first channel of unconditional transfers consists mainly of the Finance Commission formula-linked tax transfers from the Union's pool of revenues. The second channel of conditional transfers consists mainly of grants from the Finance Commission and from line ministries of the Union government (or centrally sponsored schemes). India has a three-tiered federal structure, with 29 state governments and 7 centrally administered Union Territories and more than a quarter million local self-governments in states, in both rural and urban areas. The richest province is Goa, with a per-capita income of INR 270,150 and poorest province is Bihar, with a per-capita income of INR 34,168, as per the Central Statistical Office data for the year 2015–2016 (Chakraborty et al., 2018).

Among the criteria of fiscal devolution to the third tier, population turns out to be the predominant one. It is true that population criterion has an advantage of providing a summary measure of the basic needs that is free from value judgement and arbitrariness, unlike other indicators. However, heavy reliance on too broad a measure of need (like population) could be inconsistent with promoting fiscal equalization or balanced development of regions within a state. Gulati (1987) pointed out that population as a basis of distribution altogether ignores the existence of income disparities among the states. As an alternative to that, he argued, would be the distribution of resources on the basis of per capita income; this would be much more even and fiscally equalizing.

Population criteria apart, all three SFCs have considered applying other indices of socioeconomic backwardness for the horizontal distribution of resources. While selecting the criterion of backwardness, one has to be very careful so that it does not suffer from arbitrariness and excessive value judgment. The question arises at this juncture whether objective indicators of economic and social infrastructure could also be used for assessing the backwardness of a local body. The Twelfth Finance Commission (TFC) has incorporated indices of deprivation including the percentage of households fetching water from a distance and percentage of households without sanitation. Public investment in infrastructure like water supply and sanitation can have positive social externalities in terms of educating the girl child and improving the health and nutritional aspects of the household. A World Bank study (Bredie & Beehary, 1998) noted that easy accessibility to drinking water facilities might lead to an increase in school enrolment, particularly for girls; in Madagascar, 83 percent of the girls who did not go to school spent their time collecting water, while only 58 percent of the girls who attended school spent time collecting water. However, the major criticism against the use of social indicators as an index of backwardness is that it will be biassed against the regions that, despite poor resource base, have achieved relatively high levels of attainment in these sectors.

Do fiscal equalization transfers enhance gender equity? Though these transfers are not specifically targeted to the poor, the poor will benefit from the general capacity increase in the region, especially women. When unconditional transfers are made, equalization transfers aim to neutralize deficiency in fiscal capacity, but not in revenue effort. Sometimes adjustments affecting cost and need factors may also be accommodated. In many ways, the finance commission's formula-based fiscal transfers are not part of an equalization grant system, but rather part of general or unconditional funding, which might have equalization grant features. Chakraborty (2003) seeks to empirically investigate if the fiscal transfers in India follow the principles of fiscal equalization. Econometric investigation using panel data for 15 major states for the years 1990–1991 to 1999–2000 in a fixed effects model revealed a strikingly regressive element of transfers, with aggregate tax transfers per capita positively related to state per capita income. However, grant transfers showed clear progressivity, though the grant transfers are not sufficient to eliminate horizontal inequalities owing to a smaller proportion of grants in the overall transfer in comparison to tax transfers. His results echo those of previous studies, reinforcing the oft-made observation that richer states are receiving more per capita fiscal transfers than poorer states. Fiscal equalization grants can correct for spatial inequalities in the provisioning of merit goods or quasi-public goods, which have evident gender differential impacts. Considering the acute spatial disparities in service standards in the provision of health and education, the TFC has tried to bring in the equalization principle for certain specific grants for education and health on the expenditure side. Although equalization should be pursued mostly, if not exclusively, by the equalization grant system in order to free up other grant instruments to pursue other objectives, this is a temporary positive move given the present need for more equalization in the system (Bahl et al., 2005). Fiscal equalization grants for health and education can redress the capability deprivation across gender.

The moot question at this juncture is whether gender criteria needs to be incorporated in the unconditional fiscal transfers. One of the arguments against incorporating gender concerns in unconditional fiscal transfers is that these transfers are meant for offsetting the fiscal disabilities and it is desirable to keep the transfer system formula simple and without perverse incentives (Rao, 2006). However, in India, given the disturbing demographic facts of the precipitous decline in the sex ratio for children in the 0–6 age group, especially in some of the prosperous states of India, there can be no valid objection to using central transfers for this purpose. A simple method for this could be to introduce some weight for the female population of the states in the tax devolution formula of the finance commission (Anand & Chakraborty, 2016; Bagchi & Chakraborty, 2004; Chakraborty, 2010, 2020a). The message would be even stronger and more appropriate if the population of girl children only, that is the number of females in the 0–6 age group, is adopted as the basis for determining the relative shares of the states in the amount carved out of the divisible pool by applying the allotted weight. A special dispensation for girls would also be justifiable in a scheme of need-based equalization transfers. The Fifteenth Finance Commission has used Total Fertility Rate as a criterion to correct for the demographic transition effects, which is indirectly a gender-related criterion (Chakraborty, 2020a).

While social mores cannot be changed by fiscal fiats, especially when prejudices run deep, state action is called for when they are blatantly oppressive to any section of the community. Indeed such action is an imperative. The transfer system can and should play a role in upholding the right to life for the females of the country (Bagchi & Chakraborty, 2004; Chakraborty, 2010, 2020c). Having said that, it needs to be mentioned that it is not plausible to incorporate more gender variables in the formula and complicate the transfer formula of the Finance Commission. In other words, inclusion of a *gender inequality index* in the transfer formula may not result in the intended results, as the variables included in the index may neutralize each other. Specifically, the empirical evidence on fiscal decentralization and gender arrives at the following four inferences. One, fiscal federalism prima facie does not ensure gender equality. Two, with the advent of federal governance and fiscal decentralization, significant expenditure functions that are important for gender equality such as health care, education, and income-support programmes are given importance in fiscal federal design. The infrastructure investment, though rich in potential, has not effectively been analyzed through a gender lens. Three, the fiscal allocations relate to the labour market that may promote women's economic empowerment need an emphasis. Four, the design of the tax system and tax policy are relevant to gender equality, however, evidence suggests that differential tax system cannot correct gender inequalities. Five, fiscal federalism arrangements such as specific-purpose grants to subnational governments can promote gender equality.

Fiscal Decentralization and Local Level Gender Budgeting: Case Studies

Despite the initiatives to integrate gender at various tiers of government within the federal structure, a major lacuna of such policy initiatives have been to integrate gender in intergovernmental fiscal transfers to the local level government. How gender budgeting can serve as a potential instrument to pursue gender equality objectives in a federal fiscal system can be twofold. One, adopting gender budgeting is usually a central component of gender equality agendas across federations. Two, in a federal context, gender budgeting needs to be adopted at all levels of government and must ideally be implemented using a common framework across subnational units to facilitate the assessment of relative performances and possibly strengthen subnational governments' incentives. A detailed comparative perspective is given by providing a few examples on gender budgeting at various tiers of government from the experiences of selected federal countries. Downes et al. (2017) provides gender budgeting initiatives in a few federal countries in OECD such as Australia, Canada, Austria, Spain, India, and South Africa. A further investigation of how selected countries have implemented gender budgeting as part of their local level budgetary framework is briefly attempted in this section for selected countries like The Philippines, Morocco, India, South Africa, Ethiopia, and Nepal.

The Philippines

The Nation-State of the Philippines is an archipelago of 7100 islands and home to people speaking as many as 87 dialects. This probably explains why historically, the political structure of the Philippines had been of a much decentralized nature—each barangay or village was ruled by its own chieftain, spoke its own dialect, and formulated its own laws based on tradition and needs. These rudiments of the decentralized system in the Philippines were strongly affected by the period of colonial domination. Centralized ruling structure has been the prominent characteristic legacy of Spaniards, the Americans, and the Japanese conquest of this country. However, since independence in 1946, the Philippines has been gravitating more towards decentralization. In the period of Third Republic (1946–1972), many laws related to the local autonomy were enacted, viz., Local Autonomy Act of 1959 and the Decentralization Act of 1967, to grant fiscal and regulatory powers to the local governments. The 1973 Constitution also made it mandatory for the state to "guarantee and promote the autonomy of the local governments to ensure their fullest development as self-reliant communities". However, twenty years of authoritarianism in the form of martial rule acted as a barrier to the attempts towards decentralization. Termination of this era saw the re-emergence of democracy through people's empowerment. Substantive process of fiscal decentralization started in the Philippines with the enactment of Local Government Code (LGC) in 1991. The LGC institutionalized systematic allocation of powers and responsibilities between the national and local governments. Though fifteen years into the implementation of the Code, integrating gender in the planning and budgetary policies at the local government is however relatively a new approach in the Philippines. At the national level, gender budgeting policy initiatives started in the Philippines with the Gender and Development (GAD) budget in 1995. The GAD budget made a provision for earmarking at least 5 percent of all departmental expenditure on programmes for women in national and subnational budgets. However, fixing the floor limits for spending on gender resulted in the misallocation of resources in various departments. It also resulted in the marginalization of gender issues in the mainstream budgeting, as floor limits have been taken as ceiling in various departments. In this context, it needs to be highlighted that earmarking a specific proportion of budgetary allocation for women is only a second best principle of gender budgeting and may not be the most appropriate tool to sensitize budget through gender lens. There was no penalty for not utilizing the GAD budget fully and efficiently, many of the departments ended up with unspent surplus in the GAD budget. Ideally, differential targeting of expenditure emanating from the identification of appropriate programmes for women in various sectors or reprioritising the expenditure based on a generic list of appropriate programmes and policies for women might be more effective than uniform targeting at 5 percent across sectors. However, with the strengthening of the fiscal decentralization process in the Philippines, local government units (LGUs) were provided with more opportunities in terms of local level gender budgeting and challenges as well. The devolution of basic functions like health, social welfare, and agricultural extension to the LGUs, created more space for the local government units (LGUs) to incorporate the gender needs at the local level. Some of the LGUs have indeed used this opportunity to initiate gender-responsive policies at local level. However, as devolved functions were largely unfunded mandates and the intergovernmental transfers and budgetary process at the local level were largely politically determined, they posed serious challenges for effective decentralization and in turn local level gender budgeting initiatives. Local level gender budgeting initiatives in the Philippines can be found in a few barangays, particularly in Sorsogon and Hilongos, where selective attempts were made to identify specific gender needs before budgeting. These initiatives, which came from the Department of Interior and Local Government (DILG) and National Commission on the Role of Filipino Women (NCRFW) along with the UNIFEM in the year 2004, moved ahead from quota-based gender budgeting to the identification of entry points for results-oriented gender-responsive budgeting. However, local level gender budgeting has been highly a sectoral process in the Philippines. In Sorsogon, the initiative is in the health sector; where gender-related MDG health goals have been identified and budgeted. In Hilongos, the initiative has been in the agriculture sector. Prima facie, agriculture sector appears to be a gender-neutral sector. But it was identified that strengthening the agricultural sector has clear gender differential impacts in terms of reducing the forced migration of women and also in enhancing their income-earning opportunities.

India

India has made history as the first country ever to integrate gender in the intergovernmental fiscal transfers (IGFT) formula. The 15th Finance Commission has taken this bold decision—during its transition to use the population data 2011 instead of 1971—not to penalize the states with better demographic performance. The 15th Finance Commission's decision to give 12.5 percent weightage to "demographic performance" is laudable. The Commission has decided to use total fertility rate (TFR)—instead of other plausible indicators like female population of the states or the sex ratio of 0–6 age group—as an indicator of "demographic performance". The 15th Finance Commission report tabled in Parliament on February 1, 2021 noted that the reduction of TFR—the average number of children that would be born to a woman over her lifetime—also reflects better performance in maternal and child health as well as education, and it reflects quality of human capital. It remains an empirical question whether incorporating TFR or a sex ratio (0–6) makes Finance

Commission transfers more progressive/equitable. Conducting a progressivity analysis is significant to know whether TFR is a better criterion than the other in capturing the "demographic performance". It is interesting to recall here that in United Nations Gender Inequality Index (GII) which has been published every year since 2010, adolescent fertility rate is incorporated as one of the parameters to reflect the "reproductive health" gender dimension. That being said, it needs to be mentioned that it is not plausible to incorporate more demographic variables in the Commission's already complex tax transfer formula. The inclusion of UN's "gender inequality index" in the tax transfer formula—instead of one single indicator—may not result in the intended results, if the variables included in the index may "neutralise" each other.

The genesis of these debates on how to translate the gender commitments into fiscal commitments can be traced to gender budgeting experiments as a tool of accountability. The pioneering study by the National Institute of Public Finance and Policy led to developing analytical matrices to "engender" the budgets. In 2004–2005, through accepting the recommendations of "Classification of Budgetary Transactions" Committee institutionalizing gender budgeting became a reality in India. As a prelude to this, the Economic Survey in 2000–2001 also, for the first time ever, carried a chapter on "gender", drawing the gender diagnosis from NIPFP study. However, integrating gender in macroeconomic policies has largely confined to the domain of public expenditure at the Centre and state levels. In a fiscal federalism like India, unless we "engender" the IGFT mechanisms, the picture remains partial. With the bold decision by the 15th Finance Commission to integrate gender criterion in general purpose transfers, a great leap forward is thus made.

In addition to incorporating gender criteria in tax transfer formula, it is argued that finance commissions should design specific purpose transfers to strengthen the gender budgeting initiatives at the subnational levels, including the third tier. With the advent of fiscal decentralization aftermath 73rd and 74th Constitutional Amendments and the feminisation of local governance in India (33 percent reservation for women), the imperative for gender equity will be even stronger if the specific purpose transfers can facilitate integrating the revealed preferences ("voice") of women in local level public expenditure decisions. Identifying transformative financing for gender equity is the clause 5c of Sustainable Development Goals (SDGs). Kerala has a rich experience on the local level gender budgeting.

State level gender budgeting in India has also used the national level analytical matrices and templates. For instance, a successful example of subnational level gender budgeting was adopted by the State of Karnataka in 2006–2007. In line with the NIPFP methodology, Karnataka has successfully institutionalized gender budgeting within its Ministry of Finance. The Comptroller and Auditor General report mentioned that the Finance Department of Karnataka has followed the Lahiri committee recommendations on fiscal matrices and classification of budgetary framework in categorizing the allocations (Government of India, CAG report [Report 1] on State Finance, Karnataka, 2013). Intense consultations with field officers of 21 Secretariat Departments and 34 Administrative departments led to the first gender budget statement in Karnataka. Data paucity was a major constraint in validating the classifications of spending. The challenge was to obtain disaggregated data and identify the flow of funds for monitoring and evaluation.

At the state level, Kerala was also a leader in institutionalizing gender budgeting in 2008. The "Kerala Model" of development which is widely referred to in the development economics literature refers to a peculiar situation where human development indicators are good compared to a low level of per capita income. Against the backdrop of the budget announcement in 2006, the state government entrusted the Centre for Development Studies Unit on Local Self Government to undertake a study of state-level gender budgeting. A report entitled "Analysis of Kerala State Budget 2007–2008 Through a Gender Lens" was prepared and submitted to the Finance Minister in February 2008. This Centre for Development Studies Report not only attempted an ex-post gender analysis of the Kerala State Budget 2007–2008, but also provided a roadmap for institutionalizing gender budgeting within the Kerala Department of Finance, thereby introducing a Statement on Gender Budgeting in the budget documents. Subsequently, a significant move in this direction began in Kerala with the announcement by the Finance Minister in his Budget Speech 2008 that from next year onwards a special Statement on Gender would be submitted to the legislature along with the Budget, as is done at the central government, along with other policy announcements for institutional mechanisms. The Centre for Development Studies analysis also highlighted that there is no separate Ministry/Department for Women Affairs in Kerala. A new institutional structure named the "Gender Board" was announced in the 2008 Budget speech.

A Gender Budget Statement of Kerala was extended by introducing allocations separately for infrastructure programmes (Government of India, 2015). It is also noted that 15–20 percent of local governments have undertaken studies on the Status of Women, as a prelude to gender planning at the local level (Government of India, 2015). In Kerala, democratic decentralization occurred in the mid-nineties, and a Women Component Plan (10 percent of State Plan Outlay) was earmarked to conduct gender budgeting at the third tier. The details of this process are provided in Isaac and Franke (2000), Isaac (2004), and Chakraborty (2004). In subsequent years, innovative projects related to gender in infrastructure projects have been consistently undertaken by the state government. For instance, in 2013, Kerala introduced She-Taxi to ensure safe mobility of women, driven by women, which has a database of all Emergency Response Systems in the city. Safe night shelters and hospitals are available for women, and vehicles are proactively monitored from a 24×7 Security Control Room. This is one of the flagship programmes of "Gender Park", introduced by the Department of Social Justice, Government of Kerala, to engage in innovative research and development, capacity building, and innovative infrastructure projects for women's security and empowerment. Gender Park was conceptualized by the former Finance Minister of Kerala, T. M. Thomas Isaac, and announced in his Budget Speech 2011–2012. Gender Park is the first such large scale initiative in India to reduce gender inequalities through innovative projects, though delayed in its full execution, it was officially inaugurated recently by the President of India in February, 2016. In 2019, Kerala has become the first state in India to implement the "She Pad" scheme aimed to distribute clean sanitary pads to all school students across the state with the support of local self-government institutions.

Kerala

In the backdrop of democratic decentralization, Kerala has been a pioneer state in India in moving towards gender-responsive planning and budgeting at local level. The simultaneous occurrence of feminization of political governance at the third tier with 33 percent representation of women created new democratic space for local level interventions by an agency of Women Elected Representatives (Isaac, 2004). Despite the remarkable achievements in terms of gender indicators in health and education, Kerala however has been experiencing extreme marginalization of women especially in the spheres of governance and work force participation. In other words, superior conditions of women in Kerala in terms of social indicators has had no impact on gender status. It was in this context that a deliberate attempt was made to incorporate the gender perspective into the process of democratic decentralization.

Though it was only in 1991 that Kerala (like the rest of India) came to have elected bodies at the district level, the civil conditions of the state have been ideal for democratic decentralization reforms, since long. Widespread literacy, sharply reduced deprivation and absolute poverty, good health performance, successfully carried out land reforms, powerful class and mass organizations etc. have acted in synergy for Kerala as an ideal state for the introduction of participatory local democracy. Popularly known as the "Kerala Model", the state has demonstrated how appropriate redistribution strategies can meet the basic needs for citizens despite low levels of economic development. However, Kerala has failed to translate high social sector achievements into comparable achievements in the material production sectors. This has resulted in economic stagnation of the state, growing unemployment, and an acute fiscal crisis thereby raising questions about the sustainability of the "Kerala Model".

Democratic decentralization, intended to accelerate economic growth and create a new model of growth with equity, has been the political response to the stagnating economy of the state. All 1214 local governments in Kerala—municipalities and the three tiers of rural local government—district, block, and gram panchayats were given new functions and powers of decision-making, and were granted discretionary budgeting authority over 35–40 percent of the state's developmental expenditures. The democratic decentralization, however, attempted more than just devolution of resources and functions. Local governments were not only charged with designing and implementing their own development plans, they were mandated to do so through an elaborate series of participatory exercises in which citizens were given a direct role in shaping policies and projects (Isaac & Franke, 2000).

Reversed Sequence of Decentralization
In Kerala, the usual sequence of decentralization has been reversed; financial devolution preceded functional devolution. In 1996, 35–40 percent of the outlay of Ninth Five Year Plan was devolved to local self-government institutions. This financial devolution took place outside

the purview of the State Finance Commission of Kerala. Given the low level of administrative capacity at the newly created third tier and the lack of experience of newly elected members of local bodies, the reversal of sequence of decentralization tended to create disequilibrium during plan implementation. However complementary reforms undertaken by the state government have created conditions for successful devolution. For instance, quite contrary to the rest of India where financial devolution took the form of schemes (tied in nature), in Kerala 75–80 percent of devolution has been in the form of untied grants-in-aid. Thus the nature of financial devolution in Kerala encourages maximum fiscal autonomy to the local governments.

New Democratic Space for Gender
Kerala reveals a paradox in terms of gender development. A much lower gender gap in social indicators and high female empowerment have accompanied Kerala's remarkable performance in human development as demonstrated by several attempts to constructing the GDI and the GEM at the regional level for India. However, high rates of literacy and the dramatic decline in fertility did not translate into rapid growth of paid employment for women nor into upward occupational mobility. One of the reasons for this phenomenon is the sex-differentiated pattern of education. The electoral arena of Kerala has also been short of women's representation. While in the state assembly the numbers elected have varied between 5 and 8 members in a house of 140 legislators since the early nineties, the proportion of women candidates hovered around 5 percent for the last two and a half decades.

The process of democratic decentralization is expected to enhance the visibility of educated women in the public sphere with 33 percent representation for women at the local level. The total number of elected representatives was 14,173 of whom 75 percent belonged to the gram panchayats, that is, around 10.8 per gram panchayats.

The analysis of characteristics of the women elected representatives revealed that only 10 percent of them had prior experience as elected representatives and only 18 percent had education above matriculation (Isaac, 2004). It is also revealed that while elected women representatives are better educated than their male counterparts (a social fact that is unique to Kerala in the Indian context), the women were on average younger, much less politically experienced, and inadequately equipped with basic knowledge of rules, regulations, and administrative issues.

Moreover, women representatives have had to bear a triple burden of public office, income-earning activities, and domestic duties (Isaac & Heller, 2002).

As part of the democratic decentralization, women elected representatives were given continuous capacity-building training programmes, which have helped them significantly to adapt to new challenges. A self-assessment survey of women elected representatives shows that their administrative knowledge and management skills, as well as their ability to officiate at public functions and interact effectively with their constituencies, have improved very significantly over the years (Isaac et al., 1999). There were two avenues through which democratic decentralization thus contributed to empowerment of women; (i) agency of women elected representatives (WER); and (ii) new democratic space for local level intervention by women. On the one- hand Kerala features extreme cases of marginalization of women despite remarkable development achievements, and on the other the state has introduced one of the most radical programmes on democratic decentralization, which makes Kerala an ideal case for studying the impact of fiscal decentralization on gender (Isaac, 2004).

Identifying Spatial Gender Needs for Budgeting

Yet another remarkable feature of democratic decentralization in Kerala was the noble attempt to incorporate the gender budgeting in the process through providing a Women's Component Plan (WCP) by earmarking 10 percent of State's Plan Outlay towards specifically targeted programmes for women. These programmes are determined by women at the local level through participatory process at gram sabhas (ward-level assemblies). The networks of neighbourhood groups and self-help groups were linked to gram sabhas to increase participation of women. With the constitutional provision for one-third reserved representation of women in Local Self Governments and the introduction of a special WCP amounting to 10 percent of the plan outlay, what has been the experience so far?

The distinctive feature of the democratic decentralization in Kerala is the planning function of the local self-governments to identify the spatial gender needs, prelude to budgeting. In other words, as a statutory precondition for receiving the WCP from the state government, local governments must prepare a comprehensive area plan. This planning process includes holding gram sabhas, and convening sectoral task forces in which non-official experts and volunteers directly prepare reports, formulate projects, and draft sectoral plans. The various stages of plan preparation in effect represent new participatory spaces in which women, elected women representatives, and officials deliberate and prioritize developmental goals and projects. In order to ensure transparency and participation without compromising the technical requirements of planning, the planning process is divided into discrete phases with distinct objectives, key activities, and associated training programmes (Isaac & Heller, 2002). Though modifications to the sequence have been made every year, the basic model for incorporating the gender component in various stages of democratic decentralization in Kerala remains the same to design the WCP.

Appraisal and Approval of Plans
The major failure with regard to this experiment of incorporating gender budgeting in the democratic decentralization process was that the WCP for the first year did not meet targets, both in terms of overall allocation and the relevance of projects. The allocation for the WCP fell far short (4.26%) of the suggested minimum of 10 percent in the annual plans for 1997–1998. The share steadily declined as one moved up the tier (i.e. from GP to block panchayat and then to district panchayat). The proportion of Plan grant-in-aid was also low in WCP projects. Besides, there was not much difference in overall projects and WCP projects. The proportion of WCP that could be genuinely described as women development projects was also debatable. A few of these shortcomings were dealt with in the second annual year plan through a series of policy initiatives. First, more than the statutory minimum requirement of 10 percent of the plan grant-in-aid was earmarked for WCP in all districts. Second, an undue emphasis on credit and beneficiary contribution in women development projects was reduced and more realistic patterns of project financing were adopted during the second year. Third, the quality of projects improved. The tendency to include the general sector projects in WCP on the basis of notional (indirect) benefits to women has declined and the number of projects that specifically address the gender status of women has significantly increased (Isaac & Heller, 2002).

It is also to be noted that changes were made in the role and functions of the WCP task forces. Clear guidelines were established to design

WCP projects, moving away from WCP investing in economic infrastructure including roads, water, and sanitation to more microfinance programmes and small-scale industries. As a result of these measures, many weaknesses were rectified. Despite the initial disequilibrium with regard to gender budgeting at local level in the year of commencement, the spurious projects on gender disappeared in due course and "practical gender needs" projects became the building block for institutionalizing "strategic gender needs".

The experience of WCP projects in Kerala of moving away from economic infrastructure to microfinance programmes generates a debate on "specifically targeted programmes for poor" versus "infrastructure programmes"; particularly in terms of gender budgeting. An IFPRI study showed that public expenditure on road infrastructure has the largest impact on poverty reduction. In this context, it is to be noted that investment in infrastructure can catalyze the fulfilment of practical needs of women; however gender budgeting is required more for addressing the financial allocation and implementation issues related to the strategic needs of women. Microfinance sector, one of the areas which was given emphasis in WCP projects in Kerala through credit-linked self help groups (SHGs) in the later years, can ensure the strategic needs of women.

Unlike in the Philippines, earmarking a definite proportion of budget for women has not led to marginalization of gender issues in the mainstream budgeting, as floor limits have not been taken as ceiling in case of Kerala. Rather, identifying the spatial gender needs ex-ante to budgeting led to allocation of more than the statutory minimum requirement of 10 percent of the plan grant-in-aid earmarked for WCP in all districts. Though WCP is considered as second best principle of gender budgeting, Kerala's experience of linking WCP ex-ante to identifying local needs through the appropriate institutional mechanisms proves that it is tantamount to designing the gender budgeting based on differential targeting of expenditure emanating from the identification of appropriate programmes for women in various sectors or reprioritizing the expenditure based on a generic list of appropriate programmes and policies for women. Therefore Kerala experience of WCP is more effective than ad hoc uniform targeting as in case of the Philippines GAD budget as well as the national level WCP designed as part of the Ninth-Five-Year-Plan in India.

Karnataka

The standardized system of fiscal decentralization came to existence in Karnataka only after the 73rd Constitutional Amendment (1992) through the Karnataka Panchayati Raj Act (1993). It provided for a three-tier structure of rural local government with 27 zilla parishads, 175 block panchayats and 5659 gram panchayats. Although the process of decentralization has been effective and created wide possibilities for integrating gender needs at local level in Karnataka, the scope has remained largely unexplored. Unlike Kerala, there has been no within government initiative to conduct gender budgeting at the third tier in Karnataka. However, there has been a civil society initiative on "Building Budgets from Below" to examine whether the increased feminization of governance [in Karnataka, 44 percent of those elected to village panchayats are women, though the constitution provides for 33 percent] could alter the public expenditure decisions at the third tier in Karnataka.

The first phase of the study revealed that devolved functions have remained largely as unfunded mandates and the elected women representatives (EWR) were not capable to explore their newfound powers in altering the budgetary priorities towards their needs. An attempt to rectify this lacuna was taken up in the second phase of the study through a technique of Janaagraha (community participation). An exclusive training was given to the EWRs as part of Janaagraha with regard to budgeting. It was revealed in the third phase of the study that EWRs were empowered to identify the spatial gender needs and arrive at the financial requirements, but their bargaining power in terms of altering the budgetary priorities remain dismal.

The study found that EWR are frequently excluded from budget discussions, and the requests they made for funding of projects in their constituencies were given less priority than those made by men elected representatives. The study concluded that this happen because of gender discrimination and gender bias shown by the authorities while allocating works and distributing benefits. As a result, most women members could not undertake development works in their respective constituencies.

The methodology adopted for this study, however, has certain limitations, due to non-inclusion of a simultaneous study of control groups to analyze the impact of Janaagraha and other training modules adopted in the second phase of the project. Also a longitudinal survey (at least two, a benchmark survey and an impact survey) would have been more beneficial to analyze the intertemporal effects of feminization of governance in determining public expenditure for gender needs. However, it is to be cautioned that even control group methodology should not be infected with problems like sample selection bias and Hawthorne effect (that is, any form of intervention may result in a short-term positive response from the treatment group).

Planning and Budgetary Process at Local Level
Are there any mechanisms in the local level planning and budgetary systems in Karnataka, which can provide scope to PRIs for catering to spatial gender priorities? It is often noted that although the planning process should ideally start at the gram panchayat level with participation from the gram sabha and the local people, it is usually the gram panchayats themselves who identify and prioritize works to be undertaken. This severely limits the scope of integrating gender needs in the local level planning in Karnataka.

Moreover, the resource envelope is drawn based on the resources the panchayat expects to generate and the estimated transfers indicated by the state government. Under the prevailing structure of decentralization in Karnataka, most of the schemes along with the personnel are transferred to the panchayats, though the financial allocation required to implement the schemes is often inadequate. This persistent dearth of funds prevents the local body from initiating plans for suitable public service provision as well as prioritization of existing schemes. As the panchayats receive funds from multiple sources (consolidated funds of the state as well as the central government, various regional development boards and other agencies) there seem to prevail a lack of coordination and transparency in implementation of various schemes which can result in misappropriation and inefficiency.

West Bengal

The origin of fiscal decentralization in West Bengal may be traced to the late nineteenth century. However, the local bodies enjoyed very limited autonomy and were dominated by rural elites given the property restrictions on franchise. After independence, as per the recommendation of Balwantrai-Mehta Committee (1957), West Bengal Panchayat Act was passed in the same year with the intention to set up a four-tier panchayati raj system.35 Subsequently with the enactment of the West Bengal Panchayati Raj Act of 1993, a three-tier system of panchayats was introduced at district, block and village levels. The organization structure of the third tier system in West Bengal comprises 16 zilla parishads, 340 block panchayats and 3314 gram panchayats.

The State Finance Commission of West Bengal constituted in aftermath to 73rd Constitutional Amendment recommended the fiscal devolution to the three tiers of PRIs in the ratio of 30:20:50. As mentioned, the fiscal devolution (16 percent of the net proceeds of the own tax revenue of the state government which go as entitlement to the PRIs) is based on two criteria; population and the index of backwardness, giving equal weight to both criteria. It is to be noted here that in order to encourage own revenue initiatives of PRIs, SFC recommended that 2 percent of the entitlement due to a district would be set aside to operate as an incentive fund. The incentive scheme proposed was that any local body raising its own income by 5 percent or more in a financial year should be entitled to a bonus of 2/3 of the incremental revenue.

The recommendation of SFC of West Bengal in terms of devolution has considerably reduced adhocism and arbitrariness in the fiscal devolution to the third tier. It guarantees a non-discretionary assured grant for each PRI that could be spent according to the priorities set by themselves, even though the dependence of PRIs on grants would continue in West Bengal. Yet another notable development is that the SFC made it a point that any scheme of devolution of resources from the state level to local bodies should be from the pool of state's own taxes instead of individual tax-based sharing, since the growth of individual taxes vary considerably from year to year.

Planning and Budgetary Process at Local Level
With the commencement of SFC, there were significant changes in the planning process at the district level. Earlier, the District Plans consisted mostly of departmental schemes drawn up by the departments, may be with the participation of lower tier officials of the departments, but independently of the elected bodies. The role of the three-tier panchayats in the District Plan largely consisted of utilization of funds provided to them for poverty alleviation programmes or as untied funds. The integration of planning at the district level was more of a formality before the SFC came. The new entitlement scheme recommended by SFC has provided the elected bodies with considerable funds to pursue their own

priorities through the plans they can draw up. The flexibility of district plans thus increased considerably. The question at this juncture is whether these changes occured in the planning and budgeting process provided any scope for the new EWR to prioritize their gender needs?

Chattopadhyay and Duflo (2001) have measured the impact of feminization of governance at local level on the outcomes of decentralization with data collected from a survey of all investments in local public goods made by the village councils in one district in West Bengal. Yet another study in the context of West Bengal on decentralized gender budgeting by UNIFEM, examining the budgetary policies with the broad objective of assessing the extent of efforts put in by the state government towards improving the relative position of women in the state, is mainly confined to state level.36 However, the analysis of local budgets under this UNIFEM study reveals that there is no information about whether or not funds given to local bodies are actually spent or not. It also makes a few reference to the fact that the local bodies are not capable of executing the functions devolved due to low technical capabilities of their staff. The study also shows that schemes are similarly loaded on the local bodies by all superior levels of government without any checks on the technical capability of the local bodies to execute the works. The result is that funds remain unspent and each PRI has a growing opening balance.

To conclude, Kerala has shown a good example in integrating both the elements through integrating gender needs in the process of decentralized planning after identifying the gender needs through participatory process through gram sabhas as well as translating it into women component plan in fiscal transfers. In Karnataka, the process of decentralization has created immense scope for incorporating gender needs at local level, though that remains substantially unexplored. In West Bengal, the women in governance at the third tier could change the types of public expenditure at local level more corresponding to the revealed preferences ('voice') by women. However, that could have little influence on gender needs as most of the expenditure even at the local level is in the nature of committed non- developmental expenditure.

Fiscal Decentralization and Local Level Gender Budgeting in Other Countries: Case Studies

This section broadly discusses the fiscal decentralization and gender budgeting at the local level of four countries, including Morocco, South Africa, Nepal, and Ethiopia.

Morocco

Morocco is a constitutional monarchy in North Africa, whose territory encompasses the coastal plain on the Atlantic, desert region of Sahara, and the Atlas mountain ranges. Morocco got independence in 1956 from French rule. It has a population of 30.1 million and the extent of urbanisation is 57 percent. As per recent estimates, the Gender Development Index (GDI) of Morocco is 0.616 as compared to its Human Development Index (HDI) at 0.631. The majority population of the country is Muslim population. It is also a patriarchal society. However, during the last few years there has been a significant attempt to change the status of women and considerable efforts have been made to incorporate mainstream gender in socio-economic policies, including gender budgeting initiatives. The decentralization process in Morocco dates back to the 1960 charter, when the charter was issued recognizing the need for local governments. Though limited in scope, the charter helped to constitute the local governments. However, it was the 1976 charter which started the real decentralization process. It enshrined "communes", the level of government closest to the people, as the core of local democracy and they were assigned a role in economic and social development. With this, the local government structure comprised of provinces and prefectures and urban and rural communes. A new tier "Region" was created in 1992 and since has a regional assembly. With the adoption of the 1997 charter, this new tier was assigned with the main objective of consolidating and coordinating the efforts of the provinces particularly in planning and land use development. The constitutional reforms in 1986 and 1992 empowered the subnational governments to exercise a number of legislative and administrative powers. The New Communal Charter, 2001 (enacted in 2003) expanded the powers of elected representatives to carry out local development particularly to rural communes, control budgets, and impose local taxes. This also attempted to enhance their financial powers and enabled greater participation of citizens in the public service provision. Thus, the local government structure in Morocco below the central level comprises 16 regions, 42 provinces, and 28 prefectures, 249 urban communes and 1298 rural communes. The national (central) government has two chambers namely, the House of Representatives and the Upper House represented by Unions, Chambers of Commerce and representatives of local governments (Mayors). The proportion of local government representatives in the Upper House is much larger than others. In the House of Representatives, 10 percent of seats are reserved for women. The legislative body for the Regional Council is elected through the electoral college and the executive head of the Region, Wali, is appointed by the Dahir (royal decree) from among the governors of the prefectures or provinces within the region. The provincial or prefectoral assembly is elected indirectly by the communal councillors and colleges of professional chambers and the governor is the executive head, appointed by the Dahir. The legislative body for the communes are the communal councils and the members of the council are directly elected by a universal suffrage. The President of the communal council is elected by the elected members of the council from among themselves. Thus, ever since 1976, when communes were formed, they constitute the basic democratic institution of decentralization. The communes are considered "core of local democracy" and are basic governmental units closest to the people. They have been assigned the responsibility of providing basic services such as providing basic infrastructure, solid waste management, transport development and preservation of markets, and public lighting. Provision of other important public services including some of the social services such as health care and hospital services, and education are still with the central government. Local governments get their resources for spending from their own revenues, devolved taxes from the central government and have recourse, to some extra-budgetary resources including loans. There are 42 taxes assigned to the local governments and most of these are collected by the communes. In terms of fiscal importance, the locally raised revenues are not important. Together, these constitute less than 5 percent of total receipts of the local governments. The regions get one percent of corporate tax and individual income tax for meeting their expenditures which, in the main, consists of coordination of the activities of provinces and prefectures. The provinces, prefectures, and communes receive 30 percent of the value added taxes (VAT) collections. Of the shareable proceeds, provinces and prefectures receive 40 percent of the shareable proceeds, the share of urban communes is 24 percent and the rural communes receive 26 percent. There are conditions on the spending of devolved tax revenues. It is stipulated that 8 percent of the proceeds should be spent on "public goods" which benefit all citizens equally, 79 percent should be spent on meeting operational expenditures and remaining 13 percent should be spent on investment expenditures. The lump sum component of distributable VAT revenues is distributed on the basis of the ratio of personnel expenditures. The operational component among the provinces is distributed on the basis of two indicators, population and the area in the ratio two-thirds, and one-third. The distribution of operational expenditures among communes is done on the basis of tax effort. Investment component is distributed on the basis of the nature of the projects. Thus, although attempt has been made to make the distribution formula based and transparent, there are opaque and discretionary elements in the transfer system. The Ministry of Interior is responsible for the administration, supervision, and coordination of local governments. The fiscal year is the calendar year. The budget cycle for the local governments begins with the guidelines issued by the Ministry of Interior in October setting out the basic ground rules for preparing revenue and expenditure. For all levels except rural communes, the local budgets prepared by respective levels of governments are sent to the Ministry of Interior after being duly approved by the respective Councils. In the case of rural communes, the approval has to be obtained from the governor of the province. After approval, these are sent to the Ministry of Finance for coordination. Despite initiatives taken to decentralize administration, Morocco has a highly centralized fiscal system. Together, all local governments incur a little over 13 percent of total expenditures or about 3.5 percent of GDP. Of this overwhelming proportion is financed through transfers from above by way of shared taxes. The share of VAT transfers alone constitutes almost 50 percent of the total current and capital receipts. Despite these significant features of decentralization, it is important to note that the fiscal system in Morocco is that local governments have very limited role. Even though there has been formal devolution of functions to the local bodies in Morocco in the backdrop of the New Communal Charter, elements of centralization are evident as local governments remain under the supervision of Ministry of Interior. The level of spending by the local governments is so low that they cannot make much difference to providing access, ensuring entitlements or enabling empowerment of women, however well disposed they are, towards achieving gender equality and mainstreaming women in organized economic activities. Nor is the sensitivity to gender issues in Morocco at the local level high enough to make significant difference to improve equality. There is no systematic attempt to mainstream gender approach in local budgets. There is no strategic planning to sensitize and educate the policymakers on gender equality. The stakeholders of local governments too are not well informed about the issues of gender sensitivity to make any significant impact on policies. Given the traditional nature of society with significant gender inequality, the approach continues to confine women to traditional roles. There is an initiative to analyze the local budgetary process, planning and implementation on the one hand, and the extent of gender equality accomplished in them in the 5 communes to initiate gender sensitive analysis of local budgets and assess the potential of gender mainstreaming in the local budgetary process on the other. The five communes included for the study are, Casablanca city council and urban commune of Sidi Moumen, one urban and rural commune each in Essaouira, a rural commune of Mohemmadia and rural commune of Zagora, which led to help the stakeholders of these communes to develop budget engendering strategies in them.

South Africa

South Africa has done the analysis of engendering the fiscal policy as an outside government initiative. Launched in 1995, it was the initiative of the post-apartheid regime, which took over the administration of the country in 1994. What distinguishes South African gender budgeting from that of other countries is the interface between racial discrimination and gender inequalities. Understandably, race constitutes an important focus of attention in the policy arena in a country, where 79 percent of the 46.9 million people are Africans. Public policy on gender cannot be built on the homogeneity assumption that all women are equal especially in a country where the overwhelming majority of the female population is African. It was felt that the dimension of race had to be recognized in gender budgeting as well, otherwise the main victims of oppression and discrimination viz., black women did not benefit to any appreciable extent. Thus emphasis moved away from the narrowly conceived gender budgeting with emphasis on budget allocations for women at the national level to affirmative actions through legislation to end discrimination against the blacks in general with special attention to women.

Further, allocations in public expenditure having potential for benefiting women were sought to be provided more at levels of government closer to the people i.e., through decentralization. In all these initiatives, gender figured as the focus of attention with race. Gender budget initiatives began in South Africa, immediately after the Beijing UN Conference on Women, 1995 as a collaborative venture of women parliamentarians and non-governmental organizations, known as Women's Budget Initiative (WBI). WBI emphasized that the solution to gender discrimination is mainstreaming gender issues rather than implementing separate women's programmes and policies. It is to be noted that mainstreaming gender in budget is comparatively a better approach rather than quota-based gender budgeting (of earmarking a specific proportion of each sectoral budget for women, as in the case of Philippines), which is confined to a very negligible part of the budget. Further, gender budgeting initiatives in South Africa focused more on reprioritisation of programmes rather than increasing the budgetary allocation for women. This is against the backdrop of Growth, Employment and Redistribution (GEAR) macropolicy in 1997, which emphasized the hard budget constraints. Moreover, though the environment was more favourable towards gender equality with the adoption of the final constitution in South Africa in 5 1997 as also the development of machinery to oversee implementation of measures with gender focus, such as Office of Status of Women (OSW) and Commission of Gender Equality (CGE), the gender focal points created within the government were engaged more in redressing gender imbalances among the elite of the civil service rather than attending to the needs of poor and needy women. However, the advantage of civil society (outside government) initiative of WBI in South Africa is the participatory, grassroot initiatives by the civil society to provide economic literacy among ordinary people and demystify budgets through the publication of simple budget (sectoral) booklets through a gender lens. The drawback of the WBI is that it failed to institutionalize gender budget within government in South Africa. The sustainability of gender budgeting initiatives in South Africa will depend to a great extent in creating a synergy between civil society and government, in particular with experts in the budget division of Department of Finance to strengthen the public finance lens of gender budgeting. A within government initiative on gender budgeting began in 1998 with the establishment of a women's pilot budget within Department of Finance. However, this was primarily a donor-driven initiative by the Commonwealth Secretariat, which lasted for only two years. This resulted in the inclusion of certain case studies of gender issues within the compilation of sectoral reports tabled on Budget Day in 1999. Since 1999, the initiative has been discontinued by the Department of Finance. However, in the absence of any study in this regard, what has been the impact of these initiatives in terms of gender indicators is not known. WBI took the gender budgeting initiatives to local level for the first time in 1999, though local governments were then in transition in terms of realigning the country from the racially segregated units of the apartheid regime. This was more challenging because of the difficulty in analyzing the local government budgets through a gender lens as most local government services were directed to the households and not women members of households, as such. WBI tended to focus on the poor and the way local government budgets impacted them. Revenue decentralization was one of the core thrusts of WBI in the following two years as attention was drawn to the issues related to fiscal autonomy at subnational levels. However, the within government initiative at local government on gender budgeting is almost invisible in South Africa, except in the province of Gauteng. An attempt was made in Gauteng to incorporate gender elements in its budget to which we turn in the section on budgetary process. As mentioned, though there are no direct initiatives on gender budgeting within government at the national level, several windows have been opened for affirmative action in South Africa in terms of gender, especially through legislations like the Employment Equity Act, Promotion of Equality Act, and Black Economic Empowerment Act (BEE). The Employment Equity Act, 1998 envisages non-discrimination coupled with positive measures of discrimination to accelerate women's access to employment opportunities and benefits. The provisions of this Act envisage enforcement through the labour court system, labour inspections, and broad monitoring by a statutory body, viz., Commission of Employment Equity (CEE). The Act also addresses issues such as pregnancy discrimination, sexual and other forms of harassment, discrimination on grounds of HIV and AIDS status, discrimination on grounds of family responsibility, pregnancy discrimination, and discrimination on grounds of disability, including failure to provide reasonable accommodation, as per Beijing Plus Ten Report, South Africa, 2005. The Promotion of Equality and Prevention of Unfair Discrimination Act, 2000, provides a comprehensive legal framework for the prohibition of discrimination, redressal for discrimination, progressive eradication of discrimination, and promotion of equality. The core of enforcement mechanism has the specialized equality courts. At least 60 equality courts have been established to provide relief to claimants in magistrate courts throughout the country. The government has made a conscious decision to prioritize the advancement of women along with people with disabilities, workers, and rural communities in programmes or activities that are designed to undo the legacy of apartheid in the matter of participation by the black community in the economy. This policy commitment is reflected in the key national instruments that regulate BEE. These include the Broad-based BEE, 2003 (Act 53 of 2003), and the Draft codes of Good Practice on BEE. The National Policy Framework on Gender Equality and Women's Empowerment mandates the establishment of a regular monitoring mechanism through JMC (Joint Monitoring Committee) of Parliament to ensure that gender considerations are included in all legislations. Despite these legislations and affirmative actions, within each racial group, inequalities persisted significantly. An important dimension of the interface between racial discrimination and gender inequalities in South Africa has been intra-racial income inequalities. If we decompose inequality into within-group and between-group components using the Theil-T, empirical evidence showed that 40.7 percent of inequality is owing to between-race inequality, 33 percent on account of intra-African inequality and 21 percent due to intra-White inequality (Ingrid, 2002). The point to be noted here is that affirmative action in South Africa continues to be shaped solely around racial identities, which ignores intra-racial inequalities, which is one of the emerging criteria of social differentiation in the country. In spite of the Employment Equity Act, which is aimed at improving prospects for historically disadvantaged employees, black women continue to face economic disadvantage. Labour Force Survey (2003) revealed that African women faced high rates of unemployment compared to other groups and especially in comparison to white men and women. Effective fiscal decentralization has a significant role to play in improving the access of women to the basic infrastructure and public service delivery. At the subnational level, with increasing decentralization, there is good scope for initiatives on gender budgeting; the rationale being that merit goods like education and health are the responsibility of provincial government and the provisioning of quasi-public goods like, water supply which is of crucial importance for women, is the responsibility of local governments. However, there is no meaningful decentralization at the provincial level, as the revenue powers of provinces are negligible.

Ethiopia

Ethiopia is in the process of integrating gender in intergovernmental fiscal transfers. In Ethiopia, the process has been initiated by the House of Federations (Senate) and the Terms of Reference (TOR) were moved in Parliament for public hearing. Subsequently, a majority was secured in the Senate for gender-integrated TOR and the "proclamation" by the Senate to make it a reality in their forthcoming Fiscal Commission is awaited. NIPFP, India is working in close association with House of Federation (Senate), Government of Ethiopia, and the Forum of Federation in this process of integrating gender in fiscal transfers in Ethiopia.

Nepal

In the fiscal year 2007–2008, the Ministry of Finance, Government of Nepal introduced gender budgeting. A new classification of budgetary transactions was introduced to incorporate gender budgeting into the budget. Like that of India, Bangladesh, and Sri Lanka, the new classification mainly entailed categorizing public expenditure by benefits to women. According to the government's guidelines, all line ministries, departments, project/programme units at all levels have to provide information classifying their demands for grants (on new preprograms and associated expenditure items) into the three categories, directly gender-responsive (G01), indirectly gender-responsive (G2) and neutral, scoring as per the indicators. Public budget expenditures are classified into three categories: (i) Those that are more than half related to programmes directly responsive to gender (>50 percent); (ii) Those that are indirectly gender-responsive (>20 to < 50 percent) and (iii) Those that are neutral. The scoring system takes account of different aspects of gender sensitivity, participation, capacity building, benefit sharing, and increased access to employment and income-earning opportunities and reduction in women's work load. These indicators have been allocated 20 potential percentage points each. Programmes scoring 50 percent or more are classified as directly supportive to women, those scoring 20–50 percent as indirectly supportive and scoring less than 20 percent as neutral, as per the Ministry of Finance, Government of Nepal, 2007. The complexity and subjectivity of the scoring method of gender budgeting may one of the reasons for the lack of universal acceptance of Nepal's experience with gender budgeting.

In the fiscal year 2007–2008, the Ministry of Finance, Government of Nepal introduced gender budgeting. A new classification of budgetary transactions was introduced to incorporate gender budgeting into the budget. Like that of India, Bangladesh and Sri Lanka, the new classification mainly entailed categorizing public expenditure by benefits to women. According to the government's guidelines, all line ministries, departments, project/programme units at all levels have to provide information classifying their demands for grants (on new preprograms and associated expenditure items) into the three categories, directly gender responsive (G01), indirectly gender responsive (G2) and neutral, scoring as per the indicators. The gender budgeting classification criteria and corresponding scores are given in Table 6.1.

Public budget expenditures are classified into three categories:

- Those that are more than half related to programmes directly responsive to gender (>50 percent)
- Those that are indirectly gender-responsive (>20 to < 50 percent)
- Those that are neutral (<20 percent).

The scoring system takes account of different aspects of gender sensitivity, participation, capacity building, benefit sharing, and increased access to employment and income earning opportunities and reduction in women's work load. These indicators have been allocated 20 potential percentage points each. Programs scoring 50 percent or more are classified as directly supportive to women, those scoring 20 to 50 percent as indirectly supportive and scoring less than 20 percent as neutral (Ministry

Table 6.1 Criteria of gender responsive budgeting and scores in Nepal

No	Criteria	Score
1	Women's participation in formulation and implementation of the programme	20
2	Women's capacity development	20
3	Women's share in the benefit	30
4	Promoting employment and income generation for women	20
5	Qualitative improvement of women's time use or reduced workload	10

Source *Budget Speech (2015–2016), Ministry of Finance

of Finance, Government of Nepal, 2007). The complexity and subjectivity of the scoring method of gender budgeting may one of the reasons for the lack of universal acceptance of Nepal's experience with gender budgeting. There has been criticism of this system of scoring, and Acharya et al. (2003) have put forward an alternative classification procedure.

IMF Government Finance Statistics (GFS): Analyzing "General Government" Data

The general government data is inclusive of the public finance data of all the three tiers of government—national, regional and local. The data paucity is a serious constraint to understand the expenditure and revenue assignments at various levels of government across federations. The Government Finance Statistics (GFS) of International Monetary Fund (IMF) provides data at three levels of government—the expenditure by functional and economic classification and the revenue assignments. A few countries in the Global South is selected for an illustrative analysis of general government finance. The disaggregated data on national, provincial and local governments—both expenditure and revenue—are given in Government Finance Statistics of IMF. Tables 6.2, 6.3, and 6.4 provide the general government data (including national, provincial and local)—expenditure and revenue details of four federations—Nepal, Keyna, South Africa, and Ethiopia. The IMF GFS estimates and ratios are slightly different from the estimates based on national public finance statistics.

Table 6.2 provides expenditure by "functions of government", while Table 6.3 provides expenditure by "economic classification". The transfers between different levels of government varies from 1.89 percent of GDP in Nepal to 10.35 percent of GDP in South Africa (Table 6.2). The IMF GFS data across countries on expenditure by economic classification shows that the components of expenditure as percent of GDP varies significantly across countries (Table 6.3). The grants to other levels of government varies from 6 percent of GDP in Ethiopia to 10 percent in Nepal and Keyna; to 17 percent in South Africa.

The revenue assignment shows that direct tax from income, profits, and capital gains constitutes relatively a better source of revenue in Nepal and Ethiopia, while indirect taxes on goods and services constitute a better source of revenue for Keyna and South Africa (Table 6.3). The revenue model of South Africa is like a hour glass, with thin tax handles

Table 6.2 General government finance: Expenditure (% of GDP) by functions of government, IMF GFS 2019

Expenditure	Nepal	Ethiopia	Kenya	South Africa
Expenditure on general public services	4.07	7.26	11.98	16.17
Expenditure on public debt transactions	1.77	0.48	5.50	3.49
Transfers between different levels of govt	1.89	6.21	3.69	10.35
Expenditure on Defence	1.63	0.63	1.58	1.09
Expenditure on public order and safety	2.15	0.30	1.66	2.88
Expenditure on economic affairs	10.59	3.11	5.94	2.92
Expenditure on agriculture, fishing, forestry, and hunting	2.95	1.33	0.49	0.32
Expenditure on mining, manufacturing, and construction	2.73	0.01	0.02	0.21
Expenditure on transport	3.52	1.41	3.72	1.33
Expenditure on communication	0.18	0.02	0.36	0.08
Expenditure on fuel and energy	1.20	0.12	1.01	0.32
Expenditure on environment protection	0.24	0.02	0.14	0.13
Expenditure on housing and community amenities	1.55	0.29	0.76	1.56
Expenditure on health	1.72	0.42	0.69	1.05
Of which Expenditure on outpatient services	0.14	0.00	0.14	0.00
Expenditure on hospital services	0.62	0.09	0.23	0.52
Expenditure on public health services	0.96	0.29	0.08	0.39
Expenditure on recreation, culture, and religion	0.25	0.07	0.11	0.16
Expenditure on education	4.11	2.35	3.97	1.67
Of which Expenditure on pre-primary and primary education	1.68	0.00	1.67	0.14
Expenditure on secondary education	0.44	0.00	1.14	0.01
Expenditure on tertiary education	2.00	1.91	0.98	0.96
Expenditure on social protection	1.45	0.65	1.02	3.55

Note The estimates show mild variation from national data sources
Source *Government Finance Statistics, International Monetary Fund 2019

at Provincial level—only the taxes from horse race and casino, and with significant revenue handles at national and local levels of government.

The broad conclusion of this section is that engendering fiscal policies is sustainable, but only if the Ministry of Finance owns the process. The initiatives on gender budgeting should begin from the Ministry of Finance with adequate support of all stakeholders including civil society,

Table 6.3 General Government Finance: Expenditure (% of GDP) by Economic Classification, IMF GFS 2019

Expenditure	Nepal	Ethiopia	Kenya	South Africa
Compensation of employees	4.50	1.27	5.12	3.30
Wages and salaries	4.50	1.14	0	2.75
Employers' social contributions*	0.00	0.13	–	0.56
Use of goods and services*	2.16	2.13	2.52	1.31
Consumption of fixed capital*	–	–	–	0.24
Interest expense	0.38	0.48	2.85	3.49
Interest expense to nonresidents*	0.12	0.23	0.76	–
Interest expense to residents other than gen govt*	0.26	0.25	2.09	–
Interest expense to other gen gov*	0.00	0.00	0.00	–
Subsidies expense	0.04	0.00	0.37	0.78
Subsidies expense to public corporations*	0.03	0.00	0.37	0.67
Subsidies expense to private enterprises*	0.01	0.00	0.00	0.11
Subsidies expense to other sectors*	0.00	0.00	0.00	0.00
Grants expense	9.23	5.99	10.42	17.75
Grants expense to foreign govts*	0.00	0.00	0.03	1.16
Grants expense to int orgs*	0.01	0.00	0.00	0.04
Grants expense to other gen govt	9.22	5.99	10.39	16.55
Grants expense to other gen govt: current*	4.52	4.06	6.08	14.87
Grants expense to other gen govt: capital*	4.70	1.93	4.32	1.68
Social benefits expense	3.30	0.00	0.81	3.39
Social security benefits expense*	0.00	0.00	0.81	2.37
Social assistance benefits expense*	1.50	0.00	0.00	0.68
Employment-related social benefits expense*	1.80	0.00	0.00	0.34
Other expense	0.00	1.53	0.06	0.68
Property expense other than interest*	0.00	0.00	0.00	0.00
Expense on other transfers	0.00	1.53	0.06	0.68
Expense on other transfers, current*	0.00	1.53	0.06	0.25
Expense on other transfers, capital*	0.00	0.00	0.00	0.43

Note The estimates show mild variation from national data sources
Source *Government Finance Statistics, International Monetary Fund 2019

parliamentarians, academicians, and the people. For instance, the heterogeneous stakeholders in the process who supported the Ministry of Finance in India to introduce gender budgeting include policy think tanks, the Ministry of Women and Child Development, UN entities, and civil society organizations. The prime involvement of the Ministry of Finance has provided a technical space to translate the conceptual and micro level prescriptions to a simple and practical exercise within the

Table 6.4 General Government Finance: Revenue (% of GDP), 2019

Heads	Nepal	Ethiopia	Kenya	South Africa
Tax revenue	20.95	7.71	15.58	26.11
Taxes on income, profits, and capital gains	5.49	2.29	7.66	15.30
Taxes on income, profits, and capital gains: individuals*	0.49	0.38	4.11	9.95
Taxes on income, profits, and capital gains: corporations*	4.06	1.75	3.52	5.35
Taxes on income, profits, and capital gains: other*	0.93	0.16	0.03	0.00
Taxes on payroll and workforce*	0.16	0.00	0.00	0.34
Taxes on property	0.01	0.00	0.00	0.07
Taxes on goods and services, of which	11.22	3.47	6.44	9.35
General taxes on goods and services*	6.78	2.75	4.14	6.70
Excise taxes*	3.20	0.72	2.02	2.39
Taxes on int trade and transactions*	3.90	1.95	1.38	1.05
Other taxes*	0.19	0.00	0.10	0.00
Social contributions	0.00	0.00	0.01	0.00
Social security contributions revenue*	0.00	0.00	0.01	0.00
Other social contributions revenue*	0.00	0.00	0.00	0.00
Grants revenue	1.21	0.85	0.00	0.03
Grants revenue from foreign govts*	0.15	0.15	0.00	0.03
Grants revenue from int orgs*	1.06	0.69	0.00	0.00
Grants revenue from other gen govt*	0.00	0.00	0.00	0.00
Grants revenue from other gen govt: current*	0.00	0.00	0.00	0.00
Grants revenue from other gen govt: capital*	0.00	0.00	0.00	0.00
Other revenue	2.22	1.87	1.51	0.83
Property income revenue	1.03	0.79	0.38	0.27
Revenue from sales of goods and services	1.02	0.25	1.06	0.06
Revenue from fines, penalties and forfeits	0.03	0.02	0.02	0.01
Revenue from other transfers	0.14	0.82	0.05	0.49
Revenue from NI and SGS: premiums, fees and claims	0.00	0.00	0.00	0.00

Note The estimates show mild variation from national data sources
Source *Government Finance Statistics, International Monetary Fund 2019

budget process. Though gender budgeting has the potential to transform gender equality in the region, the results are still modest in most countries except India, the Philippines, and South Korea, where the efforts have led to substantive fiscal policies. A major lacuna in the process has been to integrate a gender criterion in intergovernmental fiscal transfers.

When the review of policy space and the existing policy initiatives in this section leads to the significance of a normative framework of integrating gender in fiscal federalism, the following sections discuss the theoretical and empirical framework for advancing the policy initiatives of engendering the fiscal transfers mechanisms.

To conclude, fiscal transfers and principles of federalism prima facie do not ensure gender equality. It depends on the institutional space and transfer design. With the progress of federal governance and fiscal decentralization, significant expenditure functions important for gender equality such as health care, education, and income-support programmes are at the sub-national level. Gender-sensitive transfer design can help achieve equality of outcome. Our analysis shows that the gender differential tax system and tax policy are not the most efficient way to address gender inequality. It is argued that specific-purpose grants to subnational governments for gender-specific outcome can promote gender equality. There is no comprehensive study analyzing the link between a public employment policy, time use in care economy and female labour force participation in the market economy, the area which needs further research. There is no conclusive evidence on how women's well-being is promoted through "specific-purpose grants". The fiscal marksmanship analysis of examining the fiscal forecasting errors can be extended to gender intensive spending and tax transfers as well.

References

Acharya, M. et al. (2003). *Gender budget audit in Nepal* (Vol. 2). UNIFEM and IIDS.

Anand, A., & Chakraborty, L. (2016). *Engendering' intergovernmental transfers: Is there a case for gender-sensitive horizontal fiscal equalization?* (Working Paper 874). The Levy Economics Institute of Bard College.

Bagchi, A., & Chakraborty, L. (2004, November 19). No pride in this prejudice. *Financial Express*.

Bahl, R. (2008). *The pillars of fiscal decentralization* (CAF Working paper, 2008/07). CAF.

Bahl, R., Eunice, H.-O., Jorge, M.-V., & Mark, R. (2005). *India: Fiscal condition of the states, international experience, and options for reform: Volume 2* (Working Paper No. 05142). International Studies Program, Andrew Young School of Policy Studies, Georgia State University.

Bardhan, P. (1999). Democracy and development: A complex relationship. [~57k pdf]. In I. Shapiro & C. Hacker-Cordon (Eds.), *Democracy's values*. Cambridge University Press.

Bardhan, P., & Mookherjee, D. (1999). *Relative capture of local and central governments: An essay in the political economy of decentralization*. Boston University—Institute for Economic Development 97, Boston University.

Bird, R. M., &Vaillancourt, F. (Ed.). (2006). *Introduction and summary" in perspectives on fiscal federalism*. World Bank Institute.

Blöchliger, H. (2014). *Fiscal federalism 2014: Making decentralization work*. Organisation for Economic Co-Operation and Development.

Bredie, J., & Beehary, G. (1998). *School enrolment decline in sub-saharan Africa* (World Bank Discussion Paper No. 395). World Bank.

Breton, A., & Fraschini, A. (2004). *Intergovernmental equalization grants: Some fundamental principles* (Working Paper No. 42). Department of Public Policy and Public Choice.

Breton, A. (1996). *Competitive governments: An economic theory of politics and public finance*. Cambridge University Press.

Chakraborty, L. (2004). *Local level gender responsive budgeting international expert group meeting*. National Institute of Public Finance and Policy.

Chakraborty, L. (2010). *Determining gender equity in fiscal federalism: Analytical issues and empirical evidence from India* (Working Paper No. 590). Levy Economics Institute.

Chakraborty. L. (2014). *Gender budgeting, as fiscal innovation* (Working Paper). The Levy Economics Institute.

Chakraborty, L. (2020a). *The gender budgeting gets a leap in the fifteenth finance commission*. Business Standard.

Chakraborty, L. (2020b). *Macroeconomic policy coherence for SDG 2030: Evidence from Asia Pacific* (Working Paper No. 292). National Institute of Public Finance and Policy.

Chakraborty, L. (2020c). *Fiscal prudence for what? Analysing the state finances of Karnataka* (Working Paper No. 293). National Institute of Public Finance and Policy.

Chakraborty, L. (2020d). *Fiscal consolidation ex-post the escape clause: A call for "excessive deficit procedure* (Working Paper No. 299). National Institute of Public Finance and Policy.

Chakraborty, L., Marian, I., & Yadawendra, S. (2018). *Fiscal policy effectiveness and inequality: Efficacy of gender budgeting in Asia Pacific* (Working Paper No.224). National Institute of Public Finance and Policy.

Chakraborty, L., Nayyar, V., & Komal, J. (2020). *The political economy of gender budgeting: Empirical evidence from India* (Working Paper no. 256). National Institute of Public Finance and Policy.

Chakraborty, P. (2003, March 28–29). *Unequal fiscal capacities across Indian states: How corrective is the fiscal transfer mechanism?* Paper prepared for the UNU/WIDER Project Conference on 'Spatial Inequality in Asia, UNU Centre.

Chattopadhyay, R., & Duflo, E. (2001). *Women as policy makers: Evidence from a randomized policy experiment in India* (Working Paper No. 01-35). MIT: MIT Department of Economics.

Downes, R., Lisa, v. T., & Scherie, N. (2017). Gender budgeting in OECD countries. *OECD Journal on Budgeting, 2016/3.*

Escolano, M. J., Eyraud, L., Badia, M. M., Sarnes, M. J., & Tuladhar, M. A. (2012). *Fiscal performance, institutional design and decentralization in European Union countries* (IMF Working Paper). International Monetary Fund.

Galasso, E., & Ravallion, M. (2000). *Distributional outcomes of a decentralized welfare program* (Policy Research Working Paper Series 2316). The World Bank.

Government of India. (2015). *Gender budgeting handbook.* Ministry of Women and Child Development, Government of India.

Gulati, I. S. (Eds.). (1987). *Centre-state budgetary transfers.* Oxford University Press.

Griffith, K. (1981). Economic development in a changed world. *World Development, 9*(3), 5.

Ingrid. (2002). *The politics of gender equality policy: A study of implementation and non-implementation in three Swedish municipalities.* Monograph. Örebro University, Department of Social and Political Science.

Isaac, T. M. T. (2004). *Democratic decentralization and women empowerment: Kerala model.* Paper presented at International Expert Group Meeting on Local Level Gender Responsive Budgeting. National Institute of Public Finance and Policy.

Isaac, T. T. M., et al. (1999). *Gender and decentralised planning—The experience of people's campaign* (Unpublished Working Paper). Center for Development Studies.

Isaac, T. M. T., & Franke, R. W. (2000). *Local democracy and development.* LeftWord.

Isaac, T. T. M., & Heller, P. (2002). Decentralisation, democracy and development: People's campaign for decentralized planning in Kerala. In A. Fung & E. O. Wright (Eds.), *Deepening democracy: Institutional innovations in empowered participatory democracy.* Verso Press.

Kolovich, L. (Ed.). 2018. Fiscal policies and gender equality., ed. Lisa Kolovich, IMF, 2018 for analysis by region.

Lindahl, E. (1919). Just taxation—A positive solution. In R. A. Musgrave & A. T. Peacock (Eds.), *Classics in the theory of public finance [1964].* Macmillan.

Oates, W. E. (2001, November). *A reconsideration of environmental: Federalism.* (Discussion Paper 01–54) Resources for the Future.
Rao, M., Govinda, H. K., Amar, N., & Vani, B. P. (2004). Fiscal decentralization in Karnataka. In G. Sethi (Ed.), *Fiscal decentralization to rural governments in India.* The World Bank. Oxford University Press.
Rao, M. G. (2006, February 2). *Gender responsive budgetary policies and fiscal decentralization: Conceptual issues.* Paper presented at NIPFP-IFES-USAID Conference on Gender Budgeting, NIPFP.
Rao, M. G., & Singh, N. (2004). *Asymmetric federalism in India* (Working Paper No. 06). National Institute of Public Finance and Policy.
Ryan, R. (2017). *Women's political empowerment: Lessons for subnational levels of government—Nepal, Pakistan, Rwanda, and Indonesia.* Handbook of Research on Sub-National Governance and Development.
Reddy, Y. V., & Reddy, G. R. (2019). *Indian fiscal federalism.* Oxford University Press.
Rose-Ackerman, S. (1997). Corruption, inefficiency, and economic growth. *Nordic Journal of Political Economy, 24,* 3–20.
Salmon, P. (1987). Decentralisation as an incentive scheme. *Oxford Review of Economic Policy, 3*(2), 24–43.
Stern, N. (2002, January 10). *Public finance and policy for development: Challenges for India.* Silver Jubilee Lecture at the National Institute of Public Finance and Policy (NIPFP).
Swamy, A., Knack, S., Lee, Y., & Omar, A. (2001). Gender and corruption. *Journal of Development Economics, 64*(1), 5–55.
Tanzi, V., & Davoodi, H. R. (2000). *Corruption, growth, and public finances.* (Working Paper 00/182). International Monetary Fund.
Vickers J. (2013). Is federalism gendered? Incorporating gender into studies of federalism. *Publius: The Journal of Federalism, 43(1),* 1–23.$\e$.
Wicksell, K. (1896). c. In R. Musgrave & A. T. Peacock (Eds.), *Classics in the theory of public finance [1964].* Macmillan.

CHAPTER 7

Fiscal and Regional Context of Gender Budgeting in Asia

As a prelude to gender budgeting, it is significant to analyze the overall macroeconomic context of public finance in the region (Table 7.1). The size of the public sector varies a lot across the region, measured by the ratio of public expenditures to GDP. The low level of human development expenditure, especially in spending on health and education, presents a bleak picture of the role of public finance in social spending in the region. Public financial management is relatively weak in some countries, measured by Public Expenditure Financial Accountability (PEFA) scores, calling for strengthening fiscal administration.

There are no studies on the macroeconomic impacts of fiscal austerity and fiscal rules on gender inequality and women's development in the region. However, the plausible macroeconomic impacts of fiscal deficits have been analyzed by Chakraborty (2016). The adverse impact of rule-based fiscal deficits on gender-sensitive human development expenditure is beyond the scope of this chapter. However, a close scrutiny of gender budgeting experiences in the region has highlighted that they have contributed more to a judicious reprioritization of public expenditure than increased allocations. We will revisit this point in country-specific sections.

© The Author(s), under exclusive license to Springer Nature Singapore Pte Ltd. 2022
L. S. Chakraborty, *Fiscal Policy for Sustainable Development in Asia-Pacific*, https://doi.org/10.1007/978-981-19-3281-6_7

Table 7.1 Fiscal context of gender budgeting in Asia

Country	Fiscal Indicators[1] (Average 2010–2015)[2] (Percent of GDP)							Public Expenditure and Financial Accountability (PEFA)
	Total revenue	Total tax revenue	Total expenditure	Education expenditure	Health expenditure	Overal[3] balance	Gross[4] debt	PEFA overall score[5]
Australia	32.9	26.4	36.9	5.3	6.1	−4	25.9	n.a.6
Bangladesh	10	8.1	13	2.2*	1.2	−3	32.8	2.1
Bhutan	36.5	n.a	37.9	4.7	3.5	−1.4	71.9	3
Brunei Darussalam	47.7	31.7	32.6	3.1	2.3	15.1	1.9	n.a
Cambodia	17	n.a	20.2	2.6	1.4	−3.2	31.2	2.1
China	27	18.5	27.4	1.9*	2.9	−0.4	37	n.a
Hong Kong SAR, China	21.7	n.a	18.6	3.5	n.a	3.1	0.6	n.a
India	19.4	16.5	27.3	3.7	1.2	−7.9	67.2	2.6
Indonesia	16.8	12.1	18.1	3.3	1.1	−1.4	23.9	2.8
Japan	30.9	n.a	40	3.8	8.3	−9.1	231.2	n.a
Korea, Rep	21.6	14.3	20.2	4.9	4.1	1.4	32.4	n.a
Lao PDR	22	14.2	24.7	2.8	0.8	−2.6	57.1	n.a
Macao SAR, China	n.a	n.a	n.a	2.9	n.a	n.a	n.a	n.a
Malaysia	23.9	n.a	27.9	5.5	2.2	−4	53.8	n.a

Country	Fiscal Indicators[1] (Average 2010–2015)[2] (Percent of GDP)							Public Expenditure and Financial Accountability (PEFA)
	Total revenue	Total tax revenue	Total expenditure	Education expenditure	Health expenditure	Overall[3] balance	Gross[4] debt	PEFA overall score[5]
Maldives	25.4	15.5	35.1	6.5	5	−9.7	62.2	2
Mongolia	n.a	n.a	n.a	5.4	3.8	n.a	n.a	n.a
Myanmar	17.6	5.5	20.9	0.8	0.4	−3.4	44.2	1.5
Nepal	18.4	13.5	18.5	4.7	2.5	−0.1	33.8	2.2
New Zealand	34.3	27.3	38.5	7.2	8.3	−4.2	30.6	n.a
Pakistan	13.4	10	20.8	2.3	1	−7.4	62.4	2.5
Papua New Guinea	29.8	25.1	31.3	n.a	3.1	−1.6	27.3	n.a
Philippines	18	13.7	18.7	3.4	1.4	−0.7	41.2	2
Singapore	22.3	13.4	15.1	3.1	1.5	7.2	102.8	n.a
Sri Lanka	13.8	n.a	20.5	1.9	1.4	−6.8	79.5	n.a
Thailand	21	17.3	21.5	5.7	3.3	−0.5	40.1	3.1
Vietnam	24.7	20.6	29.2	6.3	2.7	−4.5	49	2.4

(continued)

Table 7.1 (continued)

Country	Fiscal Indicators[1] (Average 2010–2015)[2] (Percent of GDP)							Public Expenditure and Financial Accountability (PEFA)
	Total revenue	Total tax revenue	Total expenditure	Education expenditure	Health expenditure	Overall[3] balance	Gross[4] debt	PEFA overall score[5]
Regional average	23.6	16.9	25.6	4.1	2.9	−2	51.7	2.4

Sources World Economic Outlook (WEO), World Bank Development Indicators (WDI), and IMF staff calculations

Note A * reflects the value of latest year available since data were not available for the 2010–2013 period. Bangladesh (2009) and China (1999)
1/ All figures except for health and education expenditure are drawn from the latest WEO and concept of government corresponds to that in the WEO. Please see WEO for further details. Health and education expenditures are drawn from World Bank Development Indicators (WDI) and correspond to the general government concept
2/ Average over the number of years in this period for which data were available
3/ Corresponds to the concept of total revenue minus total expenditure
4/ Gross debt does not net out holdings of debt by other entities of the government
5/ PEFA is a performance monitoring framework used to assess the public financial management (PFM) systems in developing countries. It is an initiative jointly supported by the World Bank, IMF, European Commission, and other development and government institutions. The framework consists of 28 indicators with each indicator scored on a scale from A (highest) to D (lowest). PEFA scores reported above is an average of the 28 indicators and convert the four ordinal PEFA scores (A, B, C, D) to numerical scores (4, 3, 2, 1) with "+" score given 0.5 point. A higher PEFA score implies stronger administration of public finance. On a global basis, the lowest score is 1.1 and highest score is 3.6. Please see https://www.pefa.org/ for further details
6/ Data are not available

Overview of Gender Budgeting in Asia

Gender budgeting has been seen as a powerful tool to integrate gender into fiscal policy in the region to address gender inequality and women's development. Many Asian nations have undertaken gender budgeting efforts, including developed and developing countries. However, gender budgeting at the national level does not fully address the fiscal challenges to countries with heterogeneous regions and populaces. With fiscal decentralization in many countries in the region and subnational governments having important spending responsibilities for basic public services, subnational gender budgeting exercises are also important and beginning to expand, even though they are still confined to a few countries. Ng (2016a, 2016b) captures the local level processes of conducting participatory gender budgeting in the region.

The successful gender budgeting initiatives in the Asian region were "within government" exercises with the Ministry of Finance (instead of other sectoral ministries) spearheading the process, in collaboration with public policy think tanks and others. For instance, India is a leading example of gender budgeting in the Asia Pacific region, as acknowledged by the United Nations (UNDP Asia Pacific, 2010; UN Women, 2012, 2016). The Ministry of Finance has played a lead role to incorporate gender budgeting in budget circulars, expenditure budgets, and performance or outcome budgets. The technical expertise of the team working with the Ministry of Finance to integrate gender budgeting within the existing classification of budget transactions was a strength of the India initiative. The policy think tank of the Ministry of Finance, the National Institute of Public Finance and Policy (NIPFP), provided analytical templates to the Ministry of Finance to make the generic concerns from the civil society organizations were heard and translate the gender commitments into budgetary commitments.

Yet another strength of the process in the region is the so-called gender budget statements within budget papers. The gender budget statements have helped to ensure that budgets include allocations in both national and subnational governments for women's development, and this has led to more transparency and accountability in the budget exercises. The gender budget statements helped the countries to articulate how much they spend on women; and to mainstream gender budgeting in prima facie gender-neutral ministries, such as Science and Technology and others. The gender budgeting statements gave space to governments to build up sex-disaggregated or gender relevant data, though more sustained efforts are required to ensure that the data are used to guide effective programmes and policies.

In the lower-income countries in the region, the approach to budgeting is hampered by low capacity, and gender budgeting in such countries faces more challenges to achieve its intended outcomes. However, there are bold exceptions in the Asian region, where gender budgeting has been attempted by the Ministry of Finance, using gender-based analytical matrices and frameworks (for instance, in Nepal and Sri Lanka).

Gender budgeting has provided an opportunity to incorporate care economy policies into macroeconomic frameworks in the region. The valuation of work done by women using time-use data and incorporating it to gender budgeting policies came about as an offshoot of this process (Chakraborty, 2014). Exercises to incorporate time use in planning has helped governments to realize that the policies which were considered gender neutral were in fact not gender neutral. For instance, in Nepal, the gender budgeting matrix has incorporated women's time use as one criterion. In India, in the Union Budget 2016–2017, the Finance Minister has integrated gender budgeting in the energy sector by a policy initiative on care economy, to uplift poor women in the energy ladder to liquefied petroleum gas (LPG) subsidies. The Cabinet Committee on Economic Affairs, chaired by the Prime Minister, approved the scheme for providing free LPG connections to women from below

Table 7.2 Legal Fiat of Gender Budgeting

Country	*Law*	*Year of Commencement*
The Philippines	Gender and Development (GAD) Budget, earmarking 5 per cent of all sectoral budgets for women	1995
The Republic of Korea	National Finance Law (Articles 16, 26, 57, 68–2, 73–2) to introduce gender budgeting principles and statements, and to do gender-differential impacts/analyze in balance sheet, flow of funds and audits	2006

Source Author's compilation

poverty line households. This was the first time in the history of India that the Ministry of Petroleum and Natural Gas implemented a welfare scheme benefiting many women belonging to the poorest households. This is a good example of how a prima facie gender-neutral ministry like the Ministry of Petroleum and Natural Gas can design a policy to address women's needs.

Yet another challenge is to give gender budgeting legal standing in the countries in the region. Legislation supporting gender budgeting is rarely found in the region. Gender budgeting is more a fiscal fiat than a legal fiat. In the region, Korea and the Philippines have made gender budgeting mandatory through the law (Table 7.2).

Table 7.3 Revenue-Side Gender Budgeting

Content	Revenue Policy	Countries (open-ended)
Direct income taxes	Tax exemption policy	India–different tax exemption for women in the personal income tax, subsequently revoked. Vietnam–tax exemption for women entrepreneurs in small and medium enterprises
Filing of direct taxes	Personal filing of taxes instead of joint filing of direct taxes	India, Thailand (recently debated), Australia
Property taxes	Differential rates for women property owners	India (in certain Provinces including New Delhi)
Mining taxes and royalties (Non tax revenue)	Linking of mining revenue for human development	India (District Mineral Fund in latest mining regulations bill, linking coal proceeds and mining taxes to human development, is yet to be implemented)
Indirect taxes	Tax incidence analysis across income quintiles, region-wise	India (examining the incidence of different households, headed by females and males, and with children and without children)

Source Author's compilation

The revenue side of gender budgeting is still in nascent stages. Revenue policies that provide favourable treatment to women may help to improve their paid work efforts, access to land and property, and their ability to accumulate financial savings and investments, as well as enhance their children's access to education and health, and increase their "say" in intra-household decisions (Basu, 2006). Typically, the debate has centred on the role of personal income taxes (Table 7.3). However, there is more recent focus on indirect taxes as well as property and mineral taxes. These issues are discussed further in the case studies.

Sharp (2003) notes that the growth in gender budget initiatives has coincided with the introduction of reforms in budgetary processes, in both developing and advanced countries, and one of such budgetary reforms has been the introduction of "results-based" budgeting, which shifts assessment of the success of government programmes and policies away from the raising and spending of money (budgetary inputs) to the achievement of results in the form of outputs and outcomes. Gender budgeting efforts fit well into a results-based budgeting approach.

COUNTRY-SPECIFIC GENDER BUDGETING EFFORTS IN ASIA PACIFIC

We next turn to a survey and assessment of gender budgeting experiences in the region and feature those countries whose experience with gender budgeting is notable or interesting,

including the Philippines, Bangladesh, Sri Lanka, Indonesia, and Pakistan. We focus on the developing countries in the region. Australia and the Republic of Korea, both of which have had notable gender budgeting efforts, are also covered in this chapter, which features advanced economies. Indian experience on gender budgeting is given in Chapter 8.

The gender budgeting initiatives vary in scope, objectives, strategies, entry points to the budget, tools of analysis, participants, and the politics of engagement. There is no single means of assessing the success of gender budgeting and it is partly because government budgets, and gender-responsive budgets, arise as a result of multi-faceted processes leading to substantive outputs (Elson & Sharp, 2010). It is therefore difficult to identify the one particular criterion of success of gender budgeting owing to heterogeneity in the experiences of countries, but the tangible criteria of success include whether these efforts help to reduce gender inequality and lead to the advancement of women. This chapter analyzes how gender sensitive the budget making processes are, how effective countries have been in developing transparent and accountable mechanisms in revealing the gender sensitivity of budget processes and allocations, and whether the gender budgeting efforts led to specific policy actions or programmes. Although many countries in the region have begun gender-budgeting initiatives, most of them were one-off initiatives or undertaken outside government.

Australia

Australia was the pioneer in introducing gender budgeting in 1983–1984 at the national level. There were three phases of government, where gender budgeting took shape: the Hawke and Keating Labour Governments (1983–1996); the Howard Liberal-National Governments (1996–2007) and the Rudd and Gillard Labour Governments (2007–2013). This section will not address the political economy aspects of three phases, but instead highlight briefly the fiscal process and outcome of thirty years of gender budgeting in Australia, which abruptly ended in 2014. Despite this, the Australian model of gender budgeting inspired both developed and developing countries to adopt such exercises, with the aim to strengthen gender equity and women's economic empowerment.

Initial Project on Gender Budgeting

Phase I (1983–1996), under the Labour governments, is cited in a number of retrospective assessments as the most successful phase of gender budgeting. It saw the introduction of a project involving 13 departments and led to the submission of a Women's Budget Statement as part of the 1983–1984 budget documentation (Sawer, 2002). This gender budgeting framework was subsequently extended to states and territory governments, as well. The Women's Budget Statements were very comprehensive documents in Australia and were an effective first step towards transparency and accountability of budgeting in ensuring that gender equity concerns were heard.

Sawer (2002) noted that the genesis of gender budgeting discussions in Australia can be traced to the quarterly meeting of federal, state and territory "femocrats" who headed the women's policy offices established in the 1970s. Sharp and Broomhill (2002) noted that these discussions were focused on how to influence non-gender-specific public expenditure under the guidance of Dr. Anne Summers, the Head of the Office of the Status of Women[1] in the Department of the Prime Minister and Cabinet, and gained approval through the high-level coordination of federal government departmental heads–the Secretaries' Taskforce on the Status of Women. Sawer (2002) noted that the 1983 Cabinet Handbook of the new Labour government ensured that all Cabinet submissions should include a statement discussing their impact on women.

The analytical framework in which these government entities conducted gender budgeting was through categorizing public expenditure into gender allocations as follows:

> **Category 1:** Public expenditure for programmes that specifically targeted women;
> **Category 2:** public expenditure for programmes to promote employment of women and men in equal numbers, equal representation within management posts, and equal pay; and
> **Category 3:** mainstream expenditures which have components where gender might be relevant, which consisted of the bulk of the remaining expenditures not covered by the first two categories.

Sharpe's framework on gender budgeting has been the analytical framework for classifying expenditures of many countries at national and subnational levels with country-specific improvisations. Her framework is an accounting framework and not an "outcome framework" in the sense that while it helps to categorize public allocations for gender development, it does not analyze the impact of such allocations on gender outcomes.

In Australia, the categorization of gender allocations was sustained at the federal, state, and territorial level from 1984 to 1996, and despite a change of government at the federal level, some remnants of it were maintained at the state level until the early 2000s. South Australia

---

[1] The Office of the Status of Women supports the Australian Government in its commitment to strengthen the provision of gender analysis, advice and gender mainstreaming. It works in coordination with other sectoral ministries in policy and programme development and implementation towards gender equity.

published the Women's Budget Statement as an appendix to the budget papers during the early 2000s (Chakraborty, 2010; Sharp & Broomhill, 2002; Sharp & Costa, 2010). The Australian Women's Budget Statements improved the availability of sex-disaggregated data by the sectoral ministries and agencies which were essential for assessing the gender-disaggregated budgetary impacts. Despite the significant achievements in terms of an increased understanding of government officials of gender-related concerns and the need to quantify the policy impacts of budgets on women, the initial efforts failed subsequently to produce significant policy change, which was attributed to cuts in public spending (Sawer, 2002).

A Backlash: Office of Status of Women demoted from Prime Minister's Office

Phase II (1996–2007) showed some movement backward in emphasis on gender budgeting. The election of Conservative governments witnessed a shift in policy discourse towards reducing the size of government. The Office of the Status of Women was demoted from the Department of the Prime Minister and Cabinet to the Office for Women in the Department of Family and Community Services, which made it more difficult to analyze the gender-differential impact of policies and budgets.

Abrupt End to Gender Budget Statements

This practice of producing the Women's Budget Statement abruptly ceased in 2014, though the reasons why are unclear (Budlender, 2015). Nonetheless, the Australian Labour Party produced the "Women's 2014 Budget Reply Statement". The Party commissioned a micro-simulation study on the impact of the budget on different income groups which was discussed widely in the media and highlighted how single parents (85 per cent of which are women) would be particularly adversely affected by proposed budgetary policies (Budlender, 2015). The Party produced a tabular form of a Statement with Policy ("supporting family"), with measures and impact. The civil society group, the National Foundation for Australian Women, also produced a "Budget 2014–2015–a gender lens". The foundation produced detailed statements in 2014, in the absence of a government statement.

Korea

In Korea, performance-based budgeting was introduced in 2003 and the Ministry of Planning and Budget is still in the process of establishing performance indicators. In Korea, the fiscal policy reforms and the institutional structure were conducive to adopting gender budgeting. Korea adopted budget reform processes recently, which include a Medium-Term Expenditure Framework, performance-oriented budgeting, a shift from bottom-up budgeting to top-down budgeting, and a digital budgeting accounting system.

Legal Backing for Conducting Gender Budgeting

Korea's gender budgeting initiative has been substantive (Table 7.4). The legal backing for the requirement of gender-responsive budgeting is contained in legislation. The National Finance Act, legislated in 2006,

Table 7.4 Institutionalizing Gender Budgeting in Korea

Subject Details	Research Year
Development of concepts and methodology of gender budgeting	2007
Research of gender budgeting in other countries	2007, 2008
Development of gender budgeting statement (draft) and guidelines (draft) for gender budgeting	2007
Development of gender budgeting balance sheet (draft)	2008
Pilot analysis of departments and policies	2008, 2009
Development of gender budgeting mechanism and implementation methods	2008, 2009
Development of gender budgeting information database (DB) and its pilot application	2007–2009
Development of gender budgeting manual and training system targeting government officials	2009
Publication of gender budgeting guidebook and public relations brochure	2009
Institutionalization of gender budgeting in local autonomous associations	2008
Identification of budget analysis cases of local governments	2009
Analyzing taxes from a gender-sensitive approach	2008, 2009
Analyzing the mid- and long-term National Fiscal Management Plan and Programme Budget from a gender-sensitive approach	2007, 2009
Development of the gender budget performance management system	2007, 2008
Development of the monitoring and feedback system	2009

Source Adapted from Chakraborty (2016)

requires the submission of gender budgets and gender balance reports from the 2010 fiscal year onward (Kim, 2010). The Act requires the government to draw up gender budget statements which analyze the impact of the budget on women and men in advance, encompassing both spending and revenues. The government is required to produce a gender balance sheet, which assesses whether the budget benefits women and men equally and remedies gender discrimination. In all, articles of the National Finance Act relate to gender-responsive budgeting[2] as follows.

- **National Finance Law, Article 16** (the principle of budgeting): Government has to abide by the following rules in terms of budget preparation and execution. Government will evaluate how the national budget might have different effects on women and men, and make sure the evaluation results are reflected in budget preparation.
- **National Finance Law, Article 26** (gender budgeting statement): (i) The government has to prepare a report examining how the national budget will influence women and men differently. (ii) The gender-sensitive budgeting statement should include the expected outcomes in terms of enhancing gender equality, objectives related to gender budgeting, and gender analysis of programme recipients.
- **National Finance Law, Article 34** (accompanying documents to the gender budgeting plan): The budget plan submitted to the national assembly should include a gender budgeting statement.

---

[2] Article 16 states that the government should evaluate the impact of public expenditure on women and men and that the results should be reflected in the national budget. Article 26 refers to the preparation of a gender budget statement by line ministries. Article 34 specifies that the gender budget statement should be included in the Budget Bill submitted to the parliament. Article 57 mandates that a gender balance sheet is to be prepared which would indicate how identified gender imbalances are being remedied.

In addition, the Ministry of Planning and Budget, through its budget guidelines for 2006–2007, ordered that every ministry report on budget allocations with the aim of fostering gender equality as well as monitoring the impact of mainstream programmes on gender equality (Elson et al., 2009). The government set up Women's Focal Points in key ministries of government, including Justice, Labour, Health and Welfare, Agriculture and Forestry, Education and Human Resources, and Government and Home Affairs. The research methods to perform gender-sensitive fiscal planning and analysis are still a work in progress.

- **National Finance Law, Article 57** (preparation and submission of the balance sheets): (i) The government has to prepare a report that evaluates whether women and men equally receive the benefits of the budget and whether the budget was executed to reduce gender inequality. (ii) Gender-sensitive balance sheets should include budget execution records, analysis, and evaluation about the effects of gender budgeting on gender equality.
- **National Finance Law, Article 68-2** (gender sensitive funds management): (i) The government has to prepare a report examining how funds will influence women and men differently. (ii) A gender-sensitive funds management statement should include the expected outcomes in terms of enhancing gender equality, objectives related to gender-sensitive funds management, and recipient analysis based on gender.
- **National Finance Law, Article 73-2** (gender sensitive balance sheets of funds): (i) The government has to prepare a report that evaluates whether women and men equally receive the benefits of funds and whether funds were executed to reduce gender inequality. A gender-sensitive balance sheets of funds should include funds execution records, analysis, and evaluation about the effects of gender-sensitive funds on gender equality. The law states that ministries are to begin submitted gender budget statements by 2010. It also states that the Ministry for Planning and Budget is to prepare a gender budget statement about the revenue side from 2011 onwards.

Institutionalizing Gender Budgeting

In Korea, unlike in India and in Australia, the gender budgeting statement is enacted through law. However, in the first phase of knowledge building and developing methodology, India and Korea have commonalities in their approach. Like NIPFP in India, the Korean Women's Development Institute (KWDI), a policy think tank has initiated research and methodology on gender budgeting. The main objective of the KWDI is to provide a framework in which gender can be integrated in the medium-term expenditure framework, programme budgeting formats, and performance budgeting.

The KWDI has undertaken a massive consultation process by organizing international symposiums, organizing field trips abroad, and operating a Gender Budget Forum (which comprises governmental officials from line ministries and agencies, academics, journalists, and civil society groups) and shared the research and practice on Gender Budget Net, a web site developed for this purpose. The outcome of this consultation process was the 2008 pilot project on the gender budget statement. Article 26 of the National Finance Act, as mentioned above, requires the government to prepare a report on the impact that the budget is likely to have on the two genders and include its results in the national budget.

The KWDI developed a gender budgeting statement in 2008, which has two parts. The classification procedure of gender budgeting has similarities with that of India. The KWDI has classified the gender budget into expenditure those specifically targeted to women and aiming at improving gender equality and second, all the mainstream budgetary activity. For the first category of expenditure, the approach of KWDI is to calculate the total cost for these projects, calculate this as a percentage of total spending, and assess the priorities for those projects and whether they are meeting their targets. These assessments look at the needs of the target groups, recommend adjustments in budgets so as to enable the projects to better meet the target and might entail specifying new projects. For mainstream budgetary activities, guidelines for the drafting of the gender budget statement call for a gender-disaggregated breakdown of beneficiaries, analysis of the gender gap in beneficiaries, identifying a gender equality objective, and incorporating all findings of the analysis are also included in the budget.

The KWDI identified 67 projects under the first category, in 2010, which were specifically targeting for women. For the second category on mainstream expenditure or gender-based impact analysis projects, they identified 128 mainstream projects (Cho et al., 2012). These are included in a gender budget statement. In addition, a Gender Budget Balance Sheet was prepared, which evaluates the expenditure performance by conducting an impact analysis on gender equality and the overall budget expenditures.

There is a Gender Budgeting Task Force organized by both Ministries. The director of the social budget from the Ministry of Planning and the Finance and the director of the women's policy from the Ministry of

Gender Equality are co-chairs. The Task Force is comprised of the head of units from a range of ministries as well as researchers from KWDI, the Korean Institute for Gender Equality Promotion and Education (training organization on gender equality for civil servants), the Korean Development Institute, and the Korean Institute of Public Finance.

Gender Budgeting in Infrastructure

Kim (2010) noted that gender budgeting was applied to identifying needs for infrastructure, in order to reduce the average waiting time for rest rooms (the average time for men was 1 min 24 s, and for women, 2 min 30 s), which led to modifications in rest room construction to accommodate more women. Though emphasis on infrastructure is given in the Korean gender budgeting efforts, the evidence on what was accomplished is not widely available in published form. One such analysis indicated that gender budgeting led to the modification of the Act on the Public Toilet, where Article 7 (Standard for Public Toilet Construction) states that in any newly constructed public facilities the total number of toilets in women's restrooms should be the same or higher than men's (Kim, 2010).

Other substantive results relate to the funding of programmes to reduce the home care of women to enhance their labour force participation, which is important in Korea, with its rapidly ageing workforce and lower level of women's participation. Kim et al. (2014) noted that these policies would be helpful for enhancing economic growth when combined with the reduction of fundamental discrimination in the Korean labour market. The results showed that if the disparities at home and in the labour market between men and women are completely removed, the female labour force participation rate would increase from 54.4 to 67.5 per cent, and the growth rate in per capita income would rise from 3.6 per cent to 4.1 per cent on average over a generation.

Local Level Gender Budgeting

Chakraborty (2016) noted that since 2013, the local governments began to draft gender budget statements. The basis for local level gender budgeting statements was laid down in Article 36 Clause 2 and Article 53 Clause 2 ('II.3.8') of the Local Public Finance Act. The guidelines for this exercise were drafted by the Ministry of Security and Public

Administration in 2012. The lack of clear selection criteria for the target projects affected the credibility of the gender budget statements. The target projects are broadly dichotomized into "mandatory projects" and "recommended projects". Under mandatory projects, Women's Policy projects (in accordance with the Third Basic Plan for Women's Policy (2008–2012) projects and Gender Impact Assessment Projects-Government funded (projects targeted for assessment according to the Gender Impact Analysis and Assessment Act, 2016 and the other projects on which it is possible to conduct gender benefit analysis) are selected. Under "recommended projects", Gender Impact Assessment Projects-Non-Government funded and Special projects operated by the local governments were further selected.

Challenges

The KWDI has identified challenges to integrate gender budget into performance budgeting; to build capacity of the budget officials; to create regulations for consultative services for gender budgeting; and to establish a legal basis and a roadmap that lays out implementation plans (Chakraborty, 2016).

SUMMARY OF PROMINENT GENDER BUDGETING EFFORTS

India stands out for its implementation of gender budgeting at the national and subnational levels of government. It has integrated gender budget within the Expenditure Budget and also given instructions to integrate it into the Outcome Budget. However, the capacity of sectoral gender budgeting cells to carry out specific analysis of gender-related needs and advocate for policies and programmes remains a challenge. Korea, like India, with the support of think tank and other research, has formulated a framework for gender budgeting and implemented legal backing with provisions in national finance laws. The Philippines has shown the pitfalls of earmarking a floor on spending in sectoral budgets, but was later able to improve this strategy and link this spending to results-oriented budgeting. At the subnational level, the States of India like Kerala and Karnataka, and the communes in the Philippines like Sorsogon and Hilongos have provided good examples of local level gender budgeting. Australia was a pioneer of gender budgeting, but abruptly ended the Women's Budgets within budget documents and its initiative.

The Philippines

The Philippines provides an example of how gender budgeting can be applied at both national and subnational levels. Gender-responsive budget policy initiatives started at the national level in the Philippines with the Gender and Development (GAD) budget in 1995. The GAD budget made a provision for earmarking at least 5 per cent of all departmental expenditure on programmes for women in national and subnational budgets. Under quota-based gender budgeting, money was earmarked for such activities as ballroom dancing in certain government departments. As there was no penalty for not utilizing the GAD budget fully and efficiently, many departments ended up with an unspent surplus in the GAD budget. However, the 5 per cent requirement was eventually made more flexible so that departments could spend money only on what was truly needed. This "harmonized GAD" rule began in 2012 "to ensure that different concerns of men and women are addressed equally and equitably" in programmes, activities, and projects (see Philippine Budget Circular 2012).

Chakraborty (2006a, 2006b, 2010) notes that setting a floor for spending on gender-related aims resulted in a misallocation of resources in various departments. It also resulted in the marginalization of gender issues from mainstream budgeting, as floor limits were taken as ceilings in various departments. Earmarking a specific proportion of budget allocation for women is only a second-best principle of gender budgeting and is not likely to be the most appropriate tool for ensuring the effective use of public funds. By comparison, differential targeting of expenditures based on the identification of appropriate programmes for women in various sectors, or a reprioritizing of expenditures based on a generic list of appropriate programmes and policies for women might be more effective than a uniform targeting of 5 per cent across the board.

The GAD budget policy led to formulation of annual gender plans and budgets in all government departments, including their attached agencies, bureaus, state universities and colleges, government owned and controlled corporations, and local government units. The authorities reported in

2015 that GAD planning is integrated in the regular activities of agencies and the cost of implementing such is at least five per cent (5 per cent) of their total annual appropriation based on the General Appropriations Act.[3] This Act and the Philippine Magna Carta of Women (Republic Act, 9710) guarantee that all government agencies and instrumentalities review and revise or remove gender discriminatory policies, procedures and systems and should promote gender-responsive planning and budgeting. Since 1995, the Philippine Commission on Women has been the primary agency of gender budgeting, being the national machinery on women responsible in monitoring the compliance. The public expenditure analysis of gender has been carried out at the sectoral level, including education, health, environment and climate change, social welfare and protection, peace, and security.

There have been no gender budgeting initiatives on the tax side or with respect to employment or procurement policies. Gender budgeting led to initiatives related to improving sex-disaggregated data and statistics in reports of programmes and projects. Civil society organizations act as the" watch dog" of formulation and implementation of gender budgeting, while the legislative branch and parliamentary committees play a role in gender budgeting through Conduct Committees and public hearings.

Fiscal Decentralization and Gender Budgeting

With the strengthening of the fiscal decentralization process in the Philippines subsequently, local government units were provided with more opportunities for gender budgeting, and encountered more challenges as well. The devolution of basic functions like health, social welfare, and agricultural extension to these units in 1991 created more space to address gender needs at the local level. Some units have indeed used this opportunity to initiate gender-responsive policies. Chakraborty (2006a) notes, however, that as devolved functions were largely unfunded mandates and since intergovernmental transfers and budgetary process at the local level were largely politically determined, the resource gap posed serious challenges for effective decentralization and for gender budgeting initiatives as well.

---

[3] Authorities' response to the IMF questionnaire, unpublished, 2015.

Gender budget initiatives at the local level can be found in a few local units in the Philippines, particularly in Sorsogon and Hilongos, where selective attempts were made to identify specific gender needs before drafting of the budget. These initiatives, which came from the Department of Interior and Local Government and the National Commission on the Role of Filipino Women, with the support of UNIFEM in 2004, identified entry points for results-oriented gender budgeting. In Sorsogon, the initiative was taken in the health sector, where gender-related Millennium Development Goal health goals were identified and budgeted. In Hilongos, the initiative was taken in the agriculture sector. By strengthening the agricultural sector, the goal was to reduce the forced migration of women, and enhance their income-earning opportunities, as women predominate in agriculture. For instance, since women are key contributors to intra-household food and nutrition security, decentralization has implicit gender dimensions. One component of the local gender budgeting in Hilongos was revamping the irrigation system and strengthening other policies to increase agricultural productivity. The objective was to decrease women "voting with their feet" by moving to urban areas to become domestic workers. Indeed, labour mobility may be a form of local accountability, when citizens reveal their preferences by "exiting".

There has been no direct attempt so far to incorporate gender concerns into intergovernmental fiscal relations in the Philippines. Given the asymmetries in the assignment of functions and finance, a significant prerequisite of gender budgeting is to overcome the issue of unfunded mandates (Chakraborty, 2006a).

Another important question is whether the fiscal transfer system in the Philippines has an equalizing impact. Equalization transfers improve the capacity of poorer regions to deliver standards of social and economic services. Though these transfers are not specifically targeted to the poor; the poor—in particular women—are expected to benefit from a general capacity improvement in the region. However, Chakraborty (2006a) notes that in the Philippines, though equal sharing was one of the criteria of intergovernmental transfers, with 25 per cent weight— along with population (50 per cent) and area (25 per cent)—it was also not equitable. Given the systemic economic differences between the sexes, fiscal transfers should take into account gender-specific needs. The examples of local level gender budgeting in two local units highlighted the significance of spatial mapping of gender needs before budgeting.

Bangladesh

Integrating gender-related concerns into national policies became prominent in Bangladesh with the formulation of the fifth five-year plan, 1997–2002. The adoption of a National Policy for the Advancement of Women and National Action Plan for the Advancement of Women in 1997 led to gender budgeting (Chakraborty, 2010). The Ministry of Health also piloted a gender-disaggregated beneficiary assessment of community health services. After the findings of this analysis were presented to the Ministry of Finance, it agreed to incorporate gender-related and anti-poverty concerns into the budget. The Ministry of Finance along with the Ministry of Women and Children's Affairs led the initiative. Several ministries carried out gender mainstreaming separately but the major task of gender mainstreaming was given to the Ministry of Women and Children's Affairs.

The gender budgeting effort encompassed analysis in a number of ministries of gender-related concerns and also the assignment in 47 ministries of Women in Development focal points. Sect. "Summary of Prominent Gender Budgeting Efforts" of the Budget circular instructs the ministries to assess the impact of their strategies on gender-related and anti-poverty objectives, while Sect. "Country-Specific Outcomes" requires them to assess the impact of their activities on the outlined gender and poverty goals (Sharp et al., 2009). Gender "shares" for each expenditure are also calculated using the specially developed RCGP (Recurrent, Capital, Gender and Poverty) database and methodology (Budlender, 2015). A Financial Management Reform Programme involved gender budgeting training of all ministries engaged in the Medium-Term Budgetary Framework and the programme on Policy Leadership and Advocacy for Gender Equality-Phase II (PLAGE II) and complements the work undertaken by the Ministry of Finance and the Financial Management Reform Programme by strengthening partner ministries' capacity to analyze gender-related concerns and mainstream gender across their programmes, and the capacity and position of the Ministry of Women and Children's Affairs to lead gender mainstreaming.

As such, gender budgeting in Bangladesh has focused on the analysis of ministry budgets to determine whether they are gender responsive or not. The government produces a document along with the budget which explains how different activities of various ministries/divisions have implications for women's advancement and rights. The first year, such analysis was done for four ministries and in the second year this was done for ten ministries.

Since 2009, the Bangladesh government has been producing an annual gender budget report that can be considered a form of a gender budget statement (Budlender, 2015; UN Women, 2015). In 2012, a review of 20 ministries was carried out and concluded that Bangladesh is successful in institutionalizing the gender budgeting process.

Apart from gender budgeting, in Bangladesh, its Food for Education (FFE) programme, introduced in 1993, constitutes an innovative approach to raising enrolment rates and reducing dropout rates of students in school and improving nutrition. An evaluation of this programme suggested that the government could target better the subsidies to get the maximum benefits (Ahmed & Arends-Kuenning, 2006). This entailed determining the appropriate geographical targets (i.e., focusing on communities, municipalities, urban areas, etc.) and categorical targets (i.e., girls, families, HIV orphans, displaced people, and war affected people) to generate a greater impact on school enrolment and retention rates, and nutrition. An IFPRI study finds that the enrolment increase was greater for girls than for boys, however, the quality of education remained a problem for all children (Ahmad & del Ninno, 2002).

Sri Lanka

Sri Lanka joined the Commonwealth's gender budgeting pilot projects in 1997, which was then followed by an initiative by UNIFEM in 2002 (Chakraborty, 2003). Donors have played an important role in the implementation of gender-responsive budgeting and macro policies in Sri Lanka (for details, see Government of Sri Lanka, 2003, 2000a and 2000b; Sharp et al., 2010). The gender budgeting initiative in Sri Lanka has had two phases. The initial phase was the Commonwealth initiative coordinated by the Department of National Planning and concentrated on health, education, the public sector, employment, agriculture, industry, and social services in 1997. The second round of the initiative was taken up by Ministry of Women's Affairs in coordination with UNIFEM and their aim was to prepare the ex post analysis of the budget in 2003 (Chakraborty, 2003). Women's development is referred to in the 2003 budget, with the establishment of a separate window for women to borrow special money for small businesses, in each of the special funds being set up for sectoral development (Chakraborty, 2003). A report by the Department of National Planning argued that women benefited from 48 per cent of recurrent expenditure in education, 56 per cent of recurrent expenditure in health, and 57 per cent in social services, through benefit incidence analysis, but they had had limited access and participation in government-supported programmes in the agriculture and industry sectors. The report stressed that there is no need for an increase in funding for women but an evaluation and redesign of the existing programmes was required (Chakraborty, 2003). The funds allocated for women-specific programmes changed every year. In 2004, the National Budget Statement required all ministries to allocate 10 per cent of their budgets to improve the status of women.

It is difficult to understand whether there is any focus on employment programmes for women in Sri Lanka's gender budgeting. There were no quantitative goals for employment of women but the Ministry of Social Welfare had a specifically targeted expenditure programme on employment opportunities for women. The share of specifically targeted programmes for women under the Ministry of Tertiary Education and Training were few and only a negligible share of total expenditure was allocated for women (Chakraborty, 2003). The Ministry of Employment and Labour was entrusted with the mission of formulation of policies pertaining to employment. There is a Women and Child Affairs Division under this Ministry which enforces legal enactment with the objective of serving the occupational rights of women (Chakraborty, 2003).

Indonesia

In 2008, the Ministry of Finance passed a decree providing a framework for gender budgeting at the central level of government, and a form of gender budgeting was tried at the subnational level as well. Leading these efforts is the Ministry for Women's Empowerment. A major gender-responsive budgeting programme was undertaken by the Asia Foundation involving six provinces and 15 districts. The programme increased women's participation in budget and planning meetings in 93 villages in Sulawesi, trained 4500 local government and civil society representatives in gender analysis. Also, US$1.4 million in excessive or wasteful spending was reallocated to health and education as a result of partner advocacy efforts. An initiative by the Women's Research Institute funded by the Ford Foundation to reduce the high maternity mortality rate was another success. A gender budget statement was introduced within the government in Indonesia in 2010. This was in response to the 2009 regulation which provides for an introduction of "gender-responsive budget analysis tool" in the budgeting process. Since 2009, the Ministry of Finance has issued "annual regulations" similar to "call circulars" to adopt gender budgeting (Budlender, 2015; UN Women, 2015). The 2012 circular specifies that central ministries must submit completed gender budget statements for 2012 and subsequent years to the Director General of Budget within Ministry of Finance, as well as to Bappenas (the National Planning Commission) and Ministry of Women Empowerment and Child Protection for monitoring and evaluation purposes.

Pakistan

The Ministry of Women and Development called for gender budgeting in 2001 in a paper regarding gender and poverty issues put forward as part of Pakistan's application for an IMF loan under the Poverty Reduction Growth Facility. The introduction of budget reforms and changes in public resource management processes provided opportunities for the emergence of a gender budgeting initiative (Chakraborty, 2010; Government of Pakistan, 2002; Sharp et al., 2010).

The Gender Resource Budgeting Initiative in Pakistan began in the federal government and in Punjab, in coordination with UNDP and other bilateral agencies in 2005. The Initiative was integrated in "Strengthening Poverty Reduction Strategy Monitoring" (SPRSM) funded by the UNDP (2008–2012). It was implemented in the federal government and in three provinces. However, the Initiative was not confined to SPRSM. The Medium-Term Budgetary Framework Secretariat in the federal government has integrated gender in medium-term output-based budgets. The primary objective of the Initiative was to analyze public expenditure in pro poor sectors through a gender lens. The key focal areas/priority sectors of the initiative during 2008–2012 remained in the social sector–such as health, education, women development, population welfare, and labour.

The first time-use survey in Pakistan was carried out in 2007 by the Federal Bureau of Statistics. It engaged close to 20,000 households from across the country to uncover the macroeconomic implications of unpaid care work and to strengthen public policies to support men and women to realize their productive potential. Drawing on these data, further research was commissioned, to measure the value of unpaid care work in Pakistan and the results were made available to government officials and the public (Mahbub & Budlender, 2007).

The Budget Call Circular (BCC) 2006–2007, issued by the Finance Department, Government of the Punjab, for the first time asked for some sex-disaggregated information. The data given in response to the budget call circular provided information on gender patterns in public sector employment and remuneration. These data helped in increasing women's employment in the government and reducing the gender wage gap. It also led to the publically funded day care centres to promote women's participation in paid activities.

In the second phase, 2008–2012, the initiative led to engendering targets in the output-based budgeting system at the national level, across all ministries. The Ministry of Finance reported that gender-budgeting initiatives relate neither to tax nor to government employment or procurement practices. However, the initiative provided support to strengthening the statistical function in reporting of the Millennium Development Goals.

Against the backdrop of an IMF-supported economic programme, the federal government reinvigorated the work on gender-disaggregated analysis and carried out a gender-responsive analysis of the FY2015/16 budget to ensure that fiscal policies incorporate gender equality principles and are geared to attaining inclusive economic growth. This work has contributed to a baseline for the FY2016/17 budget to foster gender equality in education and work force participation, and also has applications at the subnational level (IMF, 2017).

Country-Specific Outcomes

India: The nodal role of the Ministry of Finance with the support of policy think tanks in gender budgeting has led to the successful institutionalization of gender budgeting at both the national and subnational levels. Gender budgeting has also led to gender mainstreaming in the budget, with more and more prima facie gender-neutral sectors adopting gender budgeting and reporting to the Ministry of Finance on their efforts to address gender equality through fiscal policies. Accountability and transparency are part of the objectives of gender budgeting. However, the integration of gender budgeting statements into the budget documents for transparency; and the relevant accountability mechanisms were largely absent in the region. India is an exception.

The Philippines: The initial gender budgeting efforts suggested that earmarking a portion of budget for women in every ministry or department is a second-best principle of gender budgeting. The Philippines has moved away from this approach to results-linked gender budgeting.

Bangladesh: Though not in the name of gender budgeting, a successful Food for Education programme was introduced with the aim to improve the school enrolment and retention rates of children and improve their nutrition levels, with some evidence suggesting that it had a more meaningful effect on girls.

Nepal: The integration of time use statistics and the statistically invisible care economy in gender budgeting is almost non-existent in the Asian region except in Nepal, where it was integrated in analytical matrices of gender budgeting.

Sri Lanka: Two rich studies on gender budgeting, by the Commonwealth Secretariat and UN Women, and former study analyzed the benefit incidence analysis of public expenditure through a gender lens.

Positive Outcomes of Gender Budgeting

The overall positive outcome of the gender budgeting in the region can be summarized in the following observations.

1. Gender budgeting has led to fiscal policies that were oriented to gender equality in some countries and mainstreaming gender in prima facie gender-neutral ministries in a few others.
2. The advent of fiscal decentralization raises the importance of integrating gender budgeting at subnational levels of government. So far, local initiatives were rare in the region, except in India, Indonesia and the Philippines.
3. The revenue-side gender budgeting policies, like differential rates for men and women in property tax rates in a few States in India is an innovation. And gender budgeting has led to some reconsideration

of income tax structure. However, the analysis of the revenue side through a gender lens needs to be strengthened in the region.
4. It also led to the analysis of the effectiveness of public spending through a gender lens. The public expenditure benefit incidence analysis and expenditure tracking for flow of funds are the methodologies used to capture the gender-differential impacts of public spending.
5. Public finance management in some countries now integrates gender as a category of analysis. Monitoring outcomes rather than inputs were given emphasis.
6. It has also led to improved dialogue to integrate gender in the classification of budgetary transactions to allow better tracking and management.
7. Gender budgeting statements within budget documents helps ensure transparency in the budgetary allocations for women. However, this exist only for a few countries including India, Bangladesh, and Nepal.
8. Gender budgeting has helped women activists and civil society organizations place the call for better budgetary allocations for gender equality and equity concerns.

The need to further strengthen gender budgeting within PFM framework is crucial. The assumption that "all women are equal" may lead to partial inferences as intersectionality issues (of interface between gender and race; gender and class; displaced persons and refugees) are equally significant to be addressed within the public finance discourses while preparing the fiscal policies (Bearfield, 2009; Chakraborty, 2016; Escobar, 2021; Khalifa & Scarparo, 2020; Klatzer, 2016; Riccucci et al., 2014; Rubin and Bartle,2005; Van Helden & Uddin, 2016). From the angle of gender-responsive public financial management, differentiating between ex ante and ex post approaches to gender budgeting are also crucial (Chakraborty, 2016; Bakker, 2018; Downes et al., 2017; Nakray, 2015; Rubin & Bartle, 2005).

The broad conclusion is that gender budgeting in the region is sustainable and adds substantively to fiscal policy but succeeds only if the Ministry of Finance owns the process. The experience of the region suggests that initiatives on gender budgeting should begin with the Ministry of Finance and requires adequate support of all stakeholders including civil society, parliamentarians, academicians, and the people. For instance, the heterogeneous stakeholders in the process who supported the Ministry of Finance in India to introduce gender budgeting include policy think tanks, the Ministry of Women and Child Development, UN entities, and civil society organizations. Though gender budgeting has the potential to transform gender equality in the region, the results are still modest in most of the lower-income countries except India and the Philippines, where the efforts have led to substantive fiscal policies.

References

Ahmad, A. U., & del, Ninno, Carlo. (2002). *The food for education program in Bangladesh: An evaluation of its impact on educational attainment and food security*. (Discussion Paper Brief 138). International Food Policy Research Institute.

Ahmed, A. U., & Arends-Kuenning, M. (2006). Do crowded classrooms crowd out learning? Evidence from the food for education program in Bangladesh. *World Development, 34*, 665–684.

Bakker, I. (2018). Connecting women's human rights to public resources in Canada. *Canadian Women Studies., 33*(1/2), 71–77.

Basu, Kaushik. (2006). Gender and say: a model of household behaviour with endogenously determined balance of power. *Economic Journal, 116*, 558–580. (Working Paper No. 273). Accessed at https://www.nipfp.org.in/publicati ons/working-papers/1868/. p. 43.

Bearfield, D., & A. (2009). Equity at the intersection: Public administration and the study of gender. *Public Administration Review, 96*(3), 383–386.

Budlender, D. (2002). Gender budgets: What's in it for NGOs? *Gender and Development, 10*(3), 82–87.

Budlender, D. (2015). Budget call circulars and gender budget statements in the Asia Pacific: A Review. UN Women.

Chakraborty, Lekha, S. (2003). *Gender budgeting in Sri Lanka: Categorizing financial inputs*. UNIFEM and Government of Sri Lanka.

Chakraborty, Lekha, S. (2004a). Gender budgeting in Asia: An empirical investigation of selected seven countries. (Paper prepared for The Commonwealth Secretariat, UK).

Chakraborty, Lekha, S. (2006a). *Fiscal decentralisation and local level gender responsive budgeting in the Philippines: An empirical analysis*. (Working Paper No. 41). National Institute of Public Finance and Policy.

Chakraborty, Lekha, S. (2006b). *Fiscal decentralisation and gender responsive budgeting In Mexico: Some observations*. (Working Paper No. 40). National Institute of Public Finance and Policy.

Chakraborty, Lekha, S. (2014). Integrating time in public policy: Empirical description of gender-specific outcomes and budgeting. (Working Paper No. 785). Levy Economics Institute.

Chakraborty, Lekha, S. (2019). Indian fiscal federalism: A few empirical questions. panel on *Indian fiscal federalism*. The at the book launch by Y. V. Reddy & G. R. Reddy. India International Centre. (March 28).

Chakraborty, Lekha, S. (2020a). The gender budgeting gets a leap in the fifteenth finance commission. Business Standard.

Chakraborty, Lekha, S. (2020b). *Macroeconomic policy coherence for SDG 2030: Evidence from Asia Pacific.* (Working Paper No. 292). National Institute of Public Finance and Policy.

Chakraborty, L. (2010). *Gender-sensitive fiscal policies: experience of ex-post and ex-ante gender budgets in Asia-Pacific.* UNDP.

Chakraborty, L. (2016). *Fiscal consolidation, budget deficits and macroeconomy: Monetary- Fiscal linkages.* Sage Publications.

Cho, Sun-Joo, et al., (2012). *Analysis and evaluation on gender budgeting in Korea, (II).* Korea Women's Development Institute.

Downes, R., von Trapp, L., & Nicol, S. (2017). Gender budgeting in OECD countries. *OECD Journal on Budgeting, 16*(3), 1–38.

Elson, D. (2000a). Gender at the macroeconomic level. In J. Cook, J. Roberts, & G. Waylen (Eds.), *Towards a gendered political economy* (pp. 77–97). Macmillan.

Elson, D. (2000b). *Progress of the World's Women 2000b.* UNIFEM Biennial Report. United Nations Development Fund for Women.

Elson, D. (2006). *Budgeting for women's rights: Monitoring government budgets for compliance with CEDAW.* UNIFEM.

Elson, Diane, Reina Ichii, Rhonda Sharp, Monica Costa, & Sanjugta Vas, Dev. (2009). *Gender responsive budgeting in Asia Pacific: The Republic of Korea.* UNISA.

Elson, D., & Sharp, R. (2010). Gender-responsive budgeting and women's poverty. In S. Chant (Ed.), *The international handbook of gender and poverty: Concepts, research and policy* (pp. 522–527). Edward Elgar.

Escobar, O. (2021). Transforming lives, communities and systems? Co-production through participatory budgeting. In E. Loeffler & T. Bovaird (Eds.), *The palgrave handbook of co-production of public services and outcomes* (pp. 285–309). Palgrave Macmillan.

Government of Pakistan, (2002). *Major/Important achievements made by the ministry of women development.* Ministry of Women Development, Social Welfare and Special Education.

IMF. (2017). Gender budgeting in G7 countries. International Monetary Fund.

Judd, K. (ed.) 2002. Gender Budget Initiatives: Strategies, Concepts and Experiences. UNIFEM.

Kim Jinyoung, Jong-Wha Lee, & Kwanho, Shin. (2014). *Gender inequality and economic growth in Korea*. Paper prepared for Asian Development Bank http://econ.korea.ac.kr/~jwlee/papers/Gender%20and%20Korea%20KLS.pdf

Khalifa, R., & Scarparo, S. (2020). Gender responsive budgeting: A tool for gender equality. *Critical Perspectives on Accounting.* https://doi.org/10.1016/j.cpa.2020.102183

Kim, Young-Ock. (2010). Institutionalizing gender budgeting: the experience of Korea. *Korean Women's Development Institute*. KWDI. http://www.igs.ocha.ac.jp/igs/IGS_publication/journal/13/63-66.pdf

Klatzer, E. (2016). Integrating gender equality, women's rights and participation in the budget process: A survey of entry points and practical examples. In Ng, C (Ed.) *Gender responsive and participatory budgeting*. Imperatives for equitable public expenditure (pp. 99–123). Springer.

Mahbub, N., & Budlender, D. (2007). *Gender responsive budgeting in Pakistan: Experience and lessons learned*. UNIFEM.

Nakray, K. (2015). Gender budgeting and public policy: The challenges to operationalising gender justice in India. *Policy & Politics, 43*(4), 561–577.

Ng, C. (2016a). Gender responsive and participatory budgeting: Imperatives for equitable public expenditure. Springer International.

Ng, C. (2016b). Making public expenditures equitable: Gender responsive and participatory budgeting. In Ng, C. (ed.) *Gender responsive and participatory budgeting. Imperatives for equitable public expenditure.* (pp. 1–16). Springer.

Sharp, Rhonda, Diane Elson, Monica Costa, & Sanjugta Vas Dev, (2010) The socialist republic of Vietnam: Gender responsive budgeting in the Asia Pacific region. UNISA.

Riccucci, N., Van Ryzin, G., & Lavena, C. (2014). Representative bureaucracy in policing: Does it increase perceived legitimacy? *Journal of Public Administration Research and Theory, 24*(3), 537–551.

Rubin, M. M., & Bartle, J. R. (2005). Integrating gender into government budgets: A new perspective. *Public Administration Review, 65*(3), 259–272.

Sawer, M. (2002). Australia: The Mandarin approach to gender budgets. In D. Budlender & G. Hewitt (Eds.), *Gender budgets make more cents* (pp. 43–64). Commonwealth Secretariat.

Sharp, Rhonda, Diane Elson, and Monica Costa, (2010b). *Gender responsive budgeting in the Asia Pacific region*. UNISA.

Sharp, Rhonda, and Monica Costa, (2010a). Gender responsive budgeting in the Asia Pacific region: Commonwealth of Australia. UNISA.

Sharp, R. (2003). *Budgeting for equity: Gender budgeting initiatives within a framework of performance oriented budgeting*. UNIFEM.

Sharp, R., & Broomhill, R. (2002). Budgeting for equality: The Australian experience. *Feminist Economics, 8*(1), 25–47.

Sharp, R., Elson, D., Costa, M., Dev, S. V., & Mundkur, A. (2009). *Republic of Bangladesh: Gender responsive budgeting in the Asia Pacific region*. UNISA.

UNDP Asia Pacific. (2010). *Power, voice and rights: A turning point for gender equality in Asia and the Pacific*. Macmillan.

Van Helden, J., & Uddin, S. (2016). Public sector management accounting in emerging economies: A literature review. *Critical Perspectives on Accounting, 41*(1), 34–62.

UN Women, (2012). Gender responsive budgeting in the aid effectiveness Agenda: End-of- programme evaluation. (Revised Evaluation Report). Universalia.

UN Women, (2015). Meeting report, Asia Pacific consultation on shaping a new agenda for transformative financing on gender equality. Bangkok. (November 16–17).

Women, U. N. (2016). *Gender responsive budgeting in the Asia-Pacific region: A status report*. UN Women.

CHAPTER 8

Gender Budgeting, as Fiscal Innovation in India

Gender budgeting is a fiscal innovation (Chakraborty, 2004). India's gender-budgeting efforts stand out globally because they have not only influenced expenditure but also revenue policies and because they have extended to national and subnational government levels. The goal of gender budgeting in India is to ensure greater efficiency and gender equity in fiscal policy. Gender budgeting has been integrated into many aspects of public finance, which include informing tax reforms; revising budget classification procedures to integrate gender; shaping intergovernmental fiscal transfers, fiscal decentralization efforts, and local budgeting; and assessing the effectiveness of public expenditure through the development of benefit incidence analysis. The political economy of gender-budgeting context is significant, to provide several lessons for gender-budgeting practitioners in other countries. For instance, Finland has been using gender budgets for over 10 years; however, very little is known internationally about the Finnish gender-budgeting experience, especially the importance of clear national gender equality goals for effective GB implementation, as well as the need to pay attention to mid-term fiscal frameworks (Elomäki & Ylöstalo, 2021).

© The Author(s), under exclusive license to Springer Nature
Singapore Pte Ltd. 2022
L. S. Chakraborty, *Fiscal Policy for Sustainable Development in Asia-Pacific*, https://doi.org/10.1007/978-981-19-3281-6_8

Gender Budgeting, as a Fiscal Innovation

As a fiscal innovation, gender-budgeting efforts in India have encompassed four sequential phases (Table 8.1): (i) knowledge building and networking, (ii) institutionalizing the process, (iii) capacity building, and (iv) enhancing accountability (Chakraborty, 2014). The National Institute of Public Finance and Policy (NIPFP), an independent think tank of Ministry of Finance, was entrusted to undertake the first ever research on gender budgeting in India in the year 2000 and advise the government how to institutionalize the process. The NIPFP pioneering study on gender budgeting in India arrived at the methodology and analytical matrices for conducting gender budgeting. This study on gender diagnosis and budgeting by NIPFP formed the first chapter ever in the Economic Survey of India—a document which is tabled in the Parliament on the state of the economy a day before Union Budget in India—on "gender" in the year 2000. When Parliament went into recess after the Budget presentation, NIPFP had presented the study to the Parliamentary Standing Committee for an informed debate in the Parliament during the Vote on Account debates. Later, in 2004, the Classification of Budgetary Transactions committee constituted by the Ministry of Finance, Government of India, based on a Terms of Reference on gender budgeting, worked with NIPFP to prepare the institutional design and matrices to begin gender budgeting at the national and subnational levels. The recommendations of this committee were accepted by the national government and later announced by the Union Finance Minister in The Union Budget Speech 2004–2005, *"that the budget data should be presented in a manner that the gender sensitivities of the budgetary allocations are clearly highlighted. An expert group on "Classification System of Government Transactions" has submitted its report on July 6, 2004. It has recommended appropriate systems for data collection and representation in the budget. The group has also recommended introduction of periodic benefit-incidence analysis. Government will examine the recommendations, and I hope it will be possible for me to implement some of them in the Budget for 2005–06"*. Since 2005–2006, India has started gender budgeting, however, the periodic benefit incidence analysis—which involves allocating unit costs according to individual utilization rates of public services—needs further strengthening. Technically, benefit incidence is estimated by the following $X_j \equiv \sum_i U_{ij} (S_i/U_i) \equiv \sum_i (U_{ij}/U_i) S_i \equiv \sum_i e_{ij} S_i$ where X_j = sector-specific subsidy enjoyed by

8 GENDER BUDGETING, AS FISCAL INNOVATION IN INDIA   199

Table 8.1 Phases of gender budgeting in India

	Phases	Actors	Outcome
2000–2003	Knowledge building and networking	National Institute of Public Finance and Policy (NIPFP), a think tank of the Ministry of Finance, Ministry of Women and Child Development (MWCD), UNIFEM, Ministry of Finance	Ex post analysis of budget through a gender lens with objective "budgeting for gender equity", including a chapter in India's Economic Survey; Highlighted the need to integrate the unpaid care economy into budgetary policies; Linking public expenditure and gender development
2004–2005	Institutionalizing	Ministry of Finance; NIPFP	Expert committee on "Classification of Budgetary Transactions" with gender budgeting in the terms of reference; Budget Announcement on India's commitment to gender budgeting; Analytical matrices to do gender budgeting were designed by the Ministry of Finance and NIPFP (examples are in Appendix A) Gender Budget Statements included in Expenditure Budgets, from 2005 to 2006 onwards
2005–present	Capacity building	Two phases. (i) Phase I: NIPFP, MWCD, and Ministry of Finance (till 2006), Phase II—MWCD, UN Women (2006–present)	Gender-Budgeting Cells (GBC) were instituted in Ministries GBC officials, Ministries, and State officers training; Charter on gender budgeting specifying the responsibilities of GRB cells

(continued)

Table 8.1 (continued)

Phases		Actors	Outcome
2012–present	Enhancing accountability	Erstwhile Planning Commission (Eleventh Five-Year Plan) incorporated a Committee on "Accountability", NIPFP has been part of this process with Planning Commission. Comptroller and Auditor General (CAG) has initiated accountability/auditing of gender budgeting at State level	Comptroller and Auditor General of India, since 2010, has been publishing a Report on Gender Budgeting in the State Finance Accounts. The accountability mechanism is yet to follow up effectively. This Report covers money "actually spent" on women

Source Chakraborty (2014)

group j; U_{ij} = utilization of service i by group j; U_i = utilization of service i by all groups combined; S_i = government net expenditure on service i; and e_{ij} = group j's share of utilization of service i. This analysis identifies the beneficiaries of public spending and can be used to differentiate incidence by gender, income quintiles, geographical units, etc., which will be revisited in Chapter 10.

The first ever Gender Budget Statement (GBS) in India in 2005–2006 was informed of this fiscal incidence approach to gender budgeting and the GBS is as follows.

> In line with the basic principles of governance to which the Government is committed under the National Common Minimum Programme, which includes empowerment of women, Government intends to gradually introduce gender budgeting. This means that the budget data will in due course be presented in a manner that the gender sensitivities of the budgetary allocations are clearly highlighted. An expert group on "Classification System of Government Transactions" had submitted its report in July, 2004 outlining the broad outline of issues and concerns involved. Now, Department of Women and Child Development and National Institute of Public Finance and Policy are being entrusted with the task of jointly undertaking a review of the public expenditure profile of the Departments of Rural Development, Health, Family Welfare, Labour, Elementary Education, Small Scale Industries, Urban Employment and Poverty Alleviation, Social Justice and Empowerment and Tribal Affairs, through the gender lens, conduct beneficiary-incidence analysis and recommend specific changes in the operational guidelines of various development schemes so as to improve coverage of women beneficiaries of the public expenditures. Village women and their associations will also be encouraged to assume responsibility for all development schemes relating to drinking water, sanitation, primary education, health, and nutrition. As part of the accounting reforms, it is the intention of the Government to consider aspects of beneficiary class identification for a meaningful analysis of the incidence of public expenditure and facilitate evaluation of beneficiary-impact for identified target groups. An initial and maiden effort has been made to present here the budget provisions that are substantially meant for welfare of women and children. This class of beneficiaries also benefits from other programmes but that is not presently segregated/quantified. This is intended to serve as a reference point for future exercises to segregate budget provisions according to the gender of beneficiaries. The Budget allocations, net of recoveries, substantially for the benefit of women and children are given (in the Statement).

—Union Budget (2005), Expenditure Budget, Volume 1, 2005–2006, p. 50.

Prior to gender budgeting, early on, the erstwhile Planning Commission, in the Ninth Plan (1997–2002), adopted a "Women's Component Plan" as one of the major strategies to achieve gender equality. One of the initiatives was, in 1997, to earmark 30% of developmental funds for women in all sectors. This "Women's Component Plan" is not gender budgeting. Gender budgeting encompassed both plan and nonplan components of the entire planning and budgeting processes. Moreover, evidence on the Women's Component Plan revealed that earmarking of Plan funds for gender development is only a second-best principle for integrating gender in macroeconomic policymaking, as the 30% was not spent effectively on women. This strengthened the case for introducing gender budgeting in India.

Subsequently, India moved away from "component plans" for women to macro level gender budgeting in 2000, encompassing the entire budget. This step ahead from planning to budgets was the formidable step taken in India to initiate genuinely gender budgeting.

In 2000, the Government of India commissioned the NIPFP to undertake a comprehensive study on gender budgeting. This pioneering study by NIPFP in 2000, analyzed the fiscal data of the entire Demand for Grants documents submitted by all the Ministries and Departments of Central Government—an extensive process—to identify the programmes and schemes which existed, if any, for women, and to analyze the fiscal marksmanship of these spending programmes (i.e. to assess the forecast errors or the deviation of budget estimates and revised estimates from actual results, which are released sequentially). This analysis was not selective, but covered all sectors.

The fiscal marksmanship analysis indicated that there was a significant deviation of budgeted from actual expenditure, and the NIPFP coordinated with the Office of Comptroller and Auditor General to understand the reasons for the deviation. One of the findings of the study was higher allocations per se had not ensured higher actual expenditure on gender-sensitive human development, and these findings led the researchers to conduct expenditure tracking analysis and benefit incidence analysis to understand the gender inequality effects of fiscal policies.

The NIPFP study assessed the benefit incidence of budget allocations and fiscal marksmanship, and traced the link between fiscal policy and gender development. The UNDP Asia Pacific (2010) highlights that based on the inputs from the NIPFP study and the recommendations from the Expert Committee on "Classification of Budgetary Transactions", the Government of India, (the Lahiri Committee, Government of India, 2003), through the Minister of Finance announced in the Union Budget speech 2005–2006, as mentioned earlier, that the recommendations would be accepted and India would institutionalize gender budgeting in the country from the 2006 Union Budget onwards.

Gender budgeting in India is not confined to an accounting exercise. The gender-budgeting framework has helped the gender-neutral ministries to design new programmes for women. For instance, the Ministry of Petroleum and Natural Gas has integrated gender-related policies in the energy area. Otherwise, a few mainstream ministries are trying to design new policies, though with insignificant allocations, based on the Lahiri Committee recommendations provided for in the Gender Budget Statements using the analytical matrices suggested by the NIPFP and Ministry of Finance. The Expert Committee also recommended opening a "budget head" on gender development in the classification of budgetary transactions. This recommendation to open a budget head has not yet been implemented.

As per the recommendations of the Expert Group, a Gender-Budgeting Secretariat was placed in the Ministry of Finance; and Gender-Budgeting Cells were constituted in the sectoral ministries. The Lahiri Committee also suggested the bureaucratic composition of the Gender-Budgeting Cells. The decision to conduct state-level gender budgeting was also included in the recommendations using the analytical matrices developed by the NIPFP and Ministry of Finance.

The NIPFP has conducted five analyses of the budget through a gender lens (for the period 2000–2005),1 which led to the formation of the "Gender Budget Statement" in the Expenditure Budget, Volume 1 of the Union Budget documents (Chakraborty, 2003; Lahiri et al., 2000, 2001, 2002). The NIPFP stopped doing the analysis after integrating the Gender Budget Statement into the budget documents, as each sectoral Ministry/Department has been instructed to undertake the analysis for the specific Demand for Grants through gender-budgeting cells using a practitioners' manual developed by the NIPFP (Chakraborty, 2005:

Gender Budgeting in Selected Ministries: Conceptual and Methodological Issues, Working Paper, NIPFP-DWCD, Ministry of HRD, Government of India, May 2005). The Ministries are mandated to do the analysis through compulsory instruction in the Budget Circular. Civil society organizations subsequently followed the NIPFP methodology for analyzing gender budget statements.

Integrating Gender in Intergovernmental Transfers

In India and in other federal countries, own resources for supporting public expenditures at the state and local levels are meagre, and the lower tiers of the government depend heavily on intergovernmental transfers from higher tiers of government.[1] There is an ongoing debate in India to integrate gender in formula-based transfers, though it has not yet materialized. The Fourteenth Finance Commission of India, which reported in January, 2015, integrated "climate change" variables in the formula-based fiscal transfers. Perhaps gender development variables may become the mandate for future Finance Commissions. In India, a radical approach in terms of devolving 42% of the tax pool of the central government to states (Chakraborty, 2015)[2] implemented by the Fourteenth Finance Commission, is a positive step in terms of flexibility of funds at the subnational level to prioritize in terms of gender-sensitive human development including health and education, which are state "subjects" in the Constitution of India. The flow of unconditional funds to the subnational governments in India to strengthen the cooperative federalism can provide space for state priorities on gender development. Earlier studies noted that lack of flexibility of intergovernmental transfers and unfunded

---

[1] The fiscal transfers and gender-budgeting experiences can be found in (Rao & Lekha, 2006) on Morocco, (Chakraborty, 2006a) on Philippines, (Chakraborty & Amaresh, 2007) on South Africa, Chakraborty (2007) on India, and Chakraborty (2006b, 2009) on Mexico, while the unequal impact of fiscal transfers can be found in P. Chakraborty (2003).

[2] P. Chakraborty (2015) at http://www.thehindu.com/opinion/lead/getting-federal-transfers-right/article7181478.ece.

mandates were two deterrents to implementing gender budgeting effectively. Anand and Chakraborty (2016) analyze whether fiscal transfers are progressive or regressive in India ex post to incorporating gender as a criterion in the formula-based intergovernmental fiscal transfers and found that the transfers are progressive.

Tax Side Gender Budgeting and Tax Incidence Analysis

The analysis of the revenue side of gender budgeting is still in the elementary stage because of a lack of sex-disaggregated tax data. The legislation defining different types of income does not make any specific provision for gender except in the personal income tax. The personal income tax system recognizes both individual taxation and the Hindu undivided family as a separate legal entity, reflecting an economic arrangement that is inherently biased against women as it assigns tax liability to the oldest male member of an extended family. However, looking at the income tax rule documents through a gender lens in the study, only one tax exemption is identified under section 88C for women under which a woman below the age of 65 was entitled to an additional rebate on taxation. Tax exemptions under section 88C marginally benefited women in India as only 4% of economically active women are in the formal sector. The 88C exemption for women was eventually phased out. Recently in India, in some provinces, women have gotten favorable treatment in stamp and transfer duties during property transfers. For instance, in New Delhi, the duties are set at 4% if the property is registered in the name of a woman and 6% if registered in the name of a man. A NIPFP study examines tax incidence of indirect taxes through a gender lens. It is part of an eight-country study on *Gender and Taxation: Improving Equity and Revenue Generation* (Grown & Valodia, 2010). The study is the first serious attempt to empirically analyze the revenue side of government budgets from a gender perspective, particularly in developing countries. It examines the impact of direct and indirect taxes on women and men in Argentina, Ghana, India, Mexico, Morocco, South Africa, Uganda, and the UK. The analysis of the data from this study suggests that equity goals should not be abandoned, but in fact broadened to include gender. The analysis also emphasizes the need to move beyond conventional notions of vertical and horizontal equity to a tax framework based on promoting substantive gender equality, as reflected in CEDAW. The detailed incidence estimates of VAT provided in the study is the only comprehensive study in the region on tax incidence through a gender lens. It finds the effective tax rate (or incidence) of indirect taxes is higher on women in low-income quintiles. A recent debate relates to the use of fiscal space generated from natural resources taxes and mining taxes and royalties. Empirical literature is scarce in this area.

Strengthening Accountability Mechanisms and Capacity Building and Gender Mainstreaming

The Gender Budget Statement has helped women activists and civil society organizations place the call for better funding and provisioning for women's rights on a much stronger ground (UN Women, 2012). Though the Lahiri Committee has provided a comprehensive framework for accounting in gender budgeting, it has not yet been completely implemented in India at the national and subnational levels (Government of India, 2015; UN Women, 2012). But further effort is required to strengthen the implementation of gender budgeting in terms of public expenditure benefit incidence in ministries and in building strong accountability mechanisms.

The gender-budgeting statement led to "gender mainstreaming in budgeting" in India (Chakraborty, 2011). For instance, initiatives on gender budgeting have been undertaken especially in gender-neutral ministries like Finance, Science and Technology, Road Transport and Highways, Communications and IT, Corporate Affairs, Ocean Development and Petroleum and Natural Gas and led to development of policies to improve gender equity and achieve women's development goals (Government of India, 2015).

Another important question is whether the fiscal transfer system in the Philippines has an equalizing impact. Equalization transfers improve the capacity of poorer regions to deliver standards of social and economic services. Though these transfers are not specifically targeted to the poor; the poor—in particular women—are expected to benefit from a general capacity improvement in the region. However, Chakraborty (2006a) notes that in the Philippines, though equal sharing was one of the criteria of intergovernmental transfers, with 25% weight—along with population (50%) and area (25%)—it was also not equitable. Given the systemic economic differences between the sexes, fiscal transfers should take into account gender-specific needs (Chapter 5). The examples of local level gender budgeting in two local units highlighted the significance of spatial mapping of gender needs before budgeting (Chapter 6).

The first ever analysis of gender budgeting as a fiscal innovation framework was by Chakraborty (2004). The main objective of the analytical template is to provide a simple and practical structure to integrate gender in fiscal policy within the country-specific context. This fiscal innovation framework of Indian gender budgeting can be used in other country-contexts, amending the structure to suit country-specific needs. For instance, later in Austria, Polzer and Seiward (2021) used the diffusion models of innovations, for two major elements of the Austrian approach to gender budgeting—regulatory gender impact assessments and gender aspects in audits—through document analyses. Polzer and Seiward (2021) analyses the significant impact of the implementation context—such as the constitutional anchoring, the preparation plan, capacity building, and methodological guidelines—on the results of the implementation.

Chakraborty's (2004) fiscal innovation framework of gender-budgeting analysis in India is a useful analytical framework to capture the processes of gender budgeting in other country-contexts as well. The four significant elements of fiscal innovation framework discussed by Chakraborty (2004) can be extended to integrate gender budgeting in intergovernmental framework models within fiscal federalism are as follows. The four phases discuss the crucial aspects to be incorporated under each component.

Phase 1: Country-Specific Gender Diagnosis and Intergovernmental Fiscal Framework Models

As a prelude to integrating gender in fiscal policy, it is significant to undertake gender diagnosis, incorporating the intersectionality perspectives. What is the demographic composition in terms of ethnicity and other factors and does the geographical distribution across constituent units need a careful examination before designing the gender-specific transfers? The gender-disaggregated trends in education, health, workforce participation, governance, wages, etc. need to be collated for analyzing the incidence. The analysis of existing legal and fiscal models of a specific country is crucial before designing the gender budgeting. It is also important to analyse the legislations supporting gender-related issues.

Phase 2: Intergovernmental Institutional Design

The institutional design is crucial for integrating gender in the intergovernmental fiscal transfers, within a specific country context. The analysis of the structure of revenue and expenditure assignments and the composition of intergovernmental fiscal transfers are required before gender design in the fiscal policy. The constitutional or legislative divisions of finance and functions are closely related to understanding the asymmetry in the finance and functional assignments, and it is crucial to identify the reasons for unfunded mandates. Fiscal decentralization of powers, responsibilities, and resources to local governments is a way to bring government closer to the people and improve the quality of services and the efficiency with which they are delivered (Litvack & Bird, 1998).

The analysis of the principle of subsidiarity—if government closest to people are effective in incorporating gender concerns than the higher levels of government—can provide useful insights into perpetuating gender inequalities across jurisdictions. It also helps to examine if there are any overlapping areas of responsibilities (concurrent) related to gender. In the existing frameworks, an analysis is required to understand if there any mandates provided by the federal government to subnational governments regarding integrating gender in the fiscal domain. If there is one, it is also crucial to analyse its efficacy. For instance, in India, the constitutionally assigned feminization of governance in institutions, earmarking a threshold number of seats for women helps in "engendering" public expenditure priorities. Apart from institutions, it is crucial to analyse what are the channels of federal influence on subnational policies to integrate gender concerns, including the "pork barrel funds". It is pertinent to examine what are areas of fiscal conflicts among different orders of government in the federation to integrate gender. As the next step, the identification of the institutional arrangements to deal with these conflicts is also crucial.

On the taxation side, an analysis of the tax assignments across the levels of government to identify whether there are overlapping gender issues in such assignments. This analysis needs to incorporate intersectionality concerns, along with the income quintiles. Are there any gender-related considerations in natural resources taxation, like earmarking the mining royalty to human development or reducing spatial inequalities (for instance, District Mineral Fund)?

Phase 3: Capacity Building

The capacity building is the third step after the identification of the country-specific models for gender in the intergovernmental frameworks and strengthening the institutions. What are the methods of capacity building of economic and fiscal policy institutions to integrate gender? Is there any fiscal responsibility legislation embodying fiscal rules for fiscal discipline and coordination? And special training is required to identify gender concerns within the macro-fiscal rules framework? What is the capacity to examine debt-deficit dynamics? Any interpretation of fiscal rules is required through a gender lens, if the path to fiscal consolidation is through expenditure compression than tax buoyancy? This includes trainings and workshops for dissemination of information and greater sensitization of integrating gender in federations. Regarding the links between fiscal consolidation and gender outcome, the point to be noted is that if fiscal consolidation leads to fiscal austerity, that can have gender differential impacts (Donald & Lusiani, 2017; Elson, 2018).

What is the fiscal marksmanship of tax transfers? Chakraborty et al. (2020) analysed the budget credibility, or the ability of governments to accurately forecast macro-fiscal variables, which is crucial for effective public finance management. Fiscal marksmanship analysis captures the extent of errors in the budgetary forecasting. The fiscal rules can determine fiscal marksmanship, as effective fiscal consolidation procedures affect the fiscal behaviour of the states in conducting the budgetary forecasts. Against this backdrop, applying Theil's technique, Chakraborty et al. (2020) analyzed the fiscal forecasting errors for 28 states in India for the period 2011–2016. There is a heterogeneity in the magnitude of errors across subnational governments in India. The forecast errors in revenue receipts have been greater than revenue expenditure. Within revenue receipts, the errors are more significantly pronounced in the grants component. Within expenditure budgets, the errors in capital spending are found to be greater than revenue spending in all the states. Partitioning the sources of errors, we identified that the errors were more broadly random than due to systematic bias, except for a few crucial macro-fiscal variables where improving the forecasting techniques can provide better estimates. This analysis can be extended to understand the fiscal marksmanship of gender-responsive tax transfers. What are the capacity issues in dealing with sectoral issues related to gender and federation, if we find fiscal marksmanship issues relate to forecasting errors in tax transfers? What is the content and frequency of training modules and institutional deliberations in gender and federalism? These are the plausible questions to be analyzed in the capacity building phase.

Phase 4: Accountability Mechanisms

Monitoring outcome than financial inputs is the final procedure, by linking the financial resources to the outcomes. What is the nature of fiscal inequalities? How it affects the gender equality? Is there an issue of fiscal marksmanship to be analysed? Is there any deviation between estimates and actuals in tax transfers and grants? What are the quantitative and qualitative indicators to be collated to analyse the credibility of tax transfers and grants—that is, on the variations in fiscal marksmanship and partitioning the sources of forecasting errors. Are fiscal inequalities a matter of political economy concern, describe if the accountability mechanisms to minimize the effects of such deals on economy, where it can lead to gender differential outcomes. Any fiscal equalization transfers based upon gender based considerations? Is there a constitutional basis for gender accountability in fiscal equalization? Who makes recommendations on the quantum and criteria of tax transfers—federal government agency, independent tax transfer commission? Is there any link between tax transfers (especially specific-purpose transfers) and intersectionality issues? These are the analytical issues to be examined in the accountability phase.

PUBLIC EXPENDITURE TRACKING

The NIPFP has conducted the public expenditure tracking analysis of the largest microfinance-linked poverty program–Swarnajayanti Gram Swarozgar Yojana (SGSY) for all the six banking zones in India in coordination with the National Institute of Bank Management (a research institute of the Reserve Bank of India) in 2003–2006, with NIPFP and NIBM researchers working at the grassroots with the self-help groups, local functionaries, local banking officials, the district level bureaucrats, and women beneficiaries of microcredit. One finding was that though government-led microfinance programme had been successful in detouring women from "bad lemons" (indigenous money lenders), the programme was not able to fully enable them as successful micro entrepreneurs. The programme led to social empowerment of women more than financial empowerment. The findings suggested that capacity building of women in maintaining the financial accounts and infrastructural support for their economic activities were essential prerequisites for the success of microfinance programmes (NIPFP-NIBM, 2006a, 2006b).

Gender Equality Outcomes Across Indian States

The following tables show the gender outcomes across Indian States. The gender inequality index is relatively poor for North Eastern States and the Union Territories. Within States, Bihar (0.682), Manipur (0.758), Mizoram (0.742), and Sikkim (0.725) have poor GII (Table 8.2). The overall GII for India is 0.462 for the year 2017–2018. Maharashtra has lowest GII at 0.340.

Table 8.3 shows Gender Development Index across Indian States, where Goa (0.994) and Himachal Pradesh (0.990) have highest GDI. The overall GDI for India is 0.876. Bihar (0.550) has lowest GDI. Using disaggregated gender indicators, Stotsky and Zaman (2016) provided evidence for the positive link between gender budgeting and gender equality outcomes across Indian States. They found that States with gender-budgeting efforts have made more progress on gender equality in primary school enrollment than those without, though economic growth appears insufficient to generate equality on its own (Stotsky & Zaman, 2016). Stotsky et al. (2017) also find that gender budgeting has a beneficial effect on education equality, controlling for fiscal transfers and economic growth. These coefficients need to be read with caution as determinants related to intra-household dynamics are not controlled for in the models.

Table 8.2 Gender Inequality Index (GII) across Indian States/Union Territories, 2017–2018

States/UTs	GII 2017–2018							
	RHI		EI		LMI			GII
	Female	Male	Female	Male	Female	Male		
							Male	
A & N Islands	0.036	0.073	0.019	0.685	0.254	0.627		0.704
Andhra Pradesh	0.053	0.12	0.139	0.52	0.344	0.604		0.361
Arunachal Pradesh	0.027	0.044	0.014	0.584	0.107	0.507		0.789
Assam	0.027	0.044	0.19	0.583	0.098	0.593		0.598
Bihar	0.038	0.069	0.119	0.556	0.028	0.454		0.682
Chandigarh	0.074	0.136	0.795	0.028	0.191	0.593		0.413
Chhattisgarh	0.034	0.063	0.149	0.535	0.365	0.573		0.44
Dadra & Nagar Haveli	0.036	0.073	0.015	0.653	0.264	0.62		0.719
Daman & Diu	0.036	0.073	0.021	0.777	0.199	0.714		0.73
Delhi	0.073	0.147	0.224	0.785	0.112	0.573		0.444
Goa	0.056	0.128	0.023	0.792	0.247	0.574		0.646
Gujarat	0.062	0.111	0.207	0.591	0.154	0.588		0.425
Haryana	0.068	0.168	0.143	0.692	0.107	0.537		0.462
Himachal Pradesh	0.078	0.084	0.237	0.712	0.397	0.587		0.373
Jammu & Kashmir	0.095	0.144	0.155	0.594	0.229	0.574		0.374
Jharkhand	0.036	0.101	0.012	0.553	0.109	0.504		0.741
Karnataka	0.046	0.112	0.124	0.651	0.204	0.597		0.464
Kerala	0.09	0.14	0.132	0.692	0.213	0.539		0.418
Lakshadweep	0.036	0.073	0.02	0.758	0.146	0.535		0.734
Madhya Pradesh	0.037	0.057	0.151	0.511	0.234	0.588		0.488
Maharashtra	0.072	0.155	0.203	0.669	0.241	0.576		0.34

States/UTs	GII 2017–2018							
	RHI		EI		LMI			GII
	Female	Male	Female	Male	Female	Male		
Manipur	0.027	0.044	0.022	0.804	0.177	0.537		0.758
Meghalaya	0.027	0.044	0.283	0.447	0.349	0.497		0.403
Mizoram	0.027	0.044	0.018	0.639	0.234	0.567		0.742
Nagaland	0.027	0.044	0.02	0.691	0.131	0.517		0.765
Odisha	0.039	0.082	0.154	0.509	0.15	0.58		0.483
Puducherry	0.081	0.125	0.022	0.795	0.14	0.536		0.688
Punjab	0.083	0.114	0.203	0.669	0.123	0.592		0.464
Rajasthan	0.035	0.064	0.059	0.543	0.193	0.516		0.589
Sikkim	0.027	0.044	0.019	0.68	0.342	0.624		0.725
Tamil Nadu	0.081	0.125	0.196	0.617	0.272	0.61		0.358
Telangana	0.053	0.147	0.114	0.682	0.261	0.582		0.415
Tripura	0.027	0.044	0.22	0.386	0.101	0.601		0.551
Uttar Pradesh	0.037	0.081	0.173	0.563	0.094	0.51		0.52
Uttarakhand	0.037	0.118	0.215	0.721	0.137	0.523		0.434
West Bengal	0.04	0.053	0.228	0.469	0.164	0.613		0.491
India	**0.044**	**0.083**	**0.174**	**0.59**	**0.175**	**0.555**		**0.462**

Source http://mospi.nic.in/sites/default/files/publication_reports/Report%20on%20Gendering%20Human%20Development.pdf

Table 8.3 HDI and GDI across Indian States/Union Territories, 2017–2018

Year/States	2017–2018										
	HI		EI		II		HDI		GDI
	M	F	M	F	M	F	M	F	
A & N Islands	0.735	0.775	0.566	0.578	0.861	0.733	0.71	0.69	0.971
Andhra Pradesh	0.743	0.788	0.472	0.451	0.846	0.628	0.667	0.606	0.909
Arunachal Pradesh	0.698	0.728	0.594	0.584	0.839	0.49	0.704	0.592	0.842
Assam	0.698	0.728	0.587	0.567	0.766	0.341	0.68	0.52	0.765
Bihar	0.757	0.748	0.461	0.406	0.619	0.118	0.6	0.33	0.55
Chandigarh	0.758	0.818	0.729	0.854	0.987	0.745	0.817	0.804	0.984
Chhattisgarh	0.674	0.717	0.545	0.488	0.769	0.536	0.656	0.572	0.873
Dadra & N. Haveli	0.735	0.775	0.513	0.505	0.805	0.57	0.672	0.607	0.903
Daman & Diu	0.735	0.775	0.577	0.631	0.788	0.561	0.694	0.65	0.936
Delhi	0.82	0.866	0.72	0.768	1	0.734	0.839	0.788	0.939
Goa	0.761	0.805	0.663	0.695	1	0.885	0.796	0.791	0.994
Gujarat	0.732	0.8	0.522	0.543	0.923	0.609	0.707	0.642	0.908
Haryana	0.732	0.805	0.562	0.61	0.94	0.607	0.729	0.668	0.917
Himachal Pradesh	0.766	0.855	0.649	0.675	0.876	0.73	0.758	0.75	0.99
Jammu & Kashmir	0.802	0.872	0.499	0.499	0.75	0.582	0.669	0.632	0.945
Jharkhand	0.751	0.745	0.506	0.471	0.74	0.334	0.655	0.489	0.747
Karnataka	0.734	0.782	0.564	0.552	0.917	0.633	0.724	0.649	0.896
Kerala	0.808	0.889	0.646	0.685	0.897	0.686	0.777	0.748	0.963
Lakshadweep	0.735	0.775	0.633	0.602	0.803	0.638	0.72	0.668	0.927
Madhya Pradesh	0.68	0.737	0.51	0.496	0.727	0.484	0.632	0.561	0.889
Maharashtra	0.788	0.829	0.612	0.64	0.911	0.65	0.76	0.701	0.923

Year/States	2017–2018										
	HI		EI		II		HDI		GDI
	M	F	M	F	M	F	M	F	
Manipur	0.698	0.728	0.703	0.7	0.713	0.484	0.705	0.627	0.889
Meghalaya	0.698	0.728	0.702	0.742	0.71	0.591	0.703	0.683	0.972
Mizoram	0.698	0.728	0.703	0.756	0.831	0.692	0.742	0.725	0.977
Nagaland	0.698	0.728	0.592	0.631	0.783	0.505	0.687	0.614	0.895
Odisha	0.725	0.768	0.519	0.508	0.817	0.398	0.675	0.537	0.796
Puducherry	0.768	0.826	0.647	0.65	0.918	0.611	0.77	0.69	0.896
Punjab	0.785	0.831	0.581	0.697	0.866	0.579	0.734	0.695	0.947
Rajasthan	0.712	0.783	0.497	0.484	0.788	0.539	0.654	0.589	0.901
Sikkim	0.698	0.728	0.652	0.672	0.972	0.856	0.762	0.748	0.982
Tamil Nadu	0.768	0.826	0.618	0.612	0.903	0.641	0.754	0.687	0.911
Telangana	0.743	0.788	0.578	0.545	0.904	0.622	0.73	0.644	0.883
Tripura	0.698	0.728	0.575	0.58	0.813	0.439	0.688	0.57	0.828
Uttar Pradesh	0.682	0.702	0.513	0.475	0.697	0.374	0.625	0.5	0.8
Uttarakhand	0.738	0.834	0.657	0.673	0.924	0.631	0.765	0.708	0.925
West Bengal	0.775	0.803	0.572	0.554	0.772	0.445	0.7	0.583	0.833
All India	**0.735**	**0.775**	**0.544**	**0.535**	**0.843**	**0.546**	**0.696**	**0.609**	**0.876**

Source http://mospi.nic.in/sites/default/files/publication_reports/Report%20on%20Gendering%20Human%20Development.pdf

REFERENCES

Anand, A., & Chakraborty. L. (2016). *Integrating gender criteria in intergovernmental transfers in India* (Working Paper). Levy Economics Institute.

Chakraborty, L. (2003). *Macroscan of union budget through a gender lens.* UNIFEM.

Chakraborty, L. (2004). *Gender budgeting in Asia: An empirical investigation of selected seven countries.* Commonwealth Secretariat.

Chakraborty, L. (2005). *Public investment and unpaid work: Selective evidence from time-use data.* Paper presented at UNDP Bureau for Development Policy- Levy Institute Conference. *Unpaid work and the economy: Gender, poverty, and the millennium development goals.* The Levy Economics Institute of Bard College, Annandale-on-Hudson (October 1–3).

Chakraborty, L. (2014). *Integrating time in public policy: Empirical description of gender-specific outcomes and budgeting* (Working Paper no. 785). Levy Economics Institute.

Chakraborty, L. S. (2006a). *Fiscal decentralisation and local level gender responsive budgeting in the Philippines: An empirical analysis* (Working Paper no. 41). National Institute of Public Finance and Policy.

Chakraborty, L. S. (2006b). *Fiscal decentralisation and gender responsive budgeting in Mexico: Some observations* (Working Paper no. 40). National Institute of Public Finance and Policy.

Chakraborty, L. S. (2007). *Fiscal decentralisation and gender budgeting in India: A preliminary appraisal* (Working Paper 45). National Institute of Public Finance and Policy.

Chakraborty, L. S. (2009). *Fiscal decentralization and gender budgeting in Mexico: An empirical analysis*, Vol. 12. Regional Development Studies. United Nations Center for Regional Development.

Chakraborty, L. S. & Bagchi, A. (2007). *Fiscal decentralisation and gender responsive budgeting in South Africa: An appraisal* (Working Paper no. 44). National Institute of Public Finance and Policy.

Chakraborty, P. (2003). *Unequal fiscal capacities across indian states: How corrective is the fiscal transfer mechanism?* Paper prepared for the UNU/WIDER Project Conference on *Spatial Inequality in Asia.* UNU Centre, Tokyo. March 28–29.

Chakraborty, P. (2015). *Getting the federal transfers right.* The Hindu.

Chakraborty, L. S., Chakraborty, P., & Shrestha, R. (2020). *Budget credibility of subnational governments: Analyzing the fiscal forecasting errors of 28 states in India* (Working Papers Series no. 964). Levy Economics Institute. Available at SSRN: https://ssrn.com/abstract=3661624 or https://doi.org/10.2139/ssrn.3661624

Donald, K., & Lusiani, N. (2017). *The IMF, gender equality and expenditure policy, CESR and Bretton Woods project.*

Elomäki, A. & Ylöstalo, H. (2021). Gender budgeting in the crossroad of gender policy and public financial management: The Finnish case. *Public Money & Management, Routledge Journal.*

Elson, D. (2018). *The impact of austerity on women.* UK Women's Budget Group (WBG).

Government of India. (2015). *Gender budgeting handbook.* Ministry of Women and Child Development.

Grown, C., & Imraan, V. (Eds.). (2010). *Taxation and gender equity: A comparative analysis of direct and indirect taxes in developing and developed countries.* Routledge.

Lahiri, A., Chakraborty, L., & Bhattacharrya. (2000). *India-gender budgeting.* Report submitted to UNIFEM, South Asia, and Ministry of Human Resource Development, Government of India.

Lahiri, A., Chakraborty, L., & Bhattacharrya. (2001). *Gender budgeting in India: Post budget assessment report 2001.* Report submitted to UNIFEM, South Asia and Ministry of Human Resource Development, Government of India.

Lahiri, A., Chakraborty, S. L., & Bhattacharryya, P. N. (2002). *Gender diagnosis and budgeting in India.* National Institute of Public Finance and Policy.

Litvack, A., & Bird. (1998). *Rethinking decentralization in developing countries.* The World Bank.

NIPFP-NIBM. (2006a). *Engendering microfinance in India: Empirical evidence.* Report prepared as a part of NIPFP-NIBM Collaborative Report on Microfinance, for Ministry of Rural Development, Government of India. National Institute of Public Finance and Policy.

NIPFP-NIBM. (2006b). *Microfinance and Empowerment.* Report prepared as a part of part of NIPFP-NIBM Collaborative Report on Microfinance, for Ministry of Rural Development, Government of India. National Institute of Public Finance and Policy.

Polzer, T., & Seiwald, J. (2021). Outcome orientation in Austria: How far can late adopters move? In Z. Hoque (Ed.), *Public sector reform and performance management in developed economies* (pp. 119–145). Routledge.

Rao, M. G., & Chakraborty, L. S. (2006). *Fiscal decentralisation and gender responsive budgeting in Morocco: Some observations* (Working Paper No. 42). National Institute of Public Finance and Policy.

UNDP Asia Pacific. (2010). *Power, voice and rights: A turning point for gender equality in Asia and the Pacific.* Macmillan.

UN Women. (2012). *Gender responsive budgeting in the aid effectiveness agenda: End-of-programme evaluation* (Revised Evaluation Report). Universalia.

UN Women. (2016). *Gender responsive budgeting in the Asia-Pacific region: A status report.* UN Women.

CHAPTER 9

The Political Economy of Gender Budgeting in India and Fiscal Marksmanship

Gender budgeting has political economy imperatives, it is not just a technical exercise. This chapter analyses the Union Budget 2021–2022 through a "gender lens" to understand the intensity of gender in the budgetary allocations. Higher budgetary allocations per se do not ensure higher spending. The deviation between what is budgeted and what is actual is significant in revenue and expenditure. This deviation is referred to as fiscal marksmanship. In India, the budget numbers are presented in three stages—Budget Estimates (on the day of Budget Speech), Revised Estimates (next year), and Actuals. The fiscal forecasting errors are evident from the deviations between BE, RE, and Actuals. Before focusing on the gender intensive budgetary allocations and their fiscal marksmanship, a macro-fiscal analysis of Union Budget 2021–2022 is undertaken to understand the overall expenditure and how it is financed. Against the backdrop of macroeconomic uncertainty due to covid pandemic, the Finance Minister has announced a high fiscal deficit of 9.5 per cent of GDP (Revised Estimates, 2020–2021). This is against the pegged deficit of 3.5 per cent in 2020–2021 (Budget Estimates). Simultaneously, the Finance Minister has also announced an excessive deficit procedure to bring down the high fiscal deficit to 4.5 per cent of GDP by FY26. High fiscal deficit is widely perceived as detrimental to the economy. The perceived economic reasoning is that deficit may crowd out private capital formation and widens "output gap". The output gap is the

© The Author(s), under exclusive license to Springer Nature Singapore Pte Ltd. 2022
L. S. Chakraborty, *Fiscal Policy for Sustainable Development in Asia-Pacific*, https://doi.org/10.1007/978-981-19-3281-6_9

difference between actual GDP and potential GDP (Chakraborty, 2016; Chakraborty & Kaur, 2021). In this chapter, the political economy backdrop of the Union Budget 2021–2022 is analysed prior to applying a "gender lens" to the budget to arrive at the magnitude of gender budgeting.

Fiscal Rules and Financing of Deficits in India

Globally there is a fundamental rethinking about the efficacy of "fiscal rules"—whether adhering to numeric threshold ratios of deficit is growth-enhancing. If the path to fiscal consolidation is through expenditure compression rather than increased tax buoyancy, the quality of fiscal consolidation gets affected. The Economic Survey 2021 in Chapter 2 on public debt sustainability highlighted the perspectives by the eminent macroeconomist Olivier Blanchard that "if the interest rate paid by the government is less than the growth rate, then the intertemporal budget constraint facing the government no longer binds". From that perspective, allowing a high fiscal deficit to GDP ratio to 9.5 per cent of GDP in 2020–2021 (RE) announced in Union Budget 2021, without significant expenditure compression, is welcome. In his Presidential Address in the American Economic Association 2019, Blanchard has explained that "public debt has no fiscal costs if real rate of interest is not greater than real rate of growth of economy". It was also highlighted that high public debt is not catastrophic if "more debt" can be justified by clear benefits like public investment or "output gap" reduction. The "hysteresis effects"—the persistent impact of short-run fluctuations on the long-term potential output—was highlighted in his analysis and he suggested that a temporary fiscal expansion during a contraction could even reduce debt on a longer horizon. These perspectives are incorporated in the Economic Survey 2021 while analyzing the debt-deficit dynamics.

The anatomy of the high fiscal deficit number announced in the Union Budget 2021 is relevant here. It is a combination of revenue shortfall, and new expenditure priorities. Strengthening of "budget transparency" by incorporating prior off-budget borrowings has also led to the rise in deficit number. The Food Corporation of India's borrowing from the National Small Savings Funds is stopped to bring in budget transparency. When FY21 fiscal deficit has reached 9.5 per cent, the government envisions to borrow another Rs. 80,000 crore in the next two months. For FY22, the fiscal deficit is pegged at 6.8% of GDP (Table 9.1). The existing

Table 9.1 Levels of deficit (Rs. crores)

Deficits	2019–2020 Actuals	2020–2021 Budget estimates	2020–2021 Revised estimates	2021–2022 Budget estimates
Fiscal deficit	933,651 (4.6)	796,337 (3.5)	1,848,655 (9.5)	1,506,812 (6.8)
Revenue deficit	666,545 (3.3)	609,219 (2.7)	1,455,989 (7.5)	1,140,576 (5.1)
Effective revenue deficit	480,904 (2.4)	402,719 (1.8)	1,225,613 (6.3)	921,464 (4.1)
Primary deficit	321,581 (1.6)	88,134 (0.4)	1,155,755 (5.9)	697,111 (3.1)

Source Government of India (2021), Union Budget documents

fiscal rules were amended to incorporate the revised threshold of deficit to GDP. In the previous amendment to FRBM, the "golden rule" of zero revenue deficit was eliminated and the clauses related to the elimination of "revenue balance" were incorporated in the Financial Bill. However, in 2021–2022 BE, revenue deficit is 5.1 per cent of GDP. Though there was a debate within the FRBM Committee regarding the choice of deficit—whether revenue deficit, fiscal deficit or primary deficit to be the "operational deficit parameter" in India—with a dissent note from Arvind Subramanian favouring the primary deficit (fiscal deficit minus interest payments), the Union Budget 2021–2022 reiterated that fiscal deficit is still the operational concept of deficit in India. However, primary deficit is a useful concept to understand the current fiscal stance of the government without the legacy of interest payments.

Extreme precaution is required when we measure "deficits" in the time of pandemic. It may be incorrect to think that "cyclically neutral fiscal deficit" is a better measure of deficit. It is important to analyse whether "disruptions" or "downturns" are just "cyclical" and transitory; or whether it "permanently" leave a scar and depress the level of output and employment. If it is a "drop" from the trend growth than a "deviation", it is incorrect to assume that an upturn in business cycle can eliminate the "cyclical" part of deficit, while such things cannot happen if there is no return of economic growth cycle to prior trend growth path and therefore the buoyancy of revenue receipts could remain below the prior-potential level.

In economic downturn, if we are worried about a "bad equilibrium" of rising debt and deficits, it is better to have a "contingent fiscal rule", however "keep the fiscal rules, but do not use it" (Blanchard, 2019). Blanchard also argued against the "steady" fiscal consolidation. Similarly, "a uniform and rigid fiscal rule not only undermine the fiscal autonomy of the States, but would also result in "public (developmental) expenditure compression" to comply with numerical threshold ratio (Reddy & Reddy, 2019).

The sources of financing the fiscal deficit in Union Budget 2012 show that gross market borrowing (Rs. 12 lakh crore at 68.9 per cent of total borrowings) is the dominant financing model. The National Small Savings Fund constitutes around 26 per cent of the total borrowings (Table 9.2). The deficit incurred through off-budget borrowings through public sector enterprises can be captured better through the construction of "Public Sector Borrowing Requirement" (PSBR) data. However, the Union Budget 2021 has not introduced this new deficit concept of PSBR. Instead, the details of such extra budget borrowings are still kept in an Annexure in the Union budget document.

In the Union Budget 2021, creating fiscal space for economic stimulus package was a matter of concern. In the regime of revenue uncertainties, the asset monetization programme was announced in the Union Budget 2021 to generate revenue proceeds. The revenue shortfalls of tax and non-tax revenue are significant (Table 9.3). The disaggregate analysis shows that the fiscal slippage from the disinvestment proceeds is the highest. In other words, the fiscal marksmanship ratio (BE to RE ratio) is highest for disinvestment proceeds (last column of Table 9.3). Though asset sale is perceived as the prominent source of fiscal proceeds, it constitutes only around 5 per cent of the entire receipts budget.

The economic stimulus packages have two components. One is the focus on measures that relate to instantaneous economic firefighting and the other is the long-term policy imperatives. On the monetary policy front, the RBI has done the heavy lifting through five consecutive lowering of repo rate adding to a total of 135 basis points from February to October 2019 along with liquidity infusion programme. However, the monetary-fiscal linkages are crucial to catalyze the demand.

Stiglitz (2020) pointed out that "today's excess liquidity may carry a high social cost. Beyond the usual fears about debt and inflation, there is

Table 9.2 Sources of Financing Fiscal Deficit (Rs. crores)

	2019–2020		2020–2021		2020–2021		2021–2022	
	Actual	% of total	Budget estimates	% of total	Revised estimates	% of total	Budget estimates	% of total
Debt deficit (Net)								
Market borrowings (G-Sec + T Bills)	624,089	66.84	535,870	67.29	1,273,788	68.9	967,708	64.22
Securities against small savings	240,000	25.71	240,000	30.14	480,574	26	391,927	26.01
State provident funds	11,635	1.25	18,000	2.26	18,000	0.97	20,000	1.33
Other receipts (internal debt and public account)	44,273	4.74	50,848	6.39	39,129	2.12	54,280	3.6
External debt	8682	0.93	4622	0.58	54,522	2.95	1514	0.1
Draw down of cash balance	4971	0.53	(–)53,003	(–)6.66	(–)17,358	(–)0.94	71,383	4.74
Grand total	933,651	100	796,337	100	1,848,655	100	1,506,812	100

Source Government of India (2021), Union Budget documents

Table 9.3 The composition and fiscal marksmanship of revenue receipts

(In ₹ crore)

	2019–2020 Actuals	2020–2021 Budget estimates	2020–2021 Revised estimates	2021–2022 Budget estimates	2019–2020 Actuals (In per cent)	2020–2021 Budget estimates (In per cent)	2020–2021 Revised estimates (In per cent)	2021–2022 Budget estimates (In per cent)	2020–2021 Fiscal marksmanship/fiscal slippage
Revenue receipts									
1. Tax revenue									
Gross tax revenue	2,010,059	2,423,020	1,900,280	2,217,059	74.96	78.28	54.8	64.98	1.28
a. Corporation tax	556,876	681,000	446,000	547,000	20.77	22	12.86	16.03	1.53
b. Taxes on income	492,654	638,000	459,000	561,000	18.37	20.61	13.24	16.44	1.39
c. Wealth tax	20	–	–	–	0				
d. Customs	109,283	138,000	112,000	136,000	4.08	4.46	3.23	3.99	1.23
e. Union excise duties	240,615	267,000	361,000	335,000	8.97	8.63	10.41	9.82	0.74
f. Service tax	6029	1020	1400	1000	0.22	0.03	0.04	0.03	0.73
g. GST	598,750	690,500	515,100	630,000	22.33	22.31	14.85	18.47	1.34
– CGST	494,072	580,000	431,000	530,000	18.43	18.74	12.43	15.53	1.35
– IGST	9125	–	–	–	0.34				
– GST compensation cess	95,553	110,500	84,100	100,000	3.56	3.57	2.43	2.93	1.31

(In ₹ crore)

	2019–2020 Actuals	2020–2021 Budget estimates	2020–2021 Revised estimates	2021–2022 Budget estimates	In per cent				2020–2021 Fiscal marksmanship/fiscal slippage
					2019–2020 Actuals	2020–2021 Budget estimates	2020–2021 Revised estimates	2021–2022 Budget estimates	
h. Taxes of union territories	5835	7500	5780	7059	0.22	0.24	0.17	0.21	1.3
Less—NCCD transferred to the NCCF/NDRF	2480	2930	5820	6100	0.09	0.09	0.17	0.18	0.5
Less—State's share	650,678	784,181	549,959	665,563	24.27	25.34	15.86	19.51	1.43
1a Centre's net tax revenue	1,356,902	1,635,909	1,344,501	1,545,397	50.6	52.85	38.77	45.29	1.22
2. Non-tax revenue	327,157	385,017	210,653	243,028	12.2	12.44	6.07	7.12	1.83
Interest receipts	12,349	11,042	14,005	11,541	0.46	0.36	0.4	0.34	0.79
Dividends and profits	186,132	155,396	96,544	103,538	6.94	5.02	2.78	3.03	1.61
External grants	373	812	1422	747	0.01	0.03	0.04	0.02	0.57

(continued)

Table 9.3 (continued)

(In ₹ crore)	2019–2020 Actuals	2020–2021 Budget estimates	2020–2021 Revised estimates	2021–2022 Budget estimates	2019–2020 Actuals	2020–2021 Budget estimates	2020–2021 Revised estimates	2021–2022 Budget estimates	2020–2021 Fiscal marksmanship/fiscal slippage
					\multicolumn{4}{c}{In per cent}	
Other non-tax revenue	126,540	215,465	96,602	124,671	4.72	6.96	2.79	3.65	2.23
Receipts of union territories	1762	2303	2081	2531	0.07	0.07	0.06	0.07	1.11
Total-revenue receipts (1a + 2)	1,684,059	2,020,926	1,555,153	1,788,424	62.81	65.29	44.85	52.42	1.3
3. Capital receipts									
A. non-debt receipts	68,620	224,967	46,497	188,000	2.56	7.27	1.34	5.51	4.84
(i) Recoveries of loans and advances@	18,316	14,967	14,497	13,000	0.68	0.48	0.42	0.38	1.03
(ii) Disinvestment receipts	50,304	210,000	32,000	175,000	1.88	6.78	0.92	5.13	6.56
B. Debt receipts	928,680	849,340	1,866,013	1,435,428	34.63	27.44	53.81	42.07	0.46

(In ₹ crore)	2019–2020 Actuals	2020–2021 Budget estimates	2020–2021 Revised estimates	2021–2022 Budget estimates	In per cent				
					2019–2020 Actuals	2020–2021 Budget estimates	2020–2021 Revised estimates	2021–2022 Budget estimates	2020–2021 Fiscal marksmanship/fiscal slippage
Total capital receipts (A + B)	997,301	1,074,306	1,912,510	1,623,428	37.19	34.71	55.15	47.58	0.56
4. Draw down of cash Balance	4970	−53,003	−17,358	71,383	0.19		−0.5	2.09	
Total receipts (1a + 2 + 3)	2,681,360	3,095,233	3,467,663	3,411,853	100	100	100	100	0.89

Source Government of India (2021), (Basic Data), Union Budget documents

also good reason to worry that the excess cash in banks will be funneled toward financial speculation", and he warned that this could lead to a "climate of increased (economic) uncertainty" and end up "discouraging both consumption and the investment needed to drive the recovery". This could lead us into a "liquidity trap" with a huge increase in the supply of money and not much for it by businesses and households.

In India, the RBI has retained status quo in the policy rate of repo at 4 per cent (Monetary Policy Committee Press release, February 2021). The CPI inflation after crossing 7 per cent has led to negative rate of interest in India. However, the CPI inflation has cooled off to 4.6 per cent in December 2020. The new monetary framework (NMF)—the agreement between the RBI and Government of India in February 2016 adopting inflation targeting in India—will be reviewed in March 2021. When monetary policy stance has limitations—through its liquidity infusion programmes and policy rate adjustments—to trigger growth, the fiscal dominance is crucial for economic recovery. The economies which rebounded fast, ex post global financial crisis, were the ones which resorted to significant fiscal stimulus.

In the Union Budget 2021, the fiscal stimulus was announced as "targeted" economic packages, especially in capital infrastructure investment. There is an increasing recognition of the fact that public investment has suffered from fiscal consolidation when the national and subnational governments have over-adjusted to the fiscal rules by capital expenditure compression. Empirical evidence suggests that public investment is one of the crucial determinants in strengthening private corporate investment in the context of emerging economies. Intertemporally, there is no financial crowding out through real interest rate mechanisms as well (Chakraborty, 2016).

The total size of the budget for FY21 has increased to Rs. 34.50 lakh crore. In FY22, total expenditure is pegged at Rs. 35 lakh crore. Out of total spending by the central government, defence constitutes around 10 per cent of the total, while interest payments constitute 23 per cent of total (Table 9.4). The food subsidy is 12.25 per cent of total central government revenue expenditure in 2021 RE as compared to only 3.80 per cent in 2020 BE. The fiscal slippage numbers above one reveal that RE is less than BE, in the sectors including agriculture, education, energy, and home affairs. Intertemporally, the budget credibility analysis of macro-fiscal variables at national and subnational government levels revealed that the reasons for fiscal forecasting errors can be bias, variation, or random.

Table 9.4 Anatomy of revenue expenditure

(In ₹ crore)	2019–2020 Actuals	2020–2021 Budget estimates	2020–2021 Revised estimates	2021–2022 Budget estimates	2019–2020 Actuals	2020–2021 Budget estimates	2020–2021 Revised estimates	2021–2022 Budget estimates	2020–2021 BE/RE Fiscal slippage (in %)
Pension					0	0	0	0	
Defence									
Subsidy									
Fertiliser	81,124	71,309	133,947	79,530	3.02	2.34	3.88	2.28	0.53
Food	108,688	115,570	422,618	242,836	4.05	3.8	12.25	6.97	0.27
Petroleum	38,529	40,915	38,790	12,995	1.43	1.34	1.12	0.37	1.05
Agriculture and allied activities	112,452	154,775	145,355	148,301	4.19	5.09	4.21	4.26	1.06
Commerce and industry	27,299	27,227	23,515	34,623	1.02	0.89	0.68	0.99	1.16
Development of North East	2658	3049	1860	2658	0.1	0.1	0.05	0.08	1.64
Education	89,437	99,312	85,089	93,224	3.33	3.26	2.47	2.68	1.17
Energy	43,542	42,725	33,440	42,824	1.62	1.4	0.97	1.23	1.28
External affairs	17,246	17,347	15,000	18,155	0.64	0.57	0.43	0.52	1.16
Finance	18,535	41,829	50,566	91,916	0.69	1.37	1.47	2.64	0.83
Health	63,425	67,484	82,445	74,602	2.36	2.22	2.39	2.14	0.82
Home affairs	119,850	114,387	98,106	113,521	4.46	3.76	2.84	3.26	1.17
Interest	612,070	708,203	692,900	809,701	22.78	23.28	20.08	23.25	1.02

(continued)

Table 9.4 (continued)

(In ₹ crore)

	2019–2020 Actuals	2020–2021 Budget estimates	2020–2021 Revised estimates	2021–2022 Budget estimates	2019–2020 Actuals	2020–2021 Budget estimates	2020–2021 Revised estimates	2021–2022 Budget estimates	2020–2021 BE/RE Fiscal slippage (in %)
IT and Telecom	20,597	59,349	32,178	53,108	0.77	1.95	0.93	1.52	1.84
Others	79,523	84,256	94,371	87,528	2.96	2.77	2.74	2.51	0.89
Planning and statistics	5479	6094	2164	2472	0.2	0.2	0.06	0.07	2.82
Rural development	142,384	144,817	216,342	194,633	5.3	4.76	6.27	5.59	0.67
Scientific departments	27,367	30,023	22,352	30,640	1.02	0.99	0.65	0.88	1.34
Social welfare	44,649	53,876	39,629	48,460	1.66	1.77	1.15	1.39	1.36
Tax administration	169,331	152,962	147,728	131,100	6.3	5.03	4.28	3.76	1.04
Of which transfer to GST compensation fund	153,910	135,368	106,317	100,000	5.73	4.45	3.08	2.87	1.27
Transfer to states	148,907	200,447	207,001	293,302	5.54	6.59	6	8.42	0.97
Transport	153,437	169,637	218,622	233,083	5.71	5.58	6.34	6.69	0.78

(In ₹ crore)

	2019–2020	2020–2021	2020–2021	2021–2022	2019–2020	2020–2021	2020–2021	2021–2022	2020–2021 BE/RE Fiscal slippage (in %)
	Actuals	Budget estimates	Revised estimates	Budget estimates	Actuals	Budget estimates	Revised estimates	Budget estimates	
Union territories	15,128	52,864	51,282	53,026	0.56	1.74	1.49	1.52	1.03
Urban development	42,054	50,040	46,791	54,581	1.57	1.64	1.36	1.57	1.07
Grand total	2,686,330	3,042,230	3,450,305	3,483,236	100	100	100	100	0.88

Source Government of India (2021), (Basic Data), Union Budget documents

The Intergovernmental Fiscal Transfers in India, 2021–2022

The Finance Minister has announced a new centrally sponsored scheme (CSS) for enhancing public health infrastructure—Prime Minister Atmanirbhar Swasth Bharat Yojana—with an outlay of Rs. 64,180 crores over the next six years. However, the Finance Minister has also announced about plausible convergence of CSS, as recommended by the Fifteenth Finance Commission report, which was tabled in the Parliament on February 1, 2021. This transition in the structure of intergovernmental fiscal transfers from conditional grants to formula-based (tax transfers) unconditional transfers (which is 41 per cent of tax pool as recommended by the Fifteenth Finance Commission) is welcome. The unconditional transfers provide greater fiscal autonomy to State governments. The disaggregate analysis also showed that there is no increased centralization in the design of fiscal transfers in India with conditional grants constituting only 22.96 per cent (BE 2021–2022) of the total transfers in India.

As per the 2020–2021 Revised Estimates, the tax transfer share (41.86 per cent), GST compensation (8.39 per cent), Finance Commission grants including the local body grants and revenue deficit grants (13.88 per cent) and centrally sponsored schemes (23.99 per cent) are the significant components of intergovernmental fiscal transfers to the States in India (Table 9.5). The rest 4 per cent is the intergovernmental fiscal transfers to the Union Territories (UT) including Delhi, Jammu and Kashmir, and Puducherry.

In the time of macroeconomic uncertainty, high fiscal deficit announced in Union Budget 2021 can be growth-enhancing as it can catalyze the public investment and reduce the output gap. The adherence to fiscal rules at 3 per cent fiscal deficit—GDP ratio would have been detrimental to economic recovery especially when the monetary policy stance has limitations in triggering growth through the liquidity infusion and the status quo policy rates. The "fiscal dominance" is crucial for sustained growth recovery. Against this backdrop, the Union Budget 2021–2022 is analysed through a "gender lens" to understand the magnitude of gender budgeting and its fiscal marksmanship in the next sections.

Table 9.5 Intergovernmental fiscal transfers—conditional and unconditional

(In ₹ crore)	2019–2020 Actuals	2020–2021 Revised estimates	2021–2022 Budget estimates	(in per cent) 2019–2020 Actuals	2020–2021 Revised estimates	2021–2022 Budget estimates
I. Devolution of States share in taxes	650,678	549,959	665,563	56.8	41.86	47.93
II. Some Important Items of Transfer	53,706	171,873	90,055	4.69	13.08	6.49
1. Assistance to States from NDRF	18,889	10,000	12,391	1.65	0.76	0.89
2. Back to Back Loans to States in lieu of GST Compensation Shortfall	–	110,208	–		8.39	
3. Central Pool of Resources for North Eastern Region and Sikkim	380	200	405	0.03	0.02	0.03
4. Externally Added Projects—Grants	2702	2500	3000	0.24	0.19	0.22
5. Externally Aided Projects—Loan	24,668	32,025	46,750	2.15	2.44	3.37
6. Schemes of North East Council	323	224	221	0.03	0.02	0.02

(continued)

Table 9.5 (continued)

(In ₹ crore)	2019–2020 Actuals	2020–2021 Revised estimates	2021–2022 Budget estimates	(in per cent) 2019–2020 Actuals	2020–2021 Revised estimates	2021–2022 Budget estimates
7. Schemes under Provision to Article 275(1) of the Constitution	2661	718	1119	0.23	0.05	0.08
8. Special Assistance as Loan to States for Capital Expenditure	–	12,000	10,000		0.91	0.72
9. Special Assistance under the demand—Transfers to States	1624	3000	15,000	0.14	0.23	1.08
10. Special Central Assistance to Scheduled Castes under Demand—Department of Social Justice and Empowerment	1115	290	–	0.1	0.02	
11. Special Central Assistance to Tribal Area under the Demand—Ministry of Tribal Affairs	1346	708	1170	0.12	0.05	0.08
III. Finance Commission Grants	123,710	182,352	220,843	10.8	13.88	15.91
1. Grant for local bodies—Urban Bodies	25,098	25,000	22,114	2.19	1.9	1.59
2. Grant for local bodies—Rural Bodies	59,361	60,750	44,901	5.18	4.62	3.23
3. Grants for Health Sector	–	–	13,192			0.95
4. Grants-in-Aid for SDRF	10,938	22,262	22,184	0.95	1.69	1.6
5. Post Devolution Revenue Deficit Grants	28,314	74,340	118,452	2.47	5.66	8.53
IV. Total Transfer to States [Other than (I) + (II) + (III)]	289,233	358,789	363,355	25.25	27.31	26.17
1. Under Centrally Sponsored Schemes (Revenue)	275,428	315,238	318,857	24.04	23.99	22.96

(In ₹ crore)	2019–2020 Actuals	2020–2021 Revised estimates	2021–2022 Budget estimates	(in per cent) 2019–2020 Actuals	2020–2021 Revised estimates	2021–2022 Budget estimates
2. Under Central Sector Schemes (Revenue)	12,864	42,374	43,016	1.12	3.22	3.1
3. Under Other Categories of Expenditure (Revenue)	927	1049	1259	0.08	0.08	0.09
4. Capital Transfers	13	128	223	0	0.01	0.02
V. Total Transfer to Delhi, Puducherry, and Jammu & Kashmir	28,161	50,963	48,686	2.46	3.88	3.51
1. Under Centrally Sponsored Schemes (Revenue)	3578	6583	8065	0.31	0.5	0.58
2. Under Central Sector Schemes (Revenue)	218	1080	177	0.02	0.08	0.01
3. Under Other Categories of Expenditure (Revenue)	24,140	43,301	40,444	2.11	3.3	2.91
4. Capital Transfers	225	–	–	0.02		
Total Transfer to States/UTs	1,145,487	1,313,937	1,388,502	100	100	100

Source Government of India (2021), (Basic Data), Union Budget documents

Applying "Gender Lens" to Union Budget 2021–2022

The trends in gender budget allocations derived from the gender budget statements during the period 2005–2006 to 2021–2022 are shown in Fig. 9.1. The fluctuating trend in the allocation in the graph is not exclusively due to an increase in the allocation of the budget on women-oriented spending because the number of Demands for Grants/programmes included in the gender-budgeting statement changed over time. Over the years, gender budgeting hovered around 5 per cent of total Union Budget (Fig. 9.1).

Gender-disaggregated public expenditure benefit incidence analysis though was stated in the first Gender Budget in India, as recommended by the Classification of Budgetary Transactions committee of Ministry of Finance, it was hardly undertaken by the Ministries for specific schemes. Chapter 10 presents an illustrative public expenditure benefit incidence analysis in health sector, which can be used as a template to conduct in other sectors, based on the data on units utilized of specific public service provisioning. The Gender Budget Statement of Union Budget presents two components of spending in terms of the intensity of gender allocations. Part A of gender budgeting presents the specifically targeted programmes for women (Table 9.6) and Part 2 of gender budget statement presents the intrinsic gender allocation of mainstream

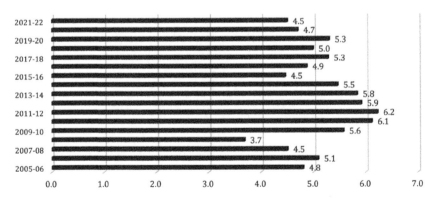

Fig. 9.1 Distribution of the Gender Budget in the Total Budget, India (*Source* [Basic Data], Expenditure Budgets Union Budget 2021–2022, Government of India [2019])

Table 9.6 Part A: Specifically Targeted programmes for Women in Union Budget 2021–2022, India

In Rs. Crores

	2019–2020 Actuals	2020–2021 Budget estimates	2020–2021 Revised estimates	2021–2022 Budget estimates
Ministries/Departments				
Agricultural Research and Education	13.04	13.04	10.64	13.25
Ayurveda, Yoga and Naturopathy, Unani, Siddha and Homoeopathy (AYUSH)		36.2	22.83	23.69
Posts				0.15
Development of North Eastern Region	18.18	7.67	7.67	3.84
School Education and Literacy	8.56	110	1	1
Higher Education	20	20	20	20
External Affairs	4.55	2.15	4.34	15.8
Health Research		40.68	36.88	41.52
Police	13	1004.07	10.28	12.25
Andaman and Nicobar Islands	26.25	29.24	27.54	28.66
Chandigarh	68.2	74.63	74.54	76.81
Dadra and Nagar Haveli and Daman and Diu	10.78	15.75	15.8	16.2
Ladakh		4.98	3.73	4.78
Lakshadweep	5.57	3.75	3.75	4.2
Law and justice		150		
Micro, Small, and Medium Enterprises		2.01		
Minority Affairs	7.1	10	6	8
Petroleum and Natural Gas	3724	1118	9690	
Railways		250		
Road Transport and Highways	66.42	174.36	140	100
Rural Development	19,890.96	21,437.79	52,981.78	21,438.8
Science and Technology	79.1	100	95	100

(continued)

Table 9.6 (continued)

In Rs. Crores				
	2019–2020 Actuals	2020–2021 Budget estimates	2020–2021 Revised estimates	2021–2022 Budget estimates
Skill Development and Entrepreneurship		45	42	42
Women and Child Development	2775.6	3919	2820.55	3310
PART A Total	26,731.31	28,568.32	66,014.33	25,260.95

Source (Basic Data), Expenditure, Union Budget 2021–2022, Government of India (2019)

spending (Table 9.7). Out of 24 Demand for Grants, in which the specifically targeted programmes were identified, around 80 per cent of the allocations pertain to rural development. The Ministry of Women and Child Development (MWCD) constitute only around 10 per cent of total specifically targeted programmes as per the BE over the years; however, there is a huge deviation between the BE and RE in the gender budget allocations in MWCD. The Ministry of Petroleum and Natural Gas also has around 14 per cent of the total Part A of gender budget as per the Budget Estimates, however the Revised Estimates revealed only 4 per cent of the total Part A of the gender budgeting in the year 2020–2021. Other than these three Departments/Ministries—rural development, women and child development and petroleum and natural gas—other departments/ministries where specifically targeted programmes were identified has constituted only less than one per cent of total Part A of gender budget. The gender budgeting in energy infrastructure is a crucial intervention by the government to provide clean fuel for the women in low-income households. The department of police allocates Rs. 1000 crores under Nirbhaya Funds in BE 2020–2021. However in the Revised Estimates for 2020–2021 it was only Rs. 10 crores. In the BE 2021–2022, Nirbhaya fund was only Rs. 12.25 crores. The Bill of Rights framed in the Justice Verma Committee Report can form the foundation for gender budgeting in a "law and order" context. Gender budgeting in criminal justice is a public good and needs effective planning and financing strategies, but it has so far been limited to the creation of the "Nirbhaya Fund" (designed to fund new schemes for the safety and

Table 9.7 Part B: Sectoral Composition of Gender Budgeting, 2021–2022

In Rs. Crores	2019–2020 Actuals	2020–2021 Budget estimates	2020–2021 Revised estimates	2021–2022 Budget estimates	2019–2020 Actuals	2020–2021 Budget estimates	2020–2021 Revised estimates	2021–2022 Budget estimates
Part B: 30% Women-specific programmes								
Demand No. 1: Department of Agriculture, Cooperation, and Farmers'		4772.18	3538.99	4813.26	0	4.15	2.51	3.76
Demand No. 3: Atomic Energy	24	30	9	30	0.02	0.03	0.01	0.02
Demand 4: (AYUSH)		49.81	17.45	21.5	0	0.04	0.01	0.02
Demand No. 10: Department of Commerce				5	0	0	0	0
Demand No. 17: Ministry of Culture	33.46	35.14	35.14	36.88	0.03	0.03	0.02	0.03
Demand No. 22: Ministry of Development of North Eastern Region	100.33	42.33	42.33	21.17	0.1	0.04	0.03	0.02
Demand No. 23: Ministry of Earth Sciences		132	60.8	129	0	0.11	0.04	0.1

(continued)

Table 9.7 (continued)

In Rs. Crores	2019–2020 Actuals	2020–2021 Budget estimates	2020–2021 Revised estimates	2021–2022 Budget estimates	2019–2020 Actuals	2020–2021 Budget estimates	2020–2021 Revised estimates	2021–2022 Budget estimates
Demand No. 24: Department of School Education and Literacy	15,559.64	17,636.1	15,325.56	15,943.05	15.79	15.35	10.85	12.45
Demand No. 25: Department of Higher Education	9524.17	11,353.04	10,133.31	12,291	9.66	9.88	7.17	9.6
Demand No. 26: Ministry of Electronics and Information Technology	2.7	3.3	2	120	0	0	0	0.09
Demand No. 28: Ministry of External Affairs	232.79	295.68	21.62	299.71	0.24	0.26	0.02	0.23
Demand No. 41: Department of Fisheries		560	700	1000	0	0.49	0.5	0.78
Demand No. 42: Department of Animal Husbandry and Dairying		370.02	425	350	0	0.32	0.3	0.27
Demand No. 44: Department of Health and Family Welfare	24,954.22	27,271.27	28,187.59	30,227.83	25.32	23.74	19.96	23.6

In Rs. Crores	2019–2020 Actuals	2020–2021 Budget estimates	2020–2021 Revised estimates	2021–2022 Budget estimates	2019–2020 Actuals	2020–2021 Budget estimates	2020–2021 Revised estimates	2021–2022 Budget estimates
Demand No. 45: Department of Health Research	9.5	55.14	67.32	82.29	0.01	0.05	0.05	0.06
Demand No. 50: Police	0.48	0.11	0.48	0.52	0	0	0	0
Demand No. 51: Andaman and Nicobar Islands	45.8	49.88	45.02	48.12	0.05	0.04	0.03	0.04
Demand No. 52 Chandigarh	28.98	14.78	32	32	0.03	0.01	0.02	0.02
Demand No. 53: Dadra and Nagar Haveli and Daman and Diu	6.33	7.02	7.02	7.02	0.01	0.01	0	0.01
Demand No. 55: Lakshadweep	6	5.34	5.34	6.02	0.01	0	0	0
Demand No. 59: Ministry of Housing and Urban Affairs		2836.67	21,245.5	7650.57	0	2.47	15.04	5.97
Demand No. 62: Department of Drinking Water and Sanitation			1546.01	2783.45	0	0	1.09	2.17
Demand No. 63: Ministry of Labour and Employment	77.48	120	50	120	0.08	0.1	0.04	0.09

(continued)

Table 9.7 (continued)

In Rs. Crores	2019–2020 Actuals	2020–2021 Budget estimates	2020–2021 Revised estimates	2021–2022 Budget estimates	2019–2020 Actuals	2020–2021 Budget estimates	2020–2021 Revised estimates	2021–2022 Budget estimates
Demand No. 69: Ministry of Minority Affairs	1239.09	1365	1108.01	1295.7	1.26	1.19	0.78	1.01
Demand No. 70: Ministry of New and Renewable Energ	98.04	60	66.5	132	0.1	0.05	0.05	0.1
Demand No. 75: Ministry of Petroleum and Natural Gas		10.14			0	0.01	0	0
Demand No. 85: Ministry of Road Transport and Highways	66.42		140	100	0.07	0	0.1	0.08
Demand No. 86: Department of Rural Development	28,387.88	25,110.9	41,777.57	30,972.13	28.81	21.86	29.58	24.18
Demand No. 90: Department of Scientific and Industrial Research	0.43		0.5	2.25	0	0	0	0
Demand No. 91: Ministry of Skill Development and Entrepreneurship		73			0	0.06	0	0

In Rs. Crores	2019–2020 Actuals	2020–2021 Budget estimates	2020–2021 Revised estimates	2021–2022 Budget estimates	2019–2020 Actuals	2020–2021 Budget estimates	2020–2021 Revised estimates	2021–2022 Budget estimates
Demand No. 92: Department of Social Justice and Empowerment	2485.8	2886.2	2347.78	2950.69	2.52	2.51	1.66	2.3
Demand No. 93: Department of Empowerment of Persons with Disabilities	298.54	352.61	262.96	342.82	0.3	0.31	0.19	0.27
Demand No. 97: Ministry of Textiles	372.52	379.7	304.59	441.3	0.38	0.33	0.22	0.34
Demand No. 99: Ministry of Tribal Affairs	2033.88	2031.57	1561.91	2106.21	2.06	1.77	1.11	1.64
Demand No. 100: Ministry of Women and Child Development	12,763.48	16,790.52	12,045.45	13,514.6	12.95	14.61	8.53	10.55
Demand No. 101: Ministry of Youth Affairs and Sports	198.92	193.95	133.94	189.24	0.2	0.17	0.09	0.15
Part B Total	98,550.88	114,893.4	141,246.69	128,065.33	100	100	100	100

Source (Basic Data), Expenditure Budgets, Union Budget 2021–2022, Government of India (2019)

security for women, with an initial allocation of Rs. 1,000 crores), which has been unused since 2013.

In the Part B of gender budgeting, the higher allocation was reported in the ministries/departments of rural development, health and family welfare, education and housing, and urban affairs. The rest of the ministries/departments identified have only less than one per cent of total gender budget allocation.

Fiscal Marksmanship

Fiscal marksmanship is the accuracy of budgetary forecasting. It can be a crucial information about how the fiscal agents form expectations. The significant variations between actual revenue and expenditure from the forecasted budgetary magnitudes could be an indicative of non-optimization or non-attainment of set objectives of fiscal policy. The difference between the budget estimates and actual expenditure gives the extent of fiscal marksmanship. Underestimation/overestimation of the budget is of critical importance to drive home the point of accountability of the government. Table 9.5 elaborates upon the budgetary estimates, revised estimates, and the fiscal marksmanship of gender budgeting. The 100% women-specific programmes implemented by Department of Agricultural Research and Education, Ministry of Women and Child development, Ministry of Petroleum and Gas had overestimated their budget. Programmes with 30% allocation for women for the above-mentioned programmes, too were having poor fiscal marksmanship. Fiscal Marksmanship—deviation between budgeted and actual—for petroleum and natural gas was as high as Rs. 988 Crore, while Ministry of External Affairs performed marvelous. The fiscal marksmanship of 1 is perfect forecast, while other deviations are either underestimates or overestimates (Table 9.8). The fiscal marksmanship is calculated through the Root Mean Square Error and Theil's U coefficients. The root mean squared error (RMSE) is a measure of the relative size of the forecast error. In this paper, to calculate the RMSE, the mean squared error (MSE) is taken over the reference period after which the square root of the MSE is calculated. While this will give us the magnitude of error, it will not give any information on the direction of the error, i.e. whether the error is positive or negative. We have taken the RMSE as a proportion of the sum of actuals of the reference period. It reflects the fact that large forecast errors are more significant than small differences.

Table 9.8 Fiscal marksmanship: The Sources of Fiscal Forecasting Errors

	Bias	Unequal variation	Random
Ex ante fiscal rules			
Revenue receipts	0.24	0.07	0.69
Capital receipts	0.45	0.14	0.41
Revenue expenditure	0.05	0.15	0.80
Capital expenditure	0.06	0.22	0.72
Revenue deficit	0.36	0.01	0.63
Fiscal deficit	0.31	0.01	0.68
Primary deficit	0.32	0.00	0.67
Ex ante fiscal rules			
Revenue receipts	0.01	0.04	0.95
Revenue expenditure	0.00	0.31	0.69
Capital expenditure	0.00	0.02	0.98
Revenue deficit	0.04	0.01	0.96
Fiscal deficit	0.02	0.01	0.97
Primary deficit	0.05	0.02	0.93

Source Chakraborty and Sinha (2020)

Theil's inequality coefficient (U) is used to analyze the measure of accuracy of the budget forecasts. Theil's inequality coefficient is based on the MSE (U1). The forecast error of Theil (1958) is defined as:

$$U_1 = \frac{\sqrt{1/n \sum (P_t - A_t)^2}}{\sqrt{1/n \sum P_t^2} + \sqrt{1/n \sum A_t^2}} \quad (9.1)$$

where U_1 = inequality coefficient, P_t = predicted value, A_t = actual value and n = the number of years.

This inequality coefficient ranges from zero to one. When $P_t = A_t$ for all observations (a perfect forecast), U_1 equals zero.[1] U_1 has been decomposed in order to indicate systematic and random sources of error. The systematic component is further divided into the proportion of the total forecast error due to bias and the proportion of total forecast error attributable to unequal variation. The derivation of Eq. 4 is given in detail in Davis (1980).

$$1 = \frac{(\overline{P} - \overline{A})^2}{1/n \sum (P_t - A_t)^2} + \frac{(Sp - Sa)^2}{1/n \sum (P_t - A_t)^2} + \frac{2(1-r)Sp.Sa}{1/n \sum (P_t - A_t)^2} \quad (9.2)$$

In Eq. (9.2), P and A are mean predicted and mean actual changes, respectively; Sp and Sa are the standard deviations of predicted and actual values, respectively; and r is the coefficient of correlation between predicted and actual values.

The first expression of RHS in Eq. (9.2) is the proportion of the total forecast error due to bias. It represents a measure of the proportion of error due to overprediction or underprediction of the average value. The second expression of the RHS in Eq. (9.2) is the proportion of total forecast error attributable to unequal variation. In other words, it measures the proportion of error due to overprediction or underprediction of the variance of the values. The third expression of

---

[1] Theil's second equation for the inequality coefficient uses a revised measure of forecast error. Theil's (1966, 1971) revised measure of inequality is as follows:

$$U_2 = \frac{\sqrt{1/n \sum (P_t - A_t)^2}}{\sqrt{1/n \sum A_t^2}}$$

This measure has the advantage that the denominator does not contain P and the inequality coefficient does not depend on the forecast. In a perfect forecast, U2 equals to zero. U2 does not have an upper bound.

A more rigorous measure of Theil's inequality statistics is also used by incorporating the lags in the actuals and the difference of the predicted value from the lag of the actuals to capture the magnitude of error:

$$U_3 = \sqrt{\frac{1/n \sum [Pt - at]^2}{1/n \sum [Pt]^2 + 1/n \sum [at]^2}}$$

where $a = A_t - A_t - 1$, $P_t = P_t - A_t - 1$, and n = number of years.

the RHS in Eq. (9.2) measures the proportion of forecasting error due to random variation. The first two sources of error are systematic; presumably they can be reduced by improved forecasting techniques, while the random component is beyond the control of the forecaster (Intriligator, 1978; Theil, 1958). Given the magnitude of each of the components of gender budgeting, a ratio of fiscal marksmanship is used instead of these elaborate Theil's U methodology. The fiscal marksmanship ratio of two departments/ministries showed wide volatility, viz, school education and literacy, and police, for the year 2020–2021. The wide deviation in the BE and RE of Nirbhaya fund was the reason for fiscal forecasting errors in the department of police.

Technically, researchers can analyze the magnitude of the macro-fiscal variable errors and the source of errors (whether it is a "random error" and beyond the control of fiscal forecaster, or whether the errors are systemic and biased) (Chakraborty & Sinha, 2020). We can also analyze whether the magnitude of the errors was greater for revenue or expenditure, as well as for the capital or revenue budget. However, as indicated in Table 9.8, the source of errors in forecasting the parameters is largely random in nature (Table 9.8), which is beyond the purview of policymakers.

In the Part B of gender budgeting, the fiscal marksmanship of the departments/ministries like External Affairs, AYUSH, Earth Sciences, Atomic Energy, and labour and employment has shown wide deviations (Table 9.9).

The gender budgeting as a fiscal innovation framework has not been effectively used in India to formulate programme design relate to ex ante identification of gender needs. Applying a gender lens to the existing budgets reveal that gender budget hovered around 5 per cent of total budget in the period 2005–2006 to 2021–2022. The fiscal marksmanship—the budget forecasting errors—is a matter of concern for macro-fiscal variables and gender budgeting. Too many programmes are designed with too little money (Table 9.10).

Table 9.9 Fiscal marksmanship of Gender Budgeting: Part A

Ministry/Department (In Rs. crores)	2019–2020 Actuals	2020–2021 Budget estimates	2020–2021 Revised estimates	2021–2022 Budget estimates	2020–2021 Fiscal marksmanship
Part A					
Agricultural Research and Education	13.04	13.04	10.64	13.25	1.23
Ayurveda, Yoga and Naturopathy, Unani, Siddha and Homoeopathy (AYUSH)		36.2	22.83	23.69	1.59
Posts				0.15	
Development of North Eastern Region	18.18	7.67	7.67	3.84	1
School Education and Literacy	8.56	110	1	1	110
Higher Education	20	20	20	20	1
External Affairs	4.55	2.15	4.34	15.8	0.5
Health Research		40.68	36.88	41.52	1.1
Police	13	1004.07	10.28	12.25	97.67
Andaman and Nicobar Islands	26.25	29.24	27.54	28.66	1.06
Chandigarh	68.2	74.63	74.54	76.81	1
Dadra and Nagar Haveli and Daman and Diu	10.78	15.75	15.8	16.2	1
Ladakh		4.98	3.73	4.78	1.34
Lakshadweep	5.57	3.75	3.75	4.2	1
Law and justice		150			

Ministry/Department (In Rs. crores)	2019–2020 Actuals	2020–2021 Budget estimates	2020–2021 Revised estimates	2021–2022 Budget estimates	2020–2021 Fiscal marksmanship
Micro, Small, and Medium Enterprises		2.01			
Minority Affairs	7.1	10	6	8	1.67
Petroleum and Natural Gas	3724	1118	9690		0.12
Railways		250			
Road Transport and Highways	66.42	174.36	140	100	1.25
Rural Development	19,890.96	21,437.79	52,981.78	21,438.8	0.4
Science and Technology	79.1	100	95	100	1.05
Skill Development and Entrepreneurship		45	42	42	1.07
Women and Child Development	2775.6	3919	2820.55	3310	1.39
Part A Total	26,731.31	28,568.32	66,014.33	25,260.95	0.43
Grand Total	125,282.19	143,461.72	207,261.02	153,326.28	0.69

Source (Basic Data), Expenditure Budgets, Union Budget 2021–2022

Table 9.10 Fiscal Marksmanship of Part B Allocations of Gender Budgeting, 2020–2021

In Rs. Crores

	2019–2020 Actuals	2020–2021 Budget estimates	2020–2021 Revised estimates	2021–2022 Budget estimates	2020–2021 FM
Part B: 30% women-specific programmes					
Demand No. 1: Department of Agriculture, Cooperation and Farmers'		4772.18	3538.99	4813.26	1.35
Demand No. 3: Atomic Energy	24	30	9	30	3.33
Demand No. 4: (AYUSH)		49.81	17.45	21.5	2.85
Demand No. 10: Department of Commerce				5	
Demand No. 17: Ministry of Culture	33.46	35.14	35.14	36.88	1
Demand No. 22: Ministry of Development of North Eastern Region	100.33	42.33	42.33	21.17	1
Demand No. 23: Ministry of Earth Sciences		132	60.8	129	2.17
Demand No. 24: Department of School Education and Literacy	15,559.64	17,636.1	15,325.56	15,943.05	1.15
Demand No. 25: Department of Higher Education	9524.17	11,353.04	10,133.31	12,291	1.12
Demand No. 26: Ministry of Electronics and Information Technology	2.7	3.3	2	120	1.65
Demand No. 28: Ministry of External Affairs	232.79	295.68	21.62	299.71	13.68

In Rs. Crores

	2019–2020 Actuals	2020–2021 Budget estimates	2020–2021 Revised estimates	2021–2022 Budget estimates	2020–2021 FM
Demand No. 41: Department of Fisheries		560	700	1000	0.8
Demand No. 42: Department of Animal Husbandry and Dairying		370.02	425	350	0.87
Demand No. 44: Department of Health and Family Welfare	24,954.22	27,271.27	28,187.59	30,227.83	0.97
Demand No. 45: Department of Health Research	9.5	55.14	67.32	82.29	0.82
Demand No. 50: Police	0.48	0.11	0.48	0.52	0.23
Demand No. 51: Andaman and Nicobar Islands	45.8	49.88	45.02	48.12	1.11
Demand No. 52: Chandigarh	28.98	14.78	32	32	0.46
Demand No. 53: Dadra and Nagar Haveli and Daman and Diu	6.33	7.02	7.02	7.02	1
Demand No. 55: Lakshadweep	6	5.34	5.34	6.02	1
Demand No. 59: Ministry of Housing and Urban Affairs		2836.67	21,245.5	7650.57	0.13
Demand No. 62: Department of Drinking Water and Sanitation			1546.01	2783.45	0
Demand No. 63: Ministry of Labour and Employment	77.48	120	50	120	2.4
Demand No. 69: Ministry of Minority Affairs	1239.09	1365	1108.01	1295.7	1.23
Demand No. 70: Ministry of New and Renewable Energy	98.04	60	66.5	132	0.9
Demand No. 75: Ministry of Petroleum and Natural Gas		10.14			
Demand No. 85: Ministry of Road Transport and Highways	66.42		140	100	0

(continued)

Table 9.10 (continued)

In Rs. Crores

	2019–2020 Actuals	2020–2021 Budget estimates	2020–2021 Revised estimates	2021–2022 Budget estimates	2020–2021 FM
Demand No. 86: Department of Rural Development	28,387.88	25,110.9	41,777.57	30,972.13	0.6
Demand No. 90: Department of Scientific and Industrial Research	0.43		0.5	2.25	0
Demand No. 91: Ministry of Skill Development and Entrepreneurship		73			
Demand No. 92: Department of Social Justice and Empowerment	2485.8	2886.2	2347.78	2950.69	1.23
Demand No. 93: Department of Empowerment of Persons with Disabilities	298.54	352.61	262.96	342.82	1.34
Demand No. 97: Ministry of Textiles	372.52	379.7	304.59	441.3	1.25
Demand No. 99: Ministry of Tribal Affairs	2033.88	2031.57	1561.91	2106.21	1.3
Demand No. 100: Ministry of Women and Child Development	12,763.48	16,790.52	12,045.45	13,514.6	1.39
Demand No. 101: Ministry of Youth Affairs and Sports	198.92	193.95	133.94	189.24	1.45
Part B total	98,550.88	114,893.4	141,246.69	128,065.33	0.81
Grand total (A + B)	125,282.19	143,461.72	207,261.02	153,326.28	0.69

Source (Basic Data), Expenditure Budgets, Union Budget 2021–2022

REFERENCES

Blanchard, O. (2019, January 6). Public debt and low interest rate. Presidential address, *Delivered at the American Economic Association Meetings, Atlanta.*

Chakraborty, L. (2016). Asia: A survey of gender budgeting experiences *(International Monetary Fund Working Paper 16/150). Washington, DC: IMF.*

Chakraborty, L., & Sinha, D. (2020). Budget credibility of subnational governments: Analyzing the fiscal forecasting errors of 28 states in India. *New York:Levy Economics Institute, working paper series, 964.*

Chakraborty, L., & Kaur, A. (2021). Why output gap is controversial? *The Financial Express.*

Davis, J. M. (1980). Fiscal marksmanship in the United Kingdom, 1951–78. *The Manchester School of Economic and Social Studies, 48*(2), 187–202.

Intriligator, M. D. (1978). *Econometric models, techniques, and applications.* Prentice-Hall.

Reddy, Y. V., & Reddy, G. R. (2019). *Indian Fiscal Federalism.* Oxford University Press.

Stiglitz, J. H. (2020, July 31). A global debt crisis is looming: How can we prevent. It? Project Syndicate. *Project Syndicate .*

Theil, H. (1958). *Economic forecasts and policy.* North Holland.

CHAPTER 10

Gender-Budgeting Outcomes and Public Expenditure Benefit Incidence

The public expenditure benefit incidence analysis (BIA), is a relatively simple and practical method to identify how well public services are targeted to certain groups in the population, across gender, ethnicity, income quintiles, and geographical units. BIA involves allocating *unit cost* according to individual utilization rates of public services. The studies on BIA revealed that a disproportionate share of the health budget benefits the elite in urban areas, or that the major part of education budget benefits schooling of boys rather than girls, which has important policy implications.

The public expenditure BIA helps in analyzing the distributional impacts of public expenditure, especially in social sector—viz, education and health sector. The behavioural approach to capture the distributional impacts of public spending—another methodology—is based on the notion that a rationed publicly provided good or service should be evaluated at the individual's own valuation of the good, which (Demery, 2000) called a "virtual price". Such prices will vary from individual to individual. This approach emphasizes the measurement of individual preferences for the publicly provided goods. The methodological complications in the valuation of revealed preferences based on the microeconomic theory and the paucity of unit record data related to the knowledge of the underlying demand functions of individuals or households led to less practicability of the behavioural approaches in estimating the distributional impact of public expenditure.

The benefit incidence analysis of public expenditure reveals the inequities in spending and the studies are broadly confined to education and health sectors (Castro-Leal et al., 1999; Davoodi et al., 2003; Demery, 2000; Filmer & Lant, 1998; Lustig, 2015; Manasan et al., 2007; Sahn & Younger, 2000). In India, the existing studies on benefit incidence of public health spending reveals a high gender (male–female) and regional (rural–urban) differentials (see Bhadra, 2016; Chakraborty et al., 2013; Mahal et al., 2001). However, these studies have not attempted the epidemiological categorization of public health expenditure benefit incidence. In this chapter, quite different from the existing literature, a meticulous disaggregation of disease-specific public health expenditure benefit incidence—based on International Classification of Diseases (ICD) by World Health Organisation (WHO)—is attempted.

The International Classification of Diseases (ICD) is the international standard diagnostic classification for all general epidemiological and many health management purposes. It is a tool for systematic recording, analysis, interpretation, and comparison of mortality and morbidity data. The ICD translates diagnoses of diseases and other health problems into an alphanumeric code, which allows storage, retrieval, and analysis of the data. According to an international treaty, the "WHO Nomenclature Regulations", adopted by the World Health Assembly, all WHO Member States are expected to use the most current version of the ICD for reporting death and illness. The new ICD codes to COVID-19 are not included in the analysis as the ICD nomenclature and the morbidity data used for analysis is prior to 2020. The mapping of ICD—10 version codes (ICD-11 will be operational only from January 2022) to Indian National Sample Survey codes on morbidity is attempted to conduct the ICD-specific benefit incidence.

The Analytical Framework

Davoodi et al. (2003) suggested a methodology consisting of comparing the resulting distribution of benefits (step for) with benchmark distributions, in order to derive useful policy recommendations, by using concentration curves. The concentration curve is explained as the cumulative proportion of individuals, ranked from poorest to richest plotting on the horizontal axis, and the (cumulative) proportion of benefits received by individuals on the vertical axis.

The benchmark for targeting a distribution of benefits is the 45° line, which is otherwise referred to as line of equality (Fig. 10.1). If the distribution lies above this line, it is considered pro-poor. A distribution is pro-rich if the curve lies under the 45° line. On the other hand, the benchmark for progressiveness is the Lorenz curve of income (or whatever welfare measure as consumption or expenditure). Thus, if the distribution curve is above the Lorenz Curve—but below the 45° line, it is considered progressive; otherwise we can say that public spending is regressive. Why progressive, (Davoodi et al., 2003) explained that it is because the proportion of the benefits from public spending for lower-income groups is larger than their participation in the total income, which is expected to have a redistributive effect. As can be seen in Fig. 10.1, when benefits from public spending are pro-poor, they are also progressive, but progressiveness does not imply pro-poor spending. The point to be noted is that although BIA is not sufficient to have a complete picture of the required

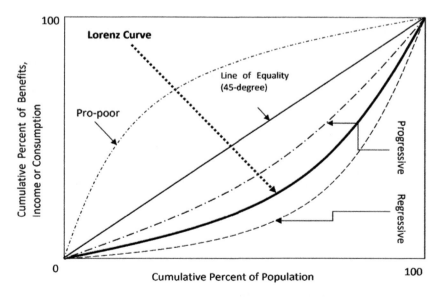

Fig. 10.1 Concentration curves, public expenditure incidence, and targeting: Pictorial representation (*Source* Davoodi et al. [2003])

pro-poor public expenditure reforms, it is still a useful methodology in order to know the distributional impacts of public spending among different categories of population, whether it is gender differentials or geographic differentials.

The earliest examples of analyses of the benefit incidence of public spending on merit goods are studies by Gillespie (1965) in Canada and the United States. Four useful surveys in the benefit incidence literature were carried out by McLure (1974) and Selden and Wasylenko (1992), and more recently by Demery (2000) and Younger (2002). The literature on benefit incidence revealed that it has been applied mainly to merit goods—in particular, health and education. The domain of BIA has been mainly confined to the International Monetary Fund (IMF) and the World Bank, in particular the studies by Davoodi et al. (2003), Demery (2000), Castro-Leal et al. (1999), and Lanjouw and Ravallion (1999). Davoodi et al. (2010) compile a large data set on the unit cost and unit utilized of the health and education spending for 56 countries between 1960 and 2000 to conduct BIA. The study found that, among other things, overall education and health spending are poorly targeted. The benefits from primary education and primary health care go disproportionately to the middle class, particularly in sub-Saharan Africa, heavily indebted poor countries (HIPCs), and the transition economies, but targeting improved in the 1990s. Second, simple measures of association show that countries with a more pro-poor incidence of education and health spending tend to have better education and health outcomes, good governance, high per capita income, and wider accessibility to information. Another important methodological lesson of this paper is that future BIA should pay more attention to recording incidence data and various breakdowns of the data (e.g. by region, gender, and ethnicity) and the necessary auxiliary identifiers that are essential for a proper analysis, which this paper intends to do in the context of India. Demery (2000) compares the public spending on education across quintiles in the context of Colombia, Côte d'Ivoire, and Indonesia. Her results revealed that the poorest quintile gained just 15% of the total education subsidy in Indonesia, only 13% in Côte d'Ivoire, and 23% in Colombia. Three factors determine these shares. First is the supply-side determinant, which is the public spending on education across the various levels of schooling. In Indonesia, the government allocated 62% of total education subsidies to primary education, while in Côte d'Ivoire, the share was under 50%. The Ivorian government spent relatively more on tertiary schooling (18%) compared with just 9% in Indonesia. Colombia's allocations were quite different, with a much lower share being allocated to primary schooling (just 41%) and a much higher share to tertiary education (26%). But surprisingly, the low allocation of the education subsidy to primary schooling in Colombia does not seem to have led to a lower share going to the poorer quintiles. Why is this? The answer, Demery (2000) argues, lies mainly with the second set of factors determining benefit incidence—the household behaviour, the demand-side factors. Differences in 9 household behaviour are reflected in the quintile shares of the subsidy at each level of education. Primary enrollments and therefore the primary subsidy in the poorest quintile represented 22% of the total primary enrollments subsidy in Indonesia, just 19% in Côte d'Ivoire, and 39% in Colombia. It is the combined influence of these enrollment shares and the allocation of government subsidies across the levels of education that yields the overall benefit incidence from education spending accruing to each of the quintiles. A third factor explaining the differences in benefit incidence is the way the quintiles were defined. For Colombia, they were defined across households rather than individuals, and this makes the benefit incidence patterns incomparable with Indonesia and Côte d'Ivoire. With total household expenditure per capita as the welfare measure, poorer households will generally be larger (Lanjouw & Ravallion, 1994). This means that when quintiles are defined for households, there will usually be more individuals in the poorer quintiles than in the richer quintiles. This can distort benefit incidence results, making it appear as though the poorer quintiles gain more, relative to the rich. In Côte d'Ivoire (as well as in Guinea, Madagascar, South Africa, Tanzania, and Uganda), the poorest 20% gain about 20% of the primary education subsidy, about 10% of the secondary education subsidy, and a minimal per cent of the tertiary level subsidy (Castro-Leal et al., 1999). In their estimation of benefit incidence in a set of African countries, they obtained that the government subsidies in education and health care are generally progressive, but are poorly targeted to the poor and favour those who are better off. Based on their analysis, the authors then suggest that unless better-off groups can be encouraged to use private service providers, especially at the secondary and tertiary levels, it is difficult to envisage how government education subsidies can be better targeted to the poor. Another study by Li et al. (1999) provided similar results. In that study, in Côte d'Ivoire, Nepal, Nicaragua, and Vietnam, the richest 20% of the population receive more than 30% of all public education expenditure. Lanjouw and Ravallion (1999) introduced the distinction between average and marginal benefit in BIA. They used cross-sectional data to assess the extent to which the marginal benefit incidence of primary school spending differs from the average incidence. They regress the "odds of enrollment" (defined as the ratio of the quintile-specific enrollment rate to that of the population as a whole) against the instrumented mean enrollment ratio (the instrument being the average enrollment rate without the quintile in question). The estimated coefficient is termed as 10 "benefit capture", which indicates the extent to which there is early capture by the rich of primary schools. Under these circumstances, any increase in the average enrollment rate is likely to come from proportionately greater increases in enrollment among the poorer quintiles. That would lead to higher marginal gains for the poor from additional primary school spending than the gains indicated by the existing enrollments across the quintiles. Whereas the poorest quintile gains just 14% of the existing primary education subsidy in rural India, they would most likely receive 22% of any additional spending. This result suggested that caution is needed in drawing policy conclusions from average benefit incidence results. The distributional impact depends on how the money is actually spent. In a recent study on BIA on education in the Philippines by Manasan et al. (2007), the results indicated that the distribution of education spending is progressive at the elementary and secondary level, using national averages. On the contrary, it is regressive for the intermediate and college-level. Extending the analysis to the local government units (LGUs) demonstrates that the urban areas usually attract higher subsidies compared to the rural areas. In the context of India, a major study on the BIA in the health sector has been carried out by Mahal et al. (2001). A broad finding by Mahal et al. (2001) was that the publicly financed health services in India continue to represent the best method for providing critical services for the poor, and that some subnational governments in India are able to ensure that public financing is not skewed to the rich. This expands the literature on benefit incidence of health spending in India. Chakraborty et al. (2013) and Bhadra (2016) analysed the benefit incidence of health spending and identified the inequities in fiscal policy related to health sector.

The Public Expenditure Benefit Incidence Analysis (BIA) Methodology

Abstract Following (Demery, 2000), there are four basic steps towards calculating benefit incidence.

Estimating Unit Cost

The unit cost of a publicly provided good is estimated by dividing the total expenditure on that particular publicly provided good by the total number of users of that good. This is synonymous to the notion of per capita expenditure, but the denominator is confined to the subset of population who are the users of the public good. For instance, the unit cost of the elementary education sector is total primary education spending per primary enrollment, while the unit cost of the health sector could be total outpatient hospital spending per outpatient visit.

Identifying the Users

Usually the information on the users of publicly provided goods are obtained from household surveys with the standard dichotomy of data into poor and non-poor, male and female headed households, rural and urban and so on.

Aggregating Users into Groups

It is important to aggregate individuals or households into groups to estimate how the benefits from public spending are distributed across the population. Empirical evidence has shown that the most frequent method of grouping is based on income quintiles or monthly per capita expenditure (mpce) quintiles. The aggregation of users based on income or mpce quintiles could reveal whether the distribution of public expenditure is progressive or regressive. The spatial differentials in the public expenditure delivery though cannot be fully captured through the rural–urban dichotomy, it can provide broad policy pointers with regard to the distributional impact of publicly provided goods across rural and urban India. Yet another significant grouping is based on gender, after or before categorizing the unit utilized based on geographical units. The grouping of users based on gender is often ignored in studies on benefit incidence analysis.

Calculating the Benefit Incidence

Benefit incidence is computed by combining information about the *unit costs* of providing the publicly provided good with information on the *use* of these goods.

Mathematically, benefit incidence is estimated by the following formula:

$$X_j \equiv \sum_i U_{ij} \left(\frac{S_i}{U_i} \right) \equiv \sum_i \left(\frac{U_{ij}}{U_i} \right) S_i \equiv \sum_i e_{ij} S_i$$

where X_j = sector-specific subsidy enjoyed by group j; U_{ij} = utilization of service i by group j; U_i = utilization of service i by all groups combined; S_i = government net expenditure on service i; and e_{ij} = group j's share of utilization of service i.

International Classification of Diseases (ICD)—Benefit Incidence

Using the CSO National Sample Survey data for units utilized and the budget data for expenditure in health sector, the benefit incidence of health sector expenditure can be calculated. The latest data on health is collated from the Household Social Consumption related to Health during the period July 2017 to June 2018 as a part of 75th round of National Sample Survey (NSS) conducted by the National Statistical Office (NSO), Ministry of Statistics and Programme Implementation. The survey covered 1,13,823 households (64,552 in rural areas and 49,271 in urban areas), covering 5,55,115 persons (3,25,883 in rural areas and 2,29,232 in urban areas), following a scientific survey methodology. The benefit incidence analysis of health sector categorized by the International Classification of Diseases (ICD) is taken up in this chapter. The mapping of International Classification of Diseases (ICD) to National Sample Survey is plausible only for a few codes. Table 10.1 provides the ICD-NSS mapping of classification of diseases.

The treatment seeking behaviour by systems of medicine revealed that in both rural and urban India, 95% of ailments were treated by allopathy. As per the 75th round 2019 National Sample Survey (NSS) round on social consumption—health round—the proportion of persons treated as inpatient (365 day period) was 2.6% for rural males and 2.7% for rural females. In urban India, 3.4% of males and 3.5% of females were

Table 10.1 WHO International Classification of Diseases (ICD) to Indian National Sample Survey Mapping

	WHO International Classification of Disease-10 version	National Sample Survey, India
I	Certain infectious and parasitic diseases	Infection (Codes 01–12)
II	Neoplasms	Cancers (Code 13)
III	Diseases of the blood and blood-forming organs and certain disorders involving the immune mechanism	Blood diseases (Codes 14 and 15)
IV	Endocrine, nutritional, and metabolic diseases	Endocrine, metabolic, nutritional (Codes 16–19)
V	Mental and behavioural disorders	Psychiatric and Neurological (Codes 20–26)
VI	Diseases of the nervous system	NA
VII	Diseases of the eye and adnexa	Eye (Codes 27–31)
VIII	Diseases of the ear and mastoid process	Ear (Codes 32 and 33)
IX	Diseases of the circulatory system	Cardio-vascular (Codes 34 and 35)
X	Diseases of the respiratory system	Respiratory (36–38)
XI	Diseases of the digestive system	Gastrointestinal (Codes 39–42)
XII	Diseases of the skin and subcutaneous tissue	Skin (Code 43)
XIII	Diseases of the musculoskeletal system and connective tissue	Musculoskeletal (Codes 44 and 45)
XIV	Diseases of the genitourinary system	Genitourinary (Codes 46–48)
XV	Pregnancy, childbirth, and the puerperium	Obstetric (Codes 49–51)
XVI	Certain conditions originating in the perinatal period	NA
XVII	Congenital malformations, deformations, and chromosomal abnormalities	NA
XVIII	Symptoms, signs, and abnormal clinical and laboratory findings, not elsewhere classified	NA
XIX	Injury, poisoning, and certain other consequences of external causes	Injuries (Codes 52–58)
XX	External causes of morbidity and mortality	Injuries (Codes 59, 60, and 88)

(continued)

Table 10.1 (continued)

	WHO International Classification of Disease-10 version	National Sample Survey, India
XXI	Factors influencing health status and contact with health services	NA
XXII	Special purposes	NA

Note The ICD-11, the eleventh revision of the International Classification of Diseases will officially come into effect on January 2021
Source WHO https://icd.who.int/en and Government of India (2019), National Sample Survey 75th Round on Health

treated as inpatient. Within the persons who did seek inpatient treatment, among persons aged above 60 years, in rural India, it was 8.6% for rural males and 6.8% for rural females. At aggregate levels, it was 7.7% for rural India and 10.2% for urban India (11.6% for urban males and 8.8% for urban females). In India, it was 8.5% in India aggregate, with 9.6% for males and 7.5% for females. Disaggregated by the type of hospital, public hospitals accounted for 42% (46% in rural areas, 35% in urban areas) and private hospitals (excluding charitable and NGO-run) accounted for 55% (52% in rural areas, 61% in urban areas) in the inpatient hospitalization (excluding childbirth). The health seeking behaviour of people as per the 2019 National Sample survey 75th round on health, showed that government hospitals formed the healthcare service provider for treatment of 30% ailments (33% in rural, 26% in urban) while private hospitals provided care for 23% ailments (21% in rural, 27% in urban). In addition to this, private doctors/clinics provided health service in case of 43% ailments (41% in rural, 44% in urban) and informal healthcare provider and charitable/trust/NGO-run hospitals provided health care in case of remaining 4.1% of ailments (5.2% in rural, 2.2% in urban). Table 10.2 shows the relative share of the public expenditure captured across different income quintiles. The quintile-wise analysis of 75th round on health by National Sample Survey 2019 data showed that 32.3% of women in q5 was hospitalized for treatment as compared to 11.6% in q1 (Table 10.3). The unit utilized in q1 is relatively higher in urban India for women (16.2).

The average medical expenditure per hospitalization case (excluding childbirth) in rural India is about Rs. 16,676 and Rs. 26,475 in urban India, as per 2019 NSS 75th round on health. In public hospitals, the

Table 10.2 Unit Utilized in Health Sector: As per income quintiles across gender, India 2019

	Rural		Urban	
	Male	Female	Male	Female
Q1	11.6	14.1	16.2	16.2
Q2	14.3	13.6	17.7	20.2
Q3	19.1	18.6	21.6	21.2
Q4	22.6	22.4	21.3	20.8
Q5	32.3	31.3	23.1	21.6
All	100	100	100	100

Source Government of India (2019), National Sample Survey 75th Round on Health

expenditure was about Rs. 4452 (approximately Rs. 4290 in rural and Rs. 4837 in urban areas). In private hospitals the expenditure was about Rs. 31,845 (about Rs. 27,347 in rural and Rs. 38,822 in urban areas). The 2019 national sample survey on health reported that only 14% of the rural population and 19% of the urban population reported that they had health expenditure coverage. Only 13% of rural and 9% of urban population reported that they were covered by Government sponsored health insurance. About 1% of rural population reported that they were covered by health insurance arranged by government/PSU as employer/employer-supported health protection schemes. Only 6% of urban population reported that they were covered by health insurance arranged by Government/PSU as employer or employer-supported health protection schemes. Only 4% of urban population reported that they were covered by health insurance arranged by the households with insurance companies. Table 10.4 shows that average medical expenses was highest in Chandigarh (Rs. 2090) and lowest in Lakshadweep (Rs. 141) for ambulatory services (non-hospitalized treatment). The all India average for medical expenses incurred by women was Rs. 621 as compared to Rs. 655 for men for non-hospitalized treatment. The gender gap is wider for rural India.

The benefit incidence analysis requires unit costs and unit utilized components. The disease-specific unit utilized analysis revealed that infections (ICD-I) and injuries (ICD-XIX) constitute the significant cause for hospitalization for men; while it was infections and gastro-intestinal (ICD-IX) cause was for women in rural and urban India (Table 10.4).

Table 10.3 Average medical expenditure for Ambulatory Health Services across Indian States, 2019 (in Rs.)

	Rural			Urban			Total		
	M	F	All	M	F	All	M	F	All
Andhra Pradesh	459	404	428	517	702	614	481	505	494
Arunachal Pradesh	1201	1233	1214	2017	2236	2097	1370	1417	1388
Assam	1064	853	963	1193	743	895	1089	816	944
Bihar	630	1015	806	739	1566	1159	644	1096	854
Chhattisgarh	342	329	335	624	573	605	434	378	406
Delhi	1	915	255	870	774	825	853	776	817
Goa	417	344	386	443	318	389	431	329	388
Gujarat	401	303	350	627	545	584	516	428	469
Haryana	922	487	665	828	886	856	880	626	740
Himachal Pradesh	638	1114	887	585	363	445	632	983	821
Jammu & Kashmir	379	375	376	306	402	368	359	383	374
Jharkhand	703	733	719	1056	973	1006	777	797	788
Karnataka	554	540	546	753	627	690	656	580	616
Kerala	467	402	432	664	466	545	545	431	480
Madhya Pradesh	795	759	775	730	1237	992	773	912	847
Maharashtra	527	529	528	679	655	666	613	599	605
Manipur	1071	1064	1067	1580	1121	1345	1270	1084	1171
Meghalaya	1240	187	661	1601	0	1162	1265	182	683
Mizoram	603	584	600	1088	1045	1065	787	942	843
Nagaland	813	164	444	1304	690	1148	1168	376	868
Odisha	561	540	550	566	499	534	562	531	547
Punjab	618	555	584	653	696	677	629	604	616
Rajasthan	740	944	842	890	778	820	774	889	836
Sikkim	707	474	545	937	630	763	805	520	620
Tamil Nadu	556	447	504	669	629	647	598	527	562
Telangana	545	535	539	692	638	671	632	573	602
Tripura	993	1092	1037	1648	1139	1339	1134	1108	1121
Uttarakhand	322	344	335	903	578	734	705	487	587
Uttar Pradesh	862	684	762	1039	1087	1065	910	785	840
West Bengal	596	542	566	621	697	662	606	598	602
A & N Islands	29	3	12	440	1028	743	213	317	276
Chandigarh	2669	1950	1968	913	2095	1490	914	2090	1497
Dadra & Nagar Haveli	107	115	113	420	619	529	266	311	294
Daman & Diu	829	419	760	347	728	601	391	725	607
Lakshadweep	44	11	22	232	175	195	197	141	160

(continued)

Table 10.3 (continued)

	Rural			Urban			Total		
	M	F	All	M	F	All	M	F	All
Puducherry	125	93	108	1469	389	783	869	285	521
All India	621	567	592	711	710	710	655	621	636

Source Government of India (2019), National Sample Survey 75th Round on Health

The unit utilized data as per 2019 NSS rounds on health showed that in rural India about 90% of childbirths were institutional (69% were in Government hospitals and about 21% in private hospital) and in urban areas it was about 96% (48% were in each of Government hospitals and private hospitals). Surgery was done in about 28% of hospital childbirths in India (24% in rural India and 41% in urban India). In public hospitals, only about 17% of childbirths were surgery cases and over 92% were provided free. In private hospitals, about 55% of childbirths were surgery cases and only 1% was provided free. As per the Sample Registration System (SRS) report by Registrar General of India (RGI), Maternal Mortality Ratio (MMR) of India has reduced from 130 per 100,000 live births in SRS 2014–2016 to 122 in SRS 2015–2017 and to 113 per 100,000 live births in SRS 2016–2018. The unit cost data based on NSS 2019 75th health rounds showed that the average expenditure per hospital childbirth was about Rs. 2404 in public and Rs. 20,788 in private hospitals in rural India. It was Rs. 3106 in public and Rs. 29,105 in private hospitals in urban areas. For a normal delivery, average expenditure per childbirth in a Government hospital was about Rs. 2084 in rural and Rs. 2459 in urban India. For a normal delivery, average expenditure per childbirth in a private hospital was about Rs. 12,931 in rural and Rs. 17,960 in urban areas. For a caesarean delivery, average expenditure in a Government hospital was around Rs. 5423 in rural and Rs. 5504 in urban areas. For a caesarean delivery, average expenditure in a private hospital was around Rs. 29,406 in rural and Rs. 37,508 in urban areas.

The NSS data on immunization as per 2019 among children aged 0–5 years showed that approximately 97% of both boys and girls had received vaccination in rural India. About 98% of boys and 97% of girls had received vaccination in urban India. About 59% of boys and 60% of girls at all India level had been fully immunized, receiving all 8 prescribed

Table 10.4 Disease-specific Morbidity: Unit Utilized Pattern of Hospitalization across Plausible ICD-10 Mapping, India 2019

International Classification of Diseases (ICD-10 version)	Rural			Urban			Total		
	M	F	All	M	F	All	M	F	All
ICD-I	31.3	31	31	31.4	32	32	31.3	32	31
ICD-XIX	16.6	7.3	12	13.1	5.9	9.6	15.3	6.8	11
ICD-IX	9.2	12	10	7.8	10	9	8.7	11	9.9
ICD-IX	8.9	7.2	8.1	12.3	9.8	11	10.1	8.1	9.1
ICD-XIV	5.2	6.2	5.7	5.7	6.8	6.3	5.4	6.5	5.9
ICD-V	6.4	5	5.7	6.1	5.4	5.7	6.3	5.1	5.7
ICD-III	4.2	4.7	4.5	3.5	5.1	4.3	4	4.8	4.4
ICD-X	4.4	3.7	4.1	4.6	4.4	4.5	4.5	3.9	4.2
ICD-VII	3	4.2	3.6	3.5	3.4	3.5	3.2	4	3.6
ICD-XV	0.8	7.5	4	0.5	4.5	2.4	0.7	6.4	3.5
Other	10	11	11	11.5	13	12	10.5	12	11
All	100	100	100	100	100	100	100	100	100

Source Government of India (2019), National Sample Survey 75th Round on Health

vaccinations. As per the 2019 NSS data, about 82% of males and 47% of females of 60 years and above were living with their spouses; and about 94% of males and 91% of females of 60 years and above were physically mobile.

Quintile-Wise Benefit Incidence and Polarization Ratio

It is difficult to measure targeting errors—type 1 (inclusion error) and type 2 (exclusion error)—of public expenditure on the health sector from a benefit incidence analysis. However, benefit incidence analysis is useful to minimize such errors in targeting. The quintile-wise benefit incidence estimates can reveal trends that support that the public health system is "seemingly" more equitable if the unit utilized figures are relatively higher for lower-income quintiles. The regressivity in the pattern of utilization of public healthcare services is observed when higher income quintiles capture significant benefits of public spending. Both these results were to be considered with caution, due to two reasons. One, the underdeveloped market for private inpatient care in some states might be the factor for disproportionate crowding-in of inpatients, which made the public healthcare system simply appear more equitable, especially among the lowest income quintiles, with the "voting with feet" to better private services seems possible only for the affordable higher income quintiles. Chakraborty et al. (2013). Two, the coexistence of well performing public and private sectors of health might be the reason that the utilization pattern of public healthcare system could be regressive.

The unit record data analysis of quintile-wise benefit incidence was conducted for the 71st National Sample Survey round on health, due to the unavailability of required unit record data for the recent round. Polarization ratio is the ratio of the share of the uppermost quintile, Q5, and the bottom quintile, Q1. It translates what is happening in terms of utilization at the two extreme tails. Polarization ratio captures the extent of the "exit" of the rich to the private sector and the access of the poorest to public provisioning of health care. The lower the polarization ratio, the higher the benefit skewed towards the lower quintiles, which means the greater the polarization. Table 10.5 provides the polarization ratio of utilization of health services across International Classification of Disease (ICD-10 version) codes. It also showed a seemingly equal utilization of services across gender, with high ratio of men comparative to women.

Table 10.5 Polarization Ratio

ICD	Rural male	Rural female	Urban male	Urban female
ICD-I: Certain infectious and parasitic diseases	2.01	2.15	1.54	1.57
ICD-II: Neoplasms	3.49	4.80	3.31	3.47
ICD-III: Diseases of the blood and blood-forming organs and certain disorders involving the immune mechanism	3.69	1.36	2.69	1.63
ICD-IV: Endocrine, nutritional, and metabolic diseases	8.33	3.65	3.53	2.57
ICD-V and VI: Mental and behavioural disorders, and Diseases of the nervous system	2.78	2.12	1.33	0.94
ICD-VII: Diseases of the eye and adnexa	1.31	2.75	2.58	1.90
ICD: VIII: Diseases of the ear and mastoid process	11.11	10.69	3.13	4.36
ICD-IX: Diseases of the circulatory system	3.64	5.65	4.39	3.53
ICD-X: Diseases of the respiratory system	2.45	1.91	1.61	1.44
ICD-XI: Diseases of the digestive system	2.40	1.81	2.83	1.75
ICD-XII: Diseases of the skin and subcutaneous tissue	0.81	2.17	9.13	0.46
ICD-XIII: Diseases of the musculoskeletal system and connective tissue	2.78	5.54	3.63	4.00
ICD-XIV: Diseases of the genitourinary system	4.07	3.68	4.42	2.26
ICD-XV and XVI: Pregnancy, childbirth and the puerperium, and Certain conditions originating in the perinatal period	0.97	0.52	0.85	0.63

(continued)

Table 10.5 (continued)

ICD	Rural male	Rural female	Urban male	Urban female
ICD-XIX: Injury, poisoning, and certain other consequences of external causes	2.86	1.10	1.02	0.03
ICD-XX: External causes of morbidity and mortality	2.50	0.84	1.84	0.65
ICD-XXI: Factors influencing health status and contact with health services	1.41	1.63	2.23	1.77
All ICD Combined	1.62	1.49	2.22	1.51

Source Government of India (2015), National Sample Survey Round on Health

Table 10.6 provides ICD-specific quintile-wise behavioural access to public health care provisioning across gender in urban and rural India. Only 1.85% of total male population in Q1 category of urban India accessed public health care (hospitalization). In rural India, 4.64% of the male population belong to Q1 category accessed health care (inpatient). Women in rural India accessed public health care (inpatient) more than in urban India, in all income quintiles. 9.74% of women in Q5 accessed public health care (Table 10.6). The disaggregated disease-specific benefit incidence across income quintiles for women and men in rural and urban India is also incorporated in detail in Table 10.6 as per the ICD codes (ICD-10 version).

Against this backdrop, the benefit incidence of public expenditure is analyzed by the depiction of concentration curves, for aggregate as well as disaggregated categories in the inpatient category as per the International Classification of Diseases—(ICD-10). The auxiliary identifiers used for the analysis are gender and geography. The ethnic groups (socio-economic categories) are not included due to lack of sufficient observations. It is clearly revealed from the concentration curves that people in the quintiles Q1 and Q2, especially in the rural areas, are utilizing the public provisioning of health care across ICD codes disproportionately from the upper income quintiles. The seemingly regressive pattern of incidence for the urban sector may reflect the utilization of private sector healthcare facilities. As the incidence lines are below the 45 degree line for almost all the ICD codes which reveals pro-poor benefit

Table 10.6 Quintile-wise Behavioural Access to Health Care in Rural and Urban India Across Gender

Quintile	Rural male	Rural female	Urban male	Urban female
All ICD Combined (per cent to total)				
Q1	4.64	6.54	1.85	3.11
Q2	4.04	6.53	2.67	3.68
Q3	4.43	6.6	2.82	4.37
Q4	6.4	8.72	3.16	4.34
Q5	7.53	9.74	4.11	4.7
Certain infectious and parasitic diseases (ICD-I) (per cent to total)				
Q1	4.83	4.07	2.44	2.35
Q2	5.47	4.86	3.7	3.26
Q3	6.61	5.19	3.96	3.54
Q4	8.18	8.25	3.75	3.69
Q5	9.71	8.72	3.76	3.67
Neoplasms (ICD-II) (per cent to total)				
Q1	2.32	3.15	1.37	1.69
Q2	3.09	5.5	2.53	2.94
Q3	2.95	3.24	1.42	2.97
Q4	4.16	20.6	3.25	5.19
Q5	8.1	15.1	4.55	5.86
Diseases of the blood and blood-forming organs and certain disorders involving the immune mechanism (ICD-III) (per cent to total)				
Q1	2.28	8.87	1.39	3.16
Q2	3.77	3.14	2.32	4.97
Q3	4.1	11.12	1.25	3.43
Q4	6.19	7.79	2.27	4.6
Q5	8.43	12.06	3.74	5.15
Endocrine, nutritional, and metabolic diseases (ICD-IV) (per cent to total)				
Q1	1.66	3.11	1.35	2.83
Q2	1.96	3.57	3.78	3.74
Q3	2.39	5.99	3.05	5.6
Q4	6.46	8.09	3.47	5.77
Q5	13.79	11.36	4.78	7.27
Mental and behavioural disorders (ICD-V), and Diseases of the nervous system (ICD-VI) (per cent to total)				
Q1	3.8	4.7	3.75	3.35
Q2	3.51	5.29	4.32	3.2
Q3	6.16	3.65	3.82	4.09
Q4	6.98	7.49	4.3	2.95
Q5	10.55	9.95	5	3.15

(continued)

Table 10.6 (continued)

Quintile	Rural male	Rural female	Urban male	Urban female
Diseases of the eye and adnexa (ICD-VII) (per cent to total)				
Q1	6.08	5.43	1.53	2
Q2	6	4.03	2.57	2.75
Q3	4.45	4.78	1.82	3.13
Q4	7.05	8	3.04	6.74
Q5	7.99	14.9	3.93	3.8
Diseases of the ear and mastoid process (ICD-VIII) (per cent to total)				
Q1	1.3	1.51	1.52	1.79
Q2	4.81	2.31	5.01	1.39
Q3	1.93	1.3	6.94	4.25
Q4	3.77	8.28	6.82	4.02
Q5	14.41	16.09	4.76	7.79
Diseases of the circulatory system (ICD-IX) (per cent to total)				
Q1	3.94	1.7	1.99	2.33
Q2	2.76	2.93	3.67	2.74
Q3	3.28	4.83	4.26	3.34
Q4	6.33	4.81	5.03	5.15
Q5	14.36	9.61	8.73	8.23
Diseases of the respiratory system (ICD-X) (per cent to total)				
Q1	4.24	5.86	2.71	2.71
Q2	5.65	4.5	2.82	3
Q3	5.93	3.96	3.34	3.13
Q4	8.03	7.14	3.74	3.38
Q5	10.39	11.21	4.37	3.9
Diseases of the digestive system (ICD-XI) (per cent to total)				
Q1	3.61	5.49	1.9	2.67
Q2	3.94	6.27	2.97	3.63
Q3	4.15	5.07	3.56	3.79
Q4	9.1	8.11	3.46	3.6
Q5	8.65	9.97	5.38	4.67
Diseases of the skin and subcutaneous tissue (ICD-XII) (per cent to total)				
Q1	7.41	4.27	0.71	8.33
Q2	7.33	4.12	2.37	2.04
Q3	6.45	2.59	3.67	2.53
Q4	7.91	7.9	3.27	3.57
Q5	5.98	9.27	6.46	3.82
Diseases of the musculoskeletal system and connective tissue (ICD-XIII) (per cent to total)				
Q1	3.93	2.63	1.34	1.61
Q2	3.39	3.33	2.89	2.57
Q3	5.18	5.66	2.98	2.19
Q4	7.98	11.08	2.62	3.87
Q5	10.94	14.55	4.85	6.41

(continued)

Table 10.6 (continued)

Quintile	Rural male	Rural female	Urban male	Urban female
Diseases of the genitourinary system (ICD-XIV) (per cent to total)				
Q1	2.65	3.56	1.02	2.61
Q2	3.07	5.19	2.48	3.49
Q3	3.63	4.2	3.11	5.49
Q4	6.28	8.41	3.33	7.2
Q5	10.79	13.1	4.49	5.92
Pregnancy, childbirth and the puerperium (ICD-XV), and Certain conditions originating in the perinatal period (ICD-XVI) (per cent to total)				
Q1	1.75	18.39	0.47	5.6
Q2	0.99	13.35	0.85	4.14
Q3	1.17	10.57	0.62	3.94
Q4	1.39	15.11	0.81	5.61
Q5	1.69	9.64	0.4	3.51
Injury, poisoning, and certain other consequences of external causes (ICD-XIX) (per cent to total)				
Q1	3.95	2.99	1.88	2.1
Q2	8.29	17.45	2.8	1.73
Q3	5.17	12.28	1.37	1.53
Q4	12.52	6.65	0.94	1.76
Q5	11.29	3.31	1.93	0.07
External causes of morbidity and mortality (ICD-XX) (per cent to total)				
Q1	1.27	13.18	0.6	5.37
Q2	1.27	12.38	1	5.6
Q3	1.54	10.77	0.95	4.85
Q4	3.07	13.78	1.24	4.23
Q5	3.17	11.13	1.11	3.48
Factors influencing health status and contact with health services (ICD-XXI) (per cent to total)				
Q1	5.49	5.67	2.05	2.79
Q2	4.52	5.72	2.86	3.44
Q3	4.86	6.13	3.05	4.5
Q4	6.79	7.78	3.44	4.34
Q5	7.74	9.26	4.58	4.95

Source Government of India (2015), National Sample Survey 75th Round on Health

capture of health services. Exception to this trend is noted for ICD-XX, ICD-XIX, ICD-XV, ICD-XVI, ICD-XII ICD-V, and ICD-VI.

Figure 10.2 revealed a pattern of concentration curves below the line of equality, which shows that the overall benefit incidence (all ICD combined) favours pro-rich. However, below the line of equality, it is

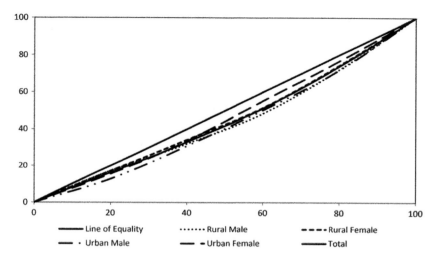

Fig. 10.2 Gender Differential in Benefit Incidence: All ICD Combined (*Source* Government of India [2015], National Sample Survey 75th Round on Health)

pertinent to dichotomize the incidence of spending into progressive and regressive patterns based on the threshold curve. The overall pattern of most of the concentration curves of ICD combined revealed that all the categories except the incidence of rural women exhibit a regressive pattern of public spending on health, as they are below the threshold curve. In the case of incidence of rural women, the striking feature of incidence is the crossover of the curve in utilizing the public health provisioning, at the aggregate level, though the case cannot be referred to as pro-poor spending as the concentration curves are not above line of equality.

It is pertinent to analyse the concentration curves at the disaggregated levels as per each ICD codes. In case of ICD-I, the pattern revealed a clear pro-rich incidence across all categories across region and gender. However rural incidence across gender showed a progressive pattern (Fig. 10.3).

In case of ICD-II also, a clear pro-rich incidence is noted for all categories. Only rural women showed a progressive pattern. This seemingly progressive pattern of rural women accessing public sector needs to be read with caution as the access to public care provisioning might have been determined by lack of access to private sector services due to high costs (Fig. 10.4).

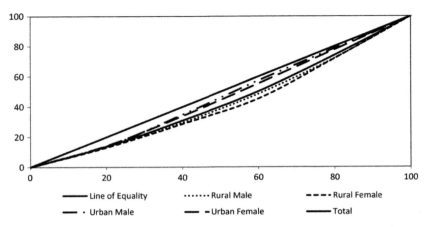

Fig. 10.3 Gender Differential in Benefit Incidence: Certain infectious and parasitic diseases (ICD-I) (*Source* Government of India [2015], National Sample Survey 75th Round on Health)

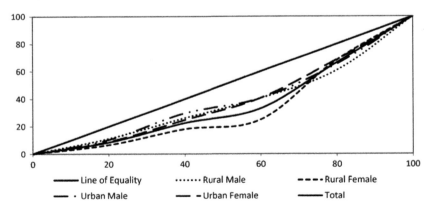

Fig. 10.4 Gender Differential in Benefit Incidence: Neoplasms (ICD-II) (*Source* Government of India [2015], National Sample Survey 75th Round on Health)

In case of ICD-III, the gender differential pattern of benefit incidence is pro-rich. A crossover is noted for the benefit incidence of public spending by rural and urban women. The incidence of rural men is clearly showing a regressive pattern of incidence (Fig. 10.5).

In case of ICD-IV, only the incidence of rural men showed a regressive pattern (Fig. 10.6). The incidence of rural men and women is above the threshold curve, which indicates progressivity. However, as no curves are above the line of equality (45 degree line), the pattern in general is highly a pro-rich incidence indicating rich quintiles accessing the benefits more than the poor income quintiles.

In case of ICD-VI, the incidence of rural women showed a crossover with the line of equality indicating a mild pro-poor incidence (Fig. 10.7). However in case of other categories, the incidence is progressive except for incidence pattern of rural men. There is a crossover with benchmark curve for incidence of rural women.

In case of ICD-VII, aggregate incidence pattern is pro-rich as there is no curve above the line of equality (Fig. 10.8). A mild crossover is noted for incidence of rural women. The pattern of benefit incidence of rural men is highly regressive as it is significantly below the benchmark curve.

In case of ICD-VIII, the broad incidence pattern is pro-rich as all curves are below the line of equality (Fig. 10.9). A regressive pattern of benefit incidence is noted for rural women in ICD-VIII.

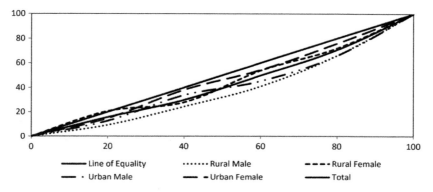

Fig. 10.5 Gender Differential in Benefit Incidence: Diseases of the blood and blood-forming organs and certain disorders involving the immune mechanism (ICD-III) (*Source* Government of India [2015], National Sample Survey 75th Round on Health)

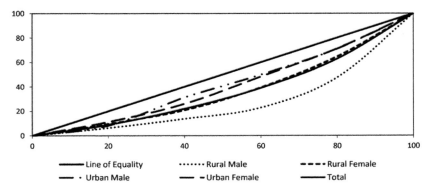

Fig. 10.6 Gender Differential in Benefit Incidence: Endocrine, nutritional, and metabolic diseases (ICD-IV) (*Source* Government of India [2015], National Sample Survey 75th Round on Health)

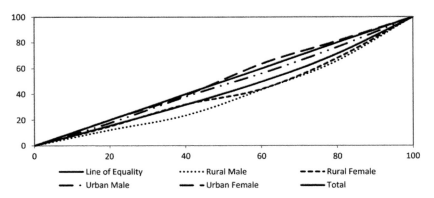

Fig. 10.7 Gender Differential in Benefit Incidence: Mental and behavioural disorders (ICD-V), and Diseases of the nervous system (ICD-VI) (*Source* Government of India [2015], National Sample Survey 75th Round on Health)

In case of ICD-IX, the benefit incidence is distinctly pro-rich (Fig. 10.10). All the curves lie below closer to the threshold curve which shows the regressivity in the pattern of incidence across urban and rural India in accessing services relate to cardio diseases.

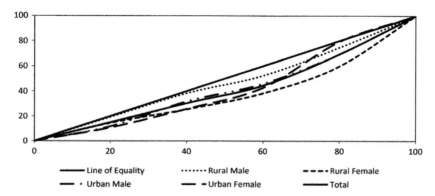

Fig. 10.8 Gender Differential in Benefit Incidence: Diseases of the eye and adnexa (ICD-VII) (*Source* Government of India [2015], National Sample Survey 75th Round on Health)

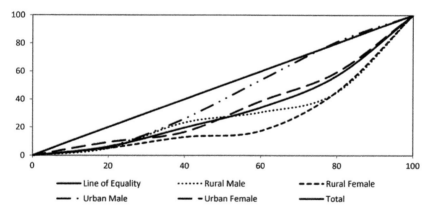

Fig. 10.9 Gender Differential in Benefit Incidence: Diseases of the ear and mastoid process (ICD-VIII) (*Source* Government of India [2015], National Sample Survey 75th Round on Health)

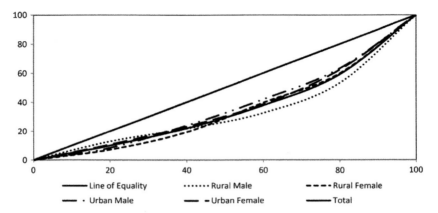

Fig. 10.10 Gender Differential in Benefit Incidence: Diseases of the circulatory system (ICD-IX) (*Source* Government of India [2015], National Sample Survey 75th Round on Health)

In case of ICD-X, the pattern is highly pro-rich (Fig. 10.11). The gender differential benefit incidence shows a regressive pattern for rural men and women in accessing health service provisioning relate to respiratory system. However, urban India showed a progressive incidence across gender.

In case of ICD-XI, the benefit incidence is highly pro-rich as all the curves are below the 45 degree line of equality. The benefit incidence pattern of rural men showed regressivity in access towards health service related to digestive system as it is below the benchmark curve (Fig. 10.12).

In case of ICD-XII, rural male and female incidence shows pro-poor pattern as these curves are above 45 degree line of equality, meaning more people in poor income quintiles are accessing the health services than the rich income quintiles (Fig. 10.13). This behavioural pattern may be due to either the lack of adequate private provisioning of the private inpatient healthcare system in rural areas or the lack of a "voting with feet" option to purchase healthcare services from private providers of health care due to cost, particularly when poor households face health costs that imply financial catastrophe (Chakraborty et al., 2013). A pro-poor pattern of health spending, however, was not revealed for urban units in most of these ten states. The urban curves show a pattern of regressivity.

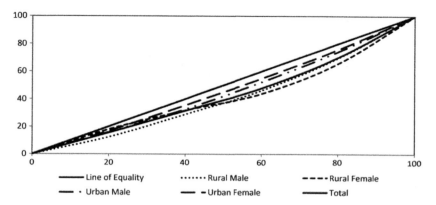

Fig. 10.11 Gender Differential in Benefit Incidence: Diseases of the respiratory system (ICD-X) (*Source* Government of India [2015], National Sample Survey 75th Round on Health)

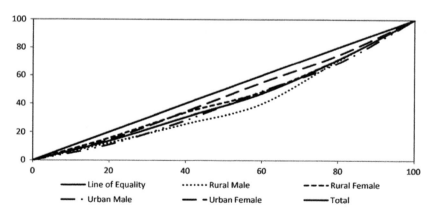

Fig. 10.12 Gender Differential in Benefit Incidence: Diseases of the digestive system (ICD-XI) (*Source* Government of India [2015], National Sample Survey 75th Round on Health)

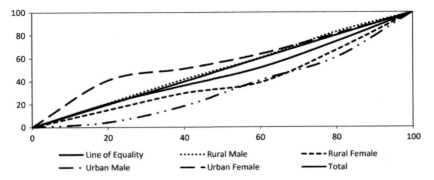

Fig. 10.13 Gender Differential in Benefit Incidence: Diseases of the skin and subcutaneous tissue (ICD-XII) (*Source* Government of India [2015], National Sample Survey 75th Round on Health)

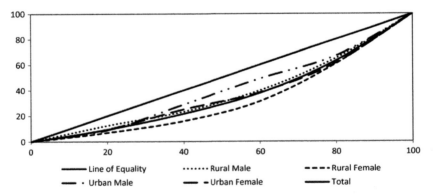

Fig. 10.14 Gender Differential in Benefit Incidence: Diseases of the musculoskeletal system and connective tissue (ICD-XIII) (*Source* Government of India [2015], National Sample Survey 75th Round on Health)

In case of ICD-XXI, the incidence across various categories revealed pro-rich capture of benefits. The rural female incidence shows that it is progressive as it is above the threshold incidence curve. However, the incidence of rural women and men showed a crossover pattern of incidence with respect to the threshold curve of incidence (Figs. 10.14–10.19).

To conclude, the analysis of concentration curves and quintile-specific ICD categories of benefit incidence broadly shows the unequal access

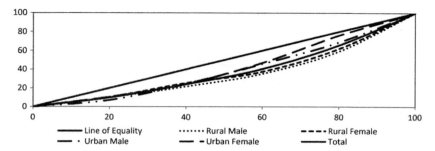

Fig. 10.15 Gender Differential in Benefit Incidence: Diseases of the genitourinary system (ICD-XIV) (*Source* Government of India [2015], National Sample Survey 75th Round on Health)

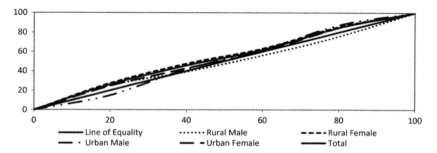

Fig. 10.16 Gender Differential in Benefit Incidence: Pregnancy, childbirth and the puerperium (ICD-XV), and Certain conditions originating in the perinatal period (ICD-XVI) (*Source* Government of India [2015], National Sample Survey 75th Round on Health)

to disease-wise health care by gender across rural and urban India. The inequality in treatment seeking behaviour has been aggravated by spurt in the average cost of inpatient care. The national health insurance scheme has not helped in improving the benefit incidence pattern towards progressivity. This is because as low as 14% of the rural population and 19% of the urban population reported that they had health expenditure coverage, as per the 2019 NSS 75th round on health. Only 13% of rural and 9% of urban population reported that they were covered by Government sponsored health insurance.

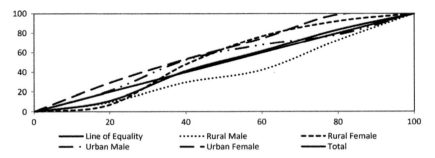

Fig. 10.17 Gender Differential in Benefit Incidence: Injury, poisoning, and certain other consequences of external causes (ICD-XIX) (*Source* Government of India [2015], National Sample Survey 75th Round on Health)

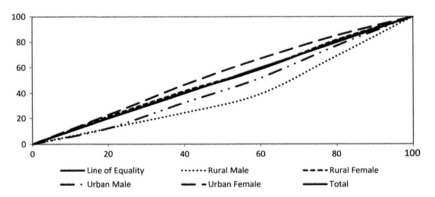

Fig. 10.18 Gender Differential in Benefit Incidence: External causes of morbidity and mortality (ICD-XX) (*Source* Government of India [2015], National Sample Survey 75th Round on Health)

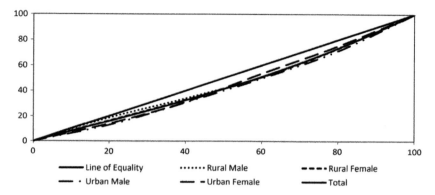

Fig. 10.19 Gender Differential in Benefit Incidence: Factors influencing health status and contact with health services (ICD-XXI) (*Source* Government of India [2015], National Sample Survey 75th Round on Health)

References

Bhadra, K. K. (2016). Inequality effects of fiscal policy: Analysing the benefit incidence on health sector in India. Working Papers. id:8433, eSocialSciences.

Castro-Leal, F., Dayton, U., Demery, L., & Mehra, K. (1999). Public social spending in Africa: Do the poor benefit? *The World Bank Research Observer, 14*(1), 49–72.

Chakraborty, L., Singh, Y., & Jacob, J. (2013). Analyzing public expenditure benefit incidence in health care: Evidence from India. (Working Papers Series no. 748). Levy Economics Institute.

Davoodi, H. R., Tiongson, E. R., & Asawanuchit, S. S. (2003). How useful are benefit incidence analysis of public education and health spending? (IMF Working Paper no. 03/227). International Monetary Fund.

Davoodi, H. R., Tiongson, E. R., & Asawanuchit, S. S. (2010). Benefit Incidence of Public Education and Health Spending Worldwide: Evidence From A New Database. *Poverty & Public Policy, 2*(2), 5–52.

Demery, L. (2000). *Benefit incidence: A practitioner's guide. Poverty and social development group.* World Bank.

Filmer, & Lant, H. P. (1998). Estimating wealth effects without expenditure data-or tears: An application to educational enrollments in states of India Deon. *Demography, 38*(1), 115–132.

Gillespie, W. I. (1965). Effect of public expenditures on the distribution of income. In R. Musgrave (Ed.), *Essays in fiscal federalism.* The Brookings Institution.

Lanjouw, P., & Ravallion, M. (1994). Poverty and Household Size (Policy Research. Working Paper Series 1332). The World Bank.

Lanjouw, P., & Ravallion, M. (1999). Benefit incidence, public spending reforms, and the timing of program capture. *World Bank Economic Review, 13*(2), 257–273.

Li, G., Steele, D., & Glewe, P. (1999). *Distribution of government education expenditures in developing countries. Preliminary estimates.* The World Bank.

Lustig, N. (2015). Fiscal policy, inequality and the poor in the developing world. Round 1. (CEQ Working Paper no. 23). Center for Inter-American Policy and Research and Department of Economics, Tulane University and Inter-American Dialogue.

Mahal, A., Singh, J., Afridi, F., Lamba, V., Gumber, A., & Selvaraju, V. (2001). *Who benefits from public sector health spending in India?* National Council for Applied Economic Research.

Manasan, R. G., Cuenca, J. S., & Villanueva, C. (2007). Benefit incidence of public spending on education in the Philippines. (Discussion Paper series no. 2007–09). Philippine Institute for Development Studies.

McLure, C. E. (1974). On the theory and methodology of estimating benefit and expenditure incidence. (Mimeo) Workshop on Income Distribution, Rice University.

Sahn, D. E., & Younger, S. (2000). Expenditure incidence in Africa: Microeconomic evidence. Fiscal Studies. *Institute for Fiscal Studies, 21*(3), 329–347.

Selden, T., & Wasylenko, M. (1992, June 17–19). Measuring the distributional effects of public education in Peru (Paper prepared for the World Bank Conference on Public Expenditure and the Poor: Incidence and Targeting).

Younger, S. (2002). Public social sector expenditures and poverty in Peru. In C. Morrisson (Ed.), Education and health expenditure, and development: The cases of Indonesia and Peru. Organization for Economic Co-operation and Development.

CHAPTER 11

COVID-19 Context and the Way Ahead

The COVID-19 pandemic has widened inequalities. As this crisis is of an unprecedented scale, it calls for unprecedented policy responses. However, it must be noted that the size of the economic stimulus largely depends upon the fiscal space. With many countries including in Asia Pacific region now preparing public finance strategies for the post-pandemic fiscal year, we now have a renewed opportunity to strengthen gender budgeting as an effective long-term public finance management (PFM) tool to redress these mounting inequalities. Gender budgeting is a fiscal policy innovation that translates gender-related commitments into fiscal commitments. Central banks and governments have responded to crisis with a range of fiscal and monetary policies. The structural reforms including labour market and lifeline infrastructure (including power sector) reforms are also strengthened across countries to avert the crisis mounting into a prolonged macroeconomic crisis. The economic stimulus packages have therefore two components; one that relates to instantaneous economic firefighting and the other on medium-term structural reforms. Applying a gender lens to these components revealed that there is a need to strengthen gender components in the social infrastructure, social protection, food security, and employment generation programmes (Chakraborty et al., 2021). Against this backdrop, the concluding chapter highlights the challenges and scope to strengthen gender budgeting as a long-term fiscal policy tool in the post-pandemic world to tackle inequalities.

Constraints of Rules-Based Policy Space

In the macro policymaking, in most countries, particularly in the emerging market economies, the fiscal and monetary policies are "rules-based". The Ministry of Finance of various countries have implemented rules-based fiscal responsibility and budget management mostly through legislations to maintain a threshold level of fiscal deficit to a fixed numerical per cent of GDP approximately at 3 per cent. In recent years, the Central Bank has moved towards a rule-based inflation targeting regime with price stability as the single objective of monetary policy. These rules may act as initial constraints to incorporate a "gender lens" in the macroeconomic policy frameworks. It is such that, when the policy framework is rules-based, there is a need to strengthen long-term PFM tools like gender budgeting for the response to the crisis.

Obsession with "Economic Growth" Frameworks

It is also an opportunity to set the macroeconomic policy response based on the beyond economic growth paradigm. It is important to go beyond GDP as economic growth per se does not translate into gender aware human development. Beyond GDP paradigm that incorporates Sustainable Development Goals (SDGs), supports inclusive development towards the 2030 SDG Agenda. The sustainability of this economic recovery from COVID-19 pandemic will depend on the fiscal policy measures a country has designed "like never before" to tackle this dual crisis—the public health crisis and the macroeconomic crisis. This macroeconomic uncertainty is hard to measure. The output gap—the gap between the potential and actual output—in times of COVID-19 pandemic is hard to measure (Chakraborty & Kaur, Why Output Gap is Controversial, 2020). The potential output is an unobserved variable. When the macroeconomic crises and recessions tend to "permanently" push down the level of a country's GDP, it is inappropriate to assume that output will bounce back to previous levels. The persistence of sluggish growth and weak macroeconomic recovery will in turn widen gender inequalities. The recessions are not followed by quick rebounds. The reasons for no quick rebound include chronic deficiency in demand, labour market challenges, legacies of debt crisis, productivity slowdown and decline in the equilibrium real interest rates.

FISCAL SUSTAINABILITY IN LOW INTEREST RATE REGIME

Fiscal sustainability rules are often based on threshold ratios of deficit to GDP, for instance, fiscal deficit to GDP ratio at 3 per cent is one of the norms for fiscal consolidation. If expenditure compression rather than tax buoyancy is the path towards fiscal consolidation, it affects the human development. It is also important to emphasise that in the low interest rate regime, high public debt has no significant fiscal costs (Blanchard, 2019). If real rate of interest is not greater than real rate of growth of economy, public debt is not catastrophic. If more public debt can be justified by clear benefits like public investment or gender aware human capital formation (Chakraborty, 2021). There is an increasing recognition of the fact that public investment has suffered from fiscal consolidation across advanced and emerging economies. Along with the upward revision of deficit threshold ratios, the countries in Asia Pacific may also think about an "excessive deficit procedure" to avoid fiscal profligacy in the long run. That is important, from the perspective of fiscal prudence in the long run. If the fiscal consolidation targets are achieved through expenditure compression rather than enhanced tax buoyancy, it will affect the quality of fiscal consolidation as it has adverse consequences on a gender-aware and rights-based fiscal policy stance in the long run.

STRENGTHENING FISCAL MARKSMANSHIP

Fiscal marksmanship—the deviation between what is announced in the budget and the actual spending—is a significant concern in Asia Pacific. The reasons for deviation can be bias or random. If the forecasting errors that led to deviations are random, then it is beyond the control of policymaker. However, if the reason for deviation is bias, then policymakers need to revise the assumptions and models they use for forecasts. The budget credibility and fiscal transparency are matters of urgent concern as it is crucial to analyse emergency pandemic programmes are translated into actual spending. The fiscal marksmanship of gender budgeting is analysed in the book using the ratios of budget estimates to actual spending. The significance of institutions like Fiscal Councils in such a context cannot be underestimated, to analyse and provide inputs relate to fiscal forecasting errors and the budget credibility. Against the backdrop of COVID-19 pandemic, as we are primarily facing a human tragedy, we may consider this crisis as an opportunity to try for establishing institutions like Fiscal Councils to monitor fiscal inputs to outcomes.

Innovative Financing of Deficits

It is not only the levels of deficits that matter for gender aware economic growth, the modes of financing the deficit is also significant. From a political economy perspective, excessive mode of financing the deficit has its own specific macroeconomic consequences. For instance, bond financing may trigger a financial crowding out. A seigniorage financing (print money to finance deficits) may be inflationary. So the choice over the financing pattern of deficits has both political economy imperatives and macroeconomic consequences. In the Asia Pacific region, fiscal conservatism determines the fiscal space for emergency pandemic programmes. A finite seigniorage financing of deficits—money financing of fiscal programmes—or a finite emergency pandemic bonds has not yet been incorporated to enhance the fiscal space in the region. Yet another method is to elongate the maturity structure of public debt to mitigate immediate refinancing risks, by changing the composition of debt from short-term bonds/securities to long term. The "operation twist" programme by the Indian central bank is one such initiative by simultaneously selling the short-term bonds and buying long-term bonds, to elongate the maturity structure of public debt. This flexibility in debt-deficit dynamics can give leverage to economic growth rather than taking an alternative route of expenditure compression. Some of the subnational governments in India has also gone for elongation of debt structure to support economic growth by shifting the refinancing risks to future.

Incorporating Unpaid Care Economy into Macro Policy

In future, it is pertinent to strengthen gender budgeting as an effective PFM tool to capture the issues in unpaid care economy. The COVID-19 pandemic has affected the lives and livelihoods of people and widened inequalities, including gender inequalities. The emergency pandemic packages are fiscal policy measures, which are short-term in nature.

The pandemic has disproportionate effects on unpaid care economy by increasing the work burden for women (D'Alessandro & Floro, 2021). The deficient public infrastructure even prior to pandemic has private costs in terms of time stress for women, which is analysed in the book. The care economy burden is one of the significant factors for low female labour force participation. The pandemic has aggravated this trend. The analysis of time-use survey statistics in the book based on 2020 Time-Use Survey published by Government of India can form a baseline analysis for capturing the covid-induced time poverty among men and women.

Acknowledging Intersectionality Issues in Gender Budgeting

In future, it is pertinent to explore long-term macro policy tools like gender budgeting in order to tackle the issues of violence against women. Gender budgeting—that integrates gender consciousness into fiscal policy frameworks—is an effective tool for accountability in Public Financial Management (PFM) in the time of the pandemic. However, gender budgeting needs to be strengthened by incorporating "intersectionality" issues. Rule of law is a public good. It is non-rival and non-excludable. The crime against women during the pandemic—a "shadow pandemic"—is increasingly acknowledged as a global problem with substantial macroeconomic costs.

Fiscal Decentralization: Move Ahead from "One Size Fits All" Gender Budgeting

It is incorrect to assume that gender budgeting is a top-down policy tool to redress gender inequalities. In future, the policy space at the local level of government needs to explore to its full potential to avoid the fallacies of "one size fits all" gender-budgeting policies. Fiscal decentralization is an essential prerequisite to gender budgeting at the local level. The policy space of feminization of governance is found to have positive impacts on designing public expenditure favouring women's revealed preferences. A few case studies of fiscal decentralization and gender budgeting are discussed in the book. The inference is that the principle of subsidiarity—the decisions to be taken at the level closest to people—is crucial in conducting gender budgeting.

Link Between Fiscal Policy and Gender Equality Outcomes

It is not the economic growth that gets translated into better gender aware human development. Using econometric models, the link between gender budgeting and gender equality outcomes are attempted in the book, controlling for economic growth, intergovernmental fiscal transfers and selected socio-economic variables. The inference reinforced the efficacy of gender budgeting on strengthening the gender equality outcomes. However these models are illustrative and the book has highlighted through case studies and qualitative analysis the significance of fiscal policy in achieving sustainable human development in Asia Pacific region.

Public Expenditure Tracking and Fiscal Incidence Analysis

It is important to track benefit incidence of public spending on human development—incorporating gender differentials—to understand the distributional impacts of fiscal policy. The public expenditure benefit incidence analysis of health sector is undertaken in the book with International Classification of Diseases (ICD) codes. The inferences clearly reveal the disease-specific access and utilization pattern across gender and geography in various income quintiles. The elements of elite benefit capture are found in benefit incidence analysis. The phenomenon of "voting with the feet" to private health sector is noted for higher income quintiles. This inference highlights that men and women in poor income quintiles depend on public health sector and strengthening health infrastructure in public sector is crucial for better health outcomes. The public expenditure tracking of a major credit-linked poverty eradication programme in India reveals that financial inclusion is crucial for women's financial empowerment. The access to credit is found to be more significant than cost of credit for women, as women prior to access to credit has engaged in Ponzi finance at exorbitant interest rates. However, in the ex post gender-budgeting analysis, the components relate to financial empowerment were relatively lesser than the budgetary allocations which reinforced the traditional roles of women like protective and social services. In future, more financial empowerment programmes need to be designed as part of gender budgeting.

Measuring Gender-Aware Human Development Outcomes

Measuring gender-aware human development outcomes is a challenge. The existing methodology of *equally distributed equivalent* was used to construct the gender development index, which was used in the econometric models in the book. This index is based on a harmonic mean construct of education, health and income, achieved by men and women with the weightage to their corresponding share in population, adjusted by a penalty to gender inequality. Another outcome variable used in the book is gender inequality index, which has technical issues as the women-specific variables are combined with gender-disaggregated variables. In future, the gender outcome indices need to be revised incorporating the care economy variables also. Strengthening gender budgeting by linking to outcomes is crucial. In the ex post framework, gender budgeting often gets confined to analysing financial inputs. Monitoring outputs rather than inputs is crucial.

Second Generation Reforms of Gender Budgeting

The second generation reforms of gender budgeting should include identification of gender needs across jurisdictions. Such spatial mapping of gender needs across jurisdictions is crucial to avoid the fallacy of aggregation. This requires a revolutionary approach across rural and urban units to link "resources to results". The existing fiscally decentralized experiments on gender budgeting are included in the book. However, such experiences are sporadic.

Integrating Gender in Intergovernmental Fiscal Mechanisms

Integrating gender in the intergovernmental fiscal transfers is an area which require more policy focus. The preliminary evidence from the analysis in the book reinforces the positive impact of such fiscal transfers on gender development outcomes. The design of such transfers can be conditional or unconditional in nature. The conditional transfers are designed for specific purpose and the funds are tied. While unconditional transfers ensure the flexibility of finances at the subnational level and strengthens fiscal autonomy as the funds are untied. However the expenditure prioritization for gender development outcome has to be done at the subnational level. The process to make this happen is to incorporate a gender criterion in the formula-based fiscal transfers. However, so far, no country has integrated gender as a criterion in statutory fiscal transfer formula. India has incorporated a gender-aware variable in the Fifteenth Finance Commission transfers while correcting for the demographic transition.

Gender Budgeting and Feminization U

Gender budgeting is a promising framework to increase women's labour force participation by designing care economy infrastructure and other supply-side interventions to ensure safe and secure mobility of women. The Feminisation U—that the female labour force participation initially decreases and then increases with economic growth—can be made operational through gender budget interventions in labour market. If the fastest and smartest way to increase GDP is to increase women's labour force participation, then gender budgeting needs to focus on care economy policies along with "employer of last resort" policies.

Strengthening Gender Budgeting on Taxation Side

Fiscal policies for sustainable development encompasses strategies for taxation, public expenditure, and intergovernmental fiscal transfers. Using taxation instruments to provide property entitlements for women is welcome. For instance, differential taxation rates for men and women in property registration across selected Indian States ideally can increase the rate of property registered in the name of women. However, tax incentives or tax exemptions for women can be suboptimal policies, as it will not lead to strengthening "agency" in women.

Fiscal Transparency and Accountability Through Gender Budgeting

Gender budget statements provide transparency and accountability to the budgetary allocations for gender development. These statements can also prevent re-appropriations of expenditure. India has time series data on gender budgeting based on NIPFP methodology. As the methodology remained the same since 2004–2005, both at national and subnational levels, it is plausible to analyse the impact of gender budgeting on gender outcomes. In future, transgender needs to be incorporated in the gender-budgeting frameworks, given the data building process on the capability deprivation of transgender is crucial.

POLITICAL WILL FOR SUSTAINABLE GENDER BUDGETING AS PFM

When pandemic economic stimulus packages are short run, it is significant to use long-term PFM tools like gender budgeting for redressing gender inequalities. Gender budgeting is not a technical exercise. As narrated in various chapters, gender budgeting has political economy aspects. Political will is a significant determinant for the sustainability of gender budgeting as a powerful PFM tool. The priority from the highest policymaking bodies for strengthening fiscal innovation like gender budgeting only can make such difference.

REFERENCES

Blanchard, O. (2019). Public debt and low interest rates. *American Economic Review, 109*(4), 1197–1229.

Chakraborty, L. (2021). Union budget 2021–22: The macroeconomic framework. *Economic and Political Weekly, 56*(9).

Chakraborty, L., & Kaur, A. (2020). Why output gap is controversial. *The Financial Express*.

Chakraborty, L., Kaur, A., Divy, R., & Jacob, J. F. (2021). *Covid 19 and economic stimulus packages: Evidence from the Asia Pacific region*.

D'Alessandro, M., & Floro, M. S. (2021, October 14). *Post pandemic recovery must include the care economy*.